D1398586

Private Property and the Constitution

Private Property and the Constitution

Private Property and the Constitution

Bruce A. Ackerman

New Haven and London, Yale University Press

Published with assistance from the foundation
established in memory of Calvin Chapin
of the Class of 1788, Yale College.

Copyright © 1977 by Susan Rose-Ackerman, Trustee.
All rights reserved. This book may not be
reproduced, in whole or in part, in any form
(beyond that copying permitted
by Sections 107 and 108 of the U.S. Copyright
Law and except by reviewers for the public press),
without written permission from the publishers.

Designed by John O. C. McCrillis
and set in Baskerville type.
Printed in the United States of America by
The Vail-Ballou Press, Inc., Binghamton, New York

Library of Congress Cataloging in Publication Data

Ackerman, Bruce A
   Private property and the Constitution.
   Includes index.
   1. Eminent domain—United States.   2. Property
—United States.   3. United States—Constitutional
law.   I. Title.
KF5599.A93   343'.73'025   76-47667
ISBN 0-300-02065-1 (cloth); 0-300-02237-9 (paper)

11   10   9   8   7   6   5   4   3

For
Alex Bickel,
who taught me
to disagree

Contents

Acknowledgments

I am deeply indebted to my research assistant, John Borgo, for an ongoing flow of criticism, as well as to my secretary, Diane McDougal, for typing a steady stream of second thoughts. Their work, as well as mine, was supported in part by the Law and Social Science Division of The National Science Foundation. The Foundation, however, should not be held responsible for the views expressed in this essay.

I am also very grateful to my many friends at Yale and elsewhere who helped me with this book. But my debts here are so numerous and diverse as to defy a comprehensive and exact accounting.

1 Two Directions for Legal Thought

THE PROBLEM OF PRIVATE PROPERTY IN AN ACTIVIST STATE

Our legal problem arises at the point where capitalist economy and activist state collide. No longer a night-watchman, the state surveys the outcome of market processes and finds them wanting. Armed with a prodigious array of legal tools, it sets about improving upon the invisible hand—taxing here, subsidizing there, regulating everywhere. The result of all this motion may well be something that clearly redounds to the public good—a cleaner environment, a safer workplace, a decent home. Nonetheless, these welfare gains can rarely be purchased without social cost—though many may gain, some will lose as a result of the new governmental initiative. And it is the fate of those called upon to sacrifice for the public good that will concern us in this essay: When may they justly demand that the state compensate them for the financial sacrifices they are called upon to make?

Consider, for example, the position of Howard B. Sibson.[1] Along with some associates, Sibson owned a four-acre tract of marshland which he was preparing to develop for modern use at the time his plans were upset by New Hampshire's water resource board. So far as the state was concerned, any land-fill activity was "bad for the marsh" and "bad for mankind";[2] hence a flat ban on development was imposed on Sibson's property. In raising Sibson's case, we are not interested in assessing the merits of the board's development ban. Instead, we shall be considering whether Sibson should be required to bear unaided the financial sacrifice involved in mankind's gain.

It is possible, of course, to assume a political position so lofty that Sibson's problem seems capable of straightforward

solution. On the one hand, one may calumniate the activist
state in all its guises and insist upon full compensation for all
those property owners who find themselves hapless victims
of the state's activist pretensions.[3] On the other hand, one
may view the political drama as a very different kind of
morality play, with the state invariably cast as the only knight
within earshot capable of saving an already ill-used damsel
from yet another dastardly assault. On this view, anyone who
takes Sibson's problem seriously thereby signals his own in-
sensitivity—for it is only the morally obtuse who can seriously
ask whether a rapist should be compensated for the frustration of his expectations.[4]

The question of just compensation, then, becomes something more than a debater's point only on a rather complicated approach to the modern state. One cannot be so taken
with the market that any effort at state intervention seems
morally bankrupt. One cannot be so caught up with the state
that the fate of those who lose by its intervention is invariably
judged of no moral significance. Instead one must move beyond a simple, all-consuming faith in state or market to a
more skeptical middle position, which concedes a place to
both, giving absolute status to neither. Just because state intervention sometimes improves upon the invisible hand does
not mean that activism is without its own moral difficulties.
Just because an individual is not always entitled to pursue
his own best interests does not mean that he is never entitled
to complain when state action destroys his pre-existing expectations. Yet to say this is not to say much. It is one thing
to insist, Polonius-like, upon the need to establish ultimate
limits upon the demands placed on the individual by the
activist state; quite another to explain the intellectual methods by which these constraints may be derived. More concretely, out of the countless interventions attempted by the
activist state, how are we to isolate those which require compensation? More concretely still, should Sibson be required
to sacrifice for mankind's gain?

These questions not only provide a fruitful source for

philosophical speculation and political pronouncement, but also serve as a focus for judicial perplexity. When all else fails, those interests that have suffered at the hands of the activist state may turn to the courts for relief, invoking nothing less than the Constitution on their behalf. The Fifth Amendment warns, "nor shall private property be taken for public use, without just compensation," thereby inviting the courts to make as much legal sense as they can of a central problem raised by the modern state.[5] Over the past generation, however, the basic questions raised by the compensation clause have not occupied the forefront of legal attention. While there has been an immense quantity of litigation and decision, our constitutional preoccupations have been elsewhere as the Warren Court struggled to give a new meaning to constitutional concepts of equality and procedural fairness. Nonetheless, recent events assure that the compensation clause will return to center stage, requiring lawyers and citizens to address the issues that lie beneath the surface of even the most prosaic dispute in which the clause is invoked. Sibson's case is no sport—the past five years have witnessed a remarkable flood of conservationist legislation that cuts deeply into traditional notions of property rights. These statutes, for the most part, have refused to compensate property owners for the sacrifices imposed upon them, sending them to the courts in droves in a last effort to obtain relief.

The result has been a set of confused judicial responses, reflecting the larger intellectual difficulty involved in setting limits on the activist state. While Sibson, for example, was denied all relief,[6] it is easy to find similar cases coming to the opposite result, where analogous regulations were invalidated so long as compensation was not forthcoming.[7] More significant than one or another judicial decision, however, is the pervasive judicial recognition that compensation law—after a long period of neglect—is in need of a fundamental reconsideration. As is often true of the early stages of constitutional reappraisal, the Supreme Court has thus far been content to stand serenely aloof from the struggle, permitting the lower

courts to glimpse its future views by consulting Delphic high
court pronouncements handed down when Warren Harding
and Calvin Coolidge were in the White House.[8] As the constitutional challenge reaches floodtide proportions, however, it
is only a matter of time before the Court will be drawn into
assessing the constitutional implications of the change in
public values wrought by the environmental revolution. And
as this constitutional moment of truth nears, I hope to convince you that there is more at stake in its resolution than
even the future shape of environmental law in this country.
Not for the first time in our constitutional law, it will be
impossible to resolve the legal issues without confronting, and
resolving as best we can, our philosophical perplexities.

My basic thesis about the compensation clause requires the
construction of two ideal types, each of which I take to em-
body a basic tendency in modern legal analysis. To put the
point extravagantly in a single line, I shall argue that, in this
corner of the law at least, almost everything depends on
whether one looks at the Constitution with the eyes of a
Scientific Policymaker or those of an Ordinary Observer. While
the varieties of Scientific Policymaking are numerous, I shall
suggest that current compensation doctrine makes very little
sense when viewed from *any* plausible Policymaking perspective. It follows that Scientific Policymakers will think current
law is in need of very substantial revision—though they will
differ among themselves in important ways when it comes to
drawing up more precise blueprints for the legal revolution.
In contrast, the Ordinary Observer has very little difficulty
seeing sense in the distinctive contours of established compensation doctrine. So far as he is concerned, only modest
and interstitial changes are required that do not call into
question the validity of the basic doctrinal structure. My
thesis, then, is this: In order to decide whether compensation
law is basically sound or ripe for sweeping change it is
necessary first to choose between two fundamentally different
ways of thinking about law, each of which has roots in our
present legal culture.

But this choice between the Scientific Policymaker and the Ordinary Observer, it will develop, turns on questions that are generally thought to be philosophical rather than legal. To put the point broadly, there can be no question here of treating philosophy as an arcane cultural product which, if applied judiciously, will provide the professional lawyer with a shiny veneer of intellectual respectability. Nor is it even proper to think of one solution to the compensation problem as legally sound while another is recognized as philosophically sound. Instead, it is only after resolving certain philosophical issues that one can make sense of the constitutional question, let alone pretend to expound a correct constitutional answer. Philosophy decides cases; and hard philosophy at that.

Now this, I confess, represents my general view of the proper relationship between philosophy and constitutional law. It is, moreover, a view that accords a role to theory far greater than that granted generally by the profession. Nevertheless, I will not now attempt to defend my thesis in the abstract, thinking it wiser to explore it first by demonstrating in terms of a concrete constitutional issue that analysts must become philosophers if they wish to remain lawyers.

THE LIMITS OF LEGAL CONVENTION

It is plain that my thesis about the compensation clause will require a good deal of hard conceptual work before it can be understood, let alone evaluated. None of my key terms —neither Scientific Policymaker nor Ordinary Observer—are currently familiar in legal discourse. As a consequence, if I am to persuade you they provide the key to the mystery of the compensation clause, their meaning and implications must be elaborated quite carefully. The prospect of a long and difficult conceptual journey, however, should be enough to raise doubts. Why blaze new trails when more familiar pathways of legal analysis beckon?

My answer is simple: however smooth and wide the conventional highways, they lead to one or another dead-end— with the principles of compensation law no less mysterious at journey's end than they were when the easy road was first taken. To see this, it is only necessary to launch a brief scouting expedition down each of the three lines of conventional inquiry that sometimes, but not always, permit lawyers to arrive at an unproblematic legal conclusion to their constitutional quest. Consider, then, how much of a sense of legal direction we can obtain, first, from the language of the clause itself; second, from the relevant history; and third, from the long series of cases in which the courts, both Supreme and inferior, have attempted to give the clause a determinate meaning.

Doubtless there are occasions even in constitutional law where the canonical words state a clear rule whose meaning leaves little room for fair dispute. Like many other fundamental provisions, however, the compensation clause is couched in language of such abstraction as to strike terror in the hearts of the literalists who imagine that the constitutional text will somehow reveal its secrets without the further intervention of human minds: "nor shall private property be taken for public use, without just compensation." At best, these words set out a number of basic questions that must be answered: when does an interest qualify as private property? under what conditions should the state be said to have "taken" the interest? when does justice demand compensation and how is the adequacy of payment to be assessed? It should be plain that there are many different ways of answering these questions—staring at the text will not assist one in choosing among them.[9]

This, of course, is no new discovery. Indeed, it is precisely because they have learned to distrust appeals to the "plain meaning" of highly abstract concepts that constitutional lawyers have developed other conventional techniques to resolve questions that arise when reading the constitutional text. Most important is the idea that one's interpretative difficulties may dissolve if the abstract text is read in the light of the concrete history in which the words were conceived and written. This appeal to history can occur at two quite different levels. First, one may search the record to find out what one or another Framer said on the very issues that perplex us today, and then argue that this grab-bag of utterance should be accepted as binding in contemporary constitutional interpretation. While I myself have very little sympathy with this approach, it is not necessary to go deeply into the question here. For the fact of the matter is that the legislative history of the compensation clause is quite unilluminating, with hardly a recorded word bespeaking sustained reflection.[10] Nor will many, I trust, be attracted to the notion that whatever the practitioners of the common law called a "taking of property" at the time of the passage of the Fifth Amendment [11] should be treated as within the scope of the compensation clause while newfangled notions should be excluded.[12] In brief, there is no indication that any individual Framer (let alone the whole bunch) had worked out a particular theory of compensation law that would suggest a determinate way of separating out those contexts in which compensation was required from those in which losers should be left to tend their wounds without communal assistance.[13]

But it is possible to appeal to history in a far more discerning spirit. Instead of searching for the final solution to our present dilemmas, one may look to history as the source of abstract principles that may provide a promising beginning for further analysis. When approached at this level the historical record speaks loud and clear. There can be little doubt that the Framers thought the protection of property rights a very important thing indeed, and that a reading of the Constitution which would render the compensation clause a dead letter would be contrary to their intentions.[14] It is, however, equally plain that the Framers were neither blind worshipers of the market nor principled opponents of active government in all its forms. Indeed, their new constitutional structure established a continental government which immediately became far more powerful than any that had come before. At this level, then, we are worthy children of the Founding Fathers. Our fundamental problem is the same as theirs: to reconcile the competing demands of state and market in a way that gives absolute priority to neither. Yet when we press beyond a perception of a common problem and demand that our Fathers provide a definite solution, they fall quite remarkably silent—requiring us to resolve the puzzle of the compensation clause in our own terms, for want of any that bear the express seal of parental approval.

This leaves the lawyer with one final hope before he must resign himself to the need for sustained reflection. It remains possible that, despite the failure of the Framers to resolve the hard questions raised by the compensation clause, generations of judges between then and now have built a doctrinal structure that will serve the purpose admirably. As has already been suggested, however, the present legal scene is of quite a different kind. Not that there aren't some rules announced in one case or another. The problem is that even the most devoted rule-fetishist would like to have a glimmer as to the reasons we have the rules we have. And it is this which is quite absent from the prevailing understanding. Moreover, in constitutional law at least, the present generation is weak on rule-fetishism. Indeed, in many conversations on the subject, I have not encountered a single lawyer, judge, or scholar who views existing case-law as anything but a chaos of confused argument which ought to be set right if one only knew how. It is difficult to imagine a setting more inhospitable to those who would invoke "settled precedent" to forestall sustained consideration of doctrinal underpinnings.

We have, then, come to the moment of truth much rhapsodized by Legal Realists of an earlier generation: the conventional techniques have failed to lead the conscientious judge beyond his starting point. Indeed, thanks largely to the Realist movement, nobody is now taken in by the claim that the Constitution's "plain meaning," together with history and precedent, will inevitably dictate answers to the basic questions of compensation law. The real question is the direction we should take once this point has been made. For the old-fashioned Realist, the answer was a straightforward one. Having established that the standard techniques were unequal to the task at hand, he would suggest that the conscientious judge had no choice but to resolve his legal problem on the basis of intuition—in which personal, professional, and political factors were inextricably intertwined. I shall argue, however, that this Realist view leaves far too much room for intuition because it has altogether too narrow a notion of legal culture. A well-trained lawyer, in America at least, need not concede defeat upon reaching the analytic limits of the pitifully small number of techniques the simple Realist allows within the conventional canon. Without in the least offending the limits of professional legal discourse, the judge may take recourse to two very different methods, each of which will cast a powerful light upon his exegetical problem. The only trouble is that these two forms of legal thought—forms that I shall associate with the Scientific Policymaker, on the one hand, and the Ordinary Observer, on the other—suggest very different ways of resolving our legal perplexities. Moreover, the different legal solutions advanced by the Scientific Policymaker and Ordinary Observer are merely symptoms of more fundamental differences in approach to compensation law. Not only will our two ideal types differ as to their legal answers to the compensation question; they will formulate the question itself in very different ways. Indeed, the choice between analytic styles runs even deeper than rival formulations of the substantive problem before the court. It alters the judge's understanding of the forms of thought appropriate to his own role. Thus, a restrained judge in one tradition will think very differently from, and may look with disdain upon, a restrained judge in the other; similarly, different sorts of judicial innovators will look upon one another with something nearing incomprehension. And the most remarkable thing of all is that lawyers (and especially sophisticated lawyers) are so adept in both styles of thought that they move effortlessly between them as suits their interest, seldom finding it necessary as advocates to reflect upon deeper analytic inconsistencies—a thoughtlessness that is carried forward to the bench when the hand of fate transforms a lawyer into a judge.

It follows that our present predicament is quite different from the one so casually attributed to the judge in the name of Realism. Instead of inhabiting an exhausted legal culture in which personal intuition reigns supreme, the sophisticated judge confronts an embarrassment of analytic riches. If he is to make sense out of the compensation question, not to speak of the compensation answer, it will be necessary to confront self-consciously a deeply rooted conflict in our present legal culture and make a choice between Scientific Policymaking and Ordinary Observing. Without clear thought on fundamental matters, the crowd of compensation cases coming to court will crush even the most refined judicial intuition—generating a mass of arbitrary decisions that will make it increasingly unclear whether there are *any* constitutional foundations for private property in the modern activist state.

FOUR DEFINITIONS

I shall define my ideal types along two different, if related, dimensions. The first basis for comparison will be the existence of a divergent understanding of the nature of legal language. It is this difference that I seek to capture by calling one type an *Ordinary* Observer, the other a *Scientific* Policymaker. According to the first approach, legal language cannot be understood unless its roots in the ordinary talk of non-lawyers are constantly kept in mind. While legal specialists, naturally enough, will sometimes be called upon to make refinements generally ignored in ordinary language, recourse to everyday, nonlegal ways of speaking can be expected to reveal the basic structure and animating concerns of legal analysis—stripped of the excessive technicality generated by special pleading and adversary confrontation. In contrast, the Scientist conceives the distinctive constituents of legal discourse to be a set of technical concepts whose meanings are set in relation to one another by clear definitions without continuing reliance upon the way similar-sounding concepts are deployed in nonlegal talk.[15] While the practitioner of Ordinary analysis will find that nonlegal discourse will provide a useful perspective upon basic concepts that may otherwise be lost in a sea of legalism, the Scientist will look upon such an appeal to ordinary talk as the surest sign of muddle.

To this first contrast, I wish to add a second, related comparison that deals with the ultimate objective of legal analysis. It is their divergence on this issue that I wish to emphasize by calling one group Policymakers, the other, Observers. On the Policymaking side, I shall place all those who understand the legal system to contain, in addition to rules,[16] a relatively small number of general principles [17] describing the abstract ideals [18] which the legal system is understood to further. It is this statement of principle, presumed by the Policymaker to form a self-consistent whole,[19] which I shall call a Comprehensive View. The rules of the system are understood to be the product of legislative and judicial efforts to implement the Comprehensive View in the best practical way. Hence, the function of the Comprehensive View is to provide a set of standards by which Policymakers may determine the proper content of legal rules and evaluate the performance of the legal system as a whole. It follows that when a Policymaker is forced to judge the merits of competing rules in the course of making a legally binding decision, he will select the rule which—in his best judgment—best conforms to the Comprehensive View he has imputed to the legal system.[20] To forestall misunderstanding, I do not want you to think a Policymaker must impute to the legal system a Comprehensive View of a Highly Moral variety—like that imagined by Immanuel Kant or Myres McDougal. For present purposes, it will be enough for the analyst to worship a more mundane—if not more intelligible—God, like Bentham's Utility or Posner's Efficiency. For the central feature of my definition is not the substantive character of the Policymaker's vision but its form: its aspiration to view seemingly disparate legal issues within a common framework provided by a *relatively* [21] small number of abstract and general principles that are assumed to permit the consistent evaluation of all the disputes the legal system is called upon to resolve.

It is this effort to evaluate particular legal rules in terms of a Comprehensive View that sets the Policymaker apart from his idealized opposite. From the Observer's point of view, it seems extraordinary to *begin* analysis by supposing, with the Policymaker, that legal rules ought to satisfy the demands of a Comprehensive View. This is not to say that our Observer is an old-fashioned Realist who argues that judges inevitably decide hard (or easy) cases on the basis of personal predilection. Rather than dealing with straw men, we shall impute a more sophisticated point of view to our ideal type. For him the test of a sound legal rule is the extent to which it vindicates the practices and expectations embedded in, and generated by, dominant social institutions. It follows that when an Observer is forced to judge the merits of competing rules in the course of making a legally binding decision, his view of the task will be quite different from that adopted by his Policymaking brethren. Rather than grounding his decision in a Comprehensive View stating the ideals the legal system is understood to serve, the Observer will instead seek to identify the norms that in fact govern proper conduct within the existing structure of social institutions. Having articulated the existing pattern of socially based expectations as sensitively as he can, the Observer will then select the legal rule which, in his best judgment, best supports these institutionally based norms.

In order to make the contrast between the two ideal types clearer, it should be emphasized that the Observer is *not* necessarily committed to deny what the Policymaker affirms and to repudiate the notion that legal rules should be understood as organized around a Comprehensive View. The relationship between the types is a bit more subtle than that—what the Policymaker asserts *must necessarily* be the case, the Observer is only willing to say *may possibly* be the case. For the Observer is quite willing to concede the possibility of a society in which institutionally based expectations formed a larger pattern which could best be understood as organized around a set of highly abstract and general principles that qualified as a Comprehensive View. If, for example, the Benthamite program had ever been thoroughly institutionalized in a concrete historical society, the Observer in such a place would be happy to accept the notion that the only socially legitimate expectations were those that could be justified by a sound utilitarian calculus. Similarly, if he lived in a Kantian Kingdom of Ends, the Observer would be prepared to concede the propriety of testing each proposed legal rule by the categorical imperative, since this basic principle served in fact as the foundation for all established social practices.

It seems quite obvious, however, that no modern society has institutionalized any single Comprehensive View with anything like this degree of success. Instead of each important social institution marching obediently to the sound of a single drummer, different clusters of social practice may often be organized along very different principles and yet coexist with one another for very long periods of time. While each of these institutional clusters may influence one another over time, it is not at all obvious that this mutual influence will result in the victory of one Comprehensive View over another as the principle for organizing all social institutions. It is also quite possible that the result of this mutual influence will be the accentuation of different Comprehensive Views in different areas of social life; or the development of social institutions organized on the basis of Comprehensive Views quite different from those that came before. Thus it would be a most remarkable coincidence if all important social institutions existing during any single generation could best be understood as organized around any *single* set of principles that would qualify as a Comprehensive View. It follows that, in real societies, Observers should be expected to disagree with Policymakers as to the degree legal principles ought to be abstract and general, as well as the extent to which consistency criteria should be used to test the soundness of a particular legal outcome. For a Policymaker, of course, the mere fact that *social practices* do not as a whole conform to a single determinate Comprehensive View does not count as a reason for giving up the enterprise of thinking about the *legal system* as if it were so organized.[22] In contrast, the Observer will insist that appropriate legal principles should be couched at a level of generality and abstraction no greater than that attained by a non-lawyer who reflectively and disinterestedly sought to identify the expectations of each social actor which have a legitimate basis in dominant institutional practices.[23]

This is not to say that consistency has *no* role to play in the Observer's conception of sound legal analysis. Once the Observer has articulated the principles that best characterize the structure of socially based expectations, he is happy to insist that they are to be *applied* consistently to all cases in which they may be invoked with equal force. That is, the Observer —like the Policymaker—will condemn a decisionmaker who breaches the most elementary principle of formal justice and discriminates between seemingly like cases without explaining why they should be treated differently by the legal order. It is only when the Policymaker uses the consistency argument to try to force the Observer to organize disparate socially based expectations into a determinate Comprehensive View that the consistency issue is joined. So far as the Observer is concerned, the Policymaker's willingness to press his concern for consistency, generality, abstraction beyond the structure of existing social expectations marks him out as an immature mind insisting on a clarity and comprehensiveness intrinsically unsuited for the subject.[24] Such lawyers will be said to lack something called "good judgment," consistently failing to take into account the endless complexity of social reality in their overly abstract formulations. In contrast, the Policymakers among us will look upon their rivals as rather superficial types who rely on their sense of the social proprieties instead of trying to ground their relatively concrete notions of socially legitimate expectation in a deeper, more abstract account of the social objectives worthy of legal support. For the Policymaker, "good judgment" comes only after deep and systematic thought about the ultimate objectives of the legal order.[25]

SOME IDEAL TYPES

Thus far we have developed two conceptual polarities in isolation from one another—Scientific has been opposed to Ordinary; Policymaker to Observer. To construct the ideal types that will serve as the principal tools for analysis, it remains only to consider the ways in which our elements may be combined to form stable compounds with interesting properties. To begin with the fundamentals, it is not very difficult to define the two ideal types that will preoccupy us in the present essay. Thus, a Scientific Policymaker is an analyst who (a) manipulates technical legal concepts so as to illuminate (b) the relationship between disputed legal rules and the Comprehensive View he understands to govern the legal system. In contrast, an Ordinary Observer is an analyst who (a) elaborates the concepts of nonlegal conversation so as to illuminate (b) the relationship between disputed legal rules and the structure of social expectations he understands to prevail in dominant institutional practice.

We shall, of course, be making a great deal of these definitions; and it is precisely because they play a central role that one should avoid placing a weight upon them they will not bear. Most important is to avoid the fallacy of misplaced concreteness. An ideal type is not a concrete person who speaks with a single voice on every question. Simply because two lawyers may be classed as Scientific Policymakers, for example, it does *not* follow that they will agree on all legal issues or even on most important questions of legal method. To the contrary, disputes within the family are often of the bitterest kind. Thus, proponents of one technical language may condemn Scientists who use a different specialized vocabulary in legal analysis; advocates of one Comprehensive View may vigorously dispute Policymakers who rely upon a different set of substantive principles to evaluate a legal conflict. On a deeper level, different groups of Scientific Policymakers may disagree about the criteria which should govern the selection of a legally relevant Scientific language or Comprehensive View. Nonetheless, so long as they agree that good legal analysis requires *some* form of specialized language and *some* determinate Comprehensive View, they will qualify as Scientific Policymakers in our sense of the word.

Similarly, a slow second reading of the definition of an Ordinary Observer should reveal any number of questions upon which members of this camp may come to blows: what is the best way to elaborate the structure of nonlegal conversation? what is one to do with the fact that laymen do not all talk alike? to what extent do social expectations have a structure? how is one to identify dominant institutional practices? and so forth. My point is not that these questions are easy; it is simply that they are *different* from the equally perplexing methodological questions which preoccupy Scientific Policymakers as they seek to justify their choice of specialized language and Comprehensive View. In short, rather than providing a detailed map of the legal terrain, our definitions serve merely to mark out two very different directions a lawyer may travel in his search for a legally satisfactory solution to his problem of constitutional interpretation. While we shall have occasion to fill in the road map as we continue our investigation, vast empty spaces will remain even at the end of the journey. In this essay we are interested in theory only so far as it directly illuminates the path to the practical solution of a pressing constitutional problem. If, in the end, I convince you that this particular trip was worth taking, there will be time enough to dream about other far-away places.

Before beginning to travel the paths to compensation law taken by Scientific Policymakers and Ordinary Observers, however, there is one final point of orientation that must be established. Thus far we have spoken of these two ideal types without trying to locate them more precisely on the larger terrain of legal discourse. Do our two models represent the only viable ways of moving beyond the simple Realist's dilemma? If there are others, are we justified in plunging headlong down only two trails, ignoring the others that may be even more fruitful?

Happily, a basis for answering these questions has already been laid by our earlier discussion of the two conceptual oppositions—Scientific v. Ordinary, Policymaking v. Observing —that provide the foundations for our two ideal types. As the simple matrix below suggests, we have in reality selected our two models from a larger scheme that defines four distinct analytic possibilities:

TABLE 1

		Objective of Legal Analysis	
		Policymaker v.	Observer
Nature of Legal Language	Scientific v.	Scientific Policymaker	Scientific Observer
	Ordinary	Ordinary Policymaker	Ordinary Observer

Given this larger framework, we can gain some added insight into our methodological premises by contrasting the two favored ideal types with the two that will remain in the background throughout this essay. Consider first the nature of the disagreement between the Ordinary Observer and the Scientific Observer inhabiting the upper right-hand cell. These two types do not disagree about the ultimate objective of good legal analysis, but rather about the kind of legal language that will best assure attainment of the goal. While the Scientific Observer agrees that the objective is to identify the legal rules that best support dominant social expectations, he thinks the patient elaboration of the structure of ordinary discourse a most unlikely means to this end. Condemning Ordinary language analysis as the idle sport of speculative dilettantes, he will propose that legal concepts be based upon a Scientific understanding of socially based expectations. Now, for present purposes, it is not a matter of great importance which of the discipline(s) the Scientist selects as the source of his superior insight—anthropology, history, psychology, and sociology are all plausible candidates. The point here is that the concepts proffered by the Scientific Observer do not gain their warrant from ordinary contemporary discourse but from a specialist's claim that his particular methods will generate superior insight—for it is this claim that distinguishes the Scientific from the Ordinary view of legal language in our theory.

It should be emphasized, moreover, that in the history of American law the viewpoint of the Scientific Observer has had many important proponents. During the half century between 1870 and 1920, legal scholarship was dominated by a group of scholars who believed that the disciplined investigation of the historical common law tradition would reveal the basic principles defining legitimate social expectations.[26] Hence the Scientific challenge to the Ordinary Observer is not a lifeless theoretical possibility but a very real force indeed. Nor can it be said that proponents of Ordinary methods in law have seriously considered, let alone resolved, the question of the proper relationship between Ordinary and Scientific methods in elaborating the structure of institutionally based expectations. Indeed, even if we move to the mainstream of philosophical debate, this issue is surprisingly undeveloped—though here it is at least possible to find some stimulating and suggestive efforts.[27]

Despite the potent claims of the Scientific Observer to attention, however, I have chosen to slight his contribution. While this gap might trouble the compleat interdiscliplinarian, it is not a serious difficulty given our purpose of demonstrating to constitutional lawyers the practical necessity of philosophical argument. For recall that it is our present thesis that the conceptual tools of Ordinary Observing are sufficiently powerful to illuminate the existing structure of compensation doctrine in a way that a lawyer would find most revealing. And if true, this would mean that the contributions of the Scientific Observer to the practical task of interpreting the compensation clause will probably be rather limited. For if the Scientist only succeeds by his more complex and expensive procedures in telling the Ordinary analyst what he already knows, this cannot count as an important contribution to substantive constitutional law, however important it may be to the development of one or another form of legal science.

It is always possible, of course, that a Scientific Observer would *not* simply confirm his Ordinary counterpart's understanding of social reality, but instead provide a very different account of the structure of social expectations. Nonetheless, I think this theoretical possibility sufficiently unlikely that I shall postpone its serious consideration until one or another Scientific Observer presents an account that makes the latent tension between the two forms of Observing a concrete problem for just compensation law. We shall have enough work in developing the Ordinary Observer's approach that we cannot afford the potentially pointless labor involved in studying his Scientific counterpart—at least until some Scientist comes forward with inconsistent findings about social practice that trumpet the coming of Judgment Day.

So much for the Scientific Observer. There is, I think, much less to say on behalf of the Ordinary Policymaker who stands in an analogous relationship to the Scientific Policymaker on the left side of our matrix. Once again these two ideal types agree as to the objective of sound legal analysis and disagree as to the kind of language that promises best to serve this goal. Only this time it is the proponent of Ordinary analysis who will be ignored in the following discussion. According to this ideal type, deep reflection upon ordinary language and practice will reveal that it can best be understood as organized around a set of self-consistent principles and policies sufficiently abstract and general to qualify as a Comprehensive View. If this were true, then it might be unnecessary to devise a Scientific vocabulary for the purpose of clearly and systematically developing the implications of the governing Comprehensive View to each kind of dispute brought before the legal system. One could then operate as an effective Policymaker by thoughtfully employing the concepts of ordinary discourse in evaluating each particular dispute.

I shall, however, ignore this view because it requires certain empirical assumptions about existing social practices that seem to me to be plainly false. While, as we have seen, it is possible to imagine a Utilitarian or Kantian paradise in which all important social practices were in fact organized around a particular Comprehensive View, I cannot believe that I live in such a world. And if social practices are not organized around a single Comprehensive View, it would be most surprising if ordinary language could be so organized. After all, ordinary talk makes sense within ordinary social structures; if these structures do not form a larger, consistent, normative pattern, there is every reason to think that common speech will reflect this underlying social disarray. Hence, I do not believe Ordinary Policymaking is a coherent mode of legal analysis in the social world as it is presently constructed.[28] If the law is to further a determinate Comprehensive View, lawyers will require a language organized on clearer normative lines than the talk generated by laymen having to deal with the tensions and inconsistencies of their common forms of life. It should be emphasized, however, that mine is a controversial view. One of our leading theorists, Ronald Dworkin, has adopted a manner of talking that sometimes—though not always—makes it seem as if he thought Ordinary Policymaking to be an intellectually sound analytic possibility.[29] Until a convincing and systematic presentation of such a view is forthcoming, however, I cannot renounce my deep skepticism on this score. At any rate, as one surveys the present legal scene, it remains true that no important Policymaking work has adopted an Ordinary vocabulary, while Scientific efforts multiply. Indeed, as I shall suggest in the concluding chapter, it is the conflict between Scientific Policymaker and Ordinary Observer that promises to provide one of the fundamental intellectual problems confronting the legal profession in the years ahead.

THE PROBLEM REVISITED

Having selected our analytic tools, it is time to test their practical utility on a concrete problem. I imagine a conscientious judge confronting the Realist's dilemma as he attempts to give meaning to the abstract pronouncements of the compensation clause. None of the standard professional techniques —neither the "plain meaning" of the text, nor the "intent" of the Framers, nor the "settled" principles of judicial decision—mark out a general method of analyzing compensation problems, much less a way of resolving particularly troublesome cases. What, then, is to save the judge from simply relying on his personal preferences when called upon to resolve the complaints pressed on him by the crowd of petitioners now streaming to the courts for relief?

Our two ideal types may be understood as alternative ways of answering this question, each marking out a distinct dimension of the present legal culture. On the one hand, a judge may respond to his perception that the standard legal cues have failed to resolve his problem in constitutional interpretation by relying on a more rigorously developed set of legal concepts than those with which he was previously content— if this path is taken, Scientific Policymaking has an obvious attraction. On the other hand, when confronted with the failure of the standard legal cues, the judge may despair of finding a solution in more elaborate forms of explicit legal analysis, exploring instead the implications of the larger pattern of social expectation and evaluation—this is the path of the Ordinary Observer. In short, the judge may seek to resolve his initial legal perplexity either by moving far more deeply *into* a specialized legal culture or moving *away* from self-consciously legal norms into the more general culture.

This essay, then, is grounded on the unsurprising hypothesis that the first step a judge takes in resolving his legal doubts carries with it commitments far more significant than may at first appear. In the next three chapters, we shall travel the road toward legal specialization with the Scientific Policy-maker. We shall then follow the opposite path with the Ordinary Observer, before attempting, in the final chapter, some tentative reflections on the nature of the conflict that has been revealed.

2 Scientific Adjudication

An Overview of the Scientific Argument

Scientific Policymaking, as we have defined it, merely marks out an abstract possibility for legal thought—it is possible to imagine a society in which not a single soul has ever thought of resolving legal disputes by consulting a Comprehensive View with the aid of a specialized language; it is equally possible to imagine a world in which the entire legal corps manipulates a single technical vocabulary to further a definite Comprehensive View. As constitutional lawyers, however, we are not interested in abstract possibilities. What is important is the state of the present legal culture in America. Are today's lawyers in fact familiar with forms of Scientific Policymaking which will cast a powerful light on the fundamental problems of compensation law?

It is true, of course, that the Scientific Policymaker is hardly a figure that American lawyers have been taught to identify by name. But this failure of explicit recognition cannot conclude the matter. It would not be the first time that lawyers have begun to build a structure of argument long before they have felt the need to understand the larger implications of their practical activities. Consequently, we cannot draw any conclusions whatever from the admitted fact that only blank stares will reward the hardy soul who, without further explanation, drops the name of Scientific Policymaking in the middle of a legal conversation. Instead of demanding instant professional recognition, we must instead take our inspiration from Molière and consider the possibility that American lawyers—like the good bourgeois gentlemen they are—have come to speak like Scientific Policymakers without becoming fully aware of it.

This will be the task of the first half of the book. In the

present chapter we shall focus upon the Scientific side of legal discourse. Have lawyers developed a specialized vocabulary—independent of ordinary language—that may be used to clarify the Delphic command of the compensation clause? Here I mean to do more than establish that Scientific concepts are in fact deeply rooted in the talk of competent lawyers. I also wish to begin the development of the larger point that these concepts, once accepted in legal analysis, will significantly shape the lawyer's perceptions both as to the nature of his constitutional problem and the character of its satisfactory legal solution. Having established the Scientific foundations in Chapter 2, we turn to consider the Policymaking aspect of present legal discourse in Chapters 3 and 4. Here, I shall build on the work of two scholars—Frank Michelman and Joseph Sax—who are generally understood to have made the most important contributions to compensation law in the past quarter-century. My aim will be to show that by thinking self-consciously like a Scientific Policymaker, it is possible to refine and broaden the existing body of compensation theory and thereby lay the basis for a body of compensation law that is both powerful and deeply grounded.

By the end of Chapter 4, then, I mean to convince you that Scientific Policymaking is in fact, if not in name, an emerging intellectual force of the first importance on the American legal scene. Yet at the same time, I mean to suggest that it is not the *only* cultural reality with which constitutional lawyers must deal. For when we turn to consider the compensation doctrine that is generated by the use of our shiny tools, the result cannot help disturb the sensibilities of anyone familiar with conventional approaches to compensation law. Although the methods of Scientific Policymaking seem familiar, and its doctrinal conclusions seem sensible, the harsh fact is that they bear very little relationship to the rules that are presently applied by the judges in the name of the Constitution. From this it follows either that the judges have been strikingly inept or that they have been thinking about compensation law in a way that is strikingly different from that characteristic of the

Scientific Policymaker. It is this second hypothesis that will provide the inspiration for our exploration, in the second half of the book, of the legal methods of the Ordinary Observer.

But I have been getting ahead of myself. It is time to get down to Scientific business. If we are to make good on the promise of Scientific method in compensation law, we must develop a technical vocabulary adequate to deal with two important, but quite different, subjects. The first, obviously enough, is the concept of property and what is involved in a taking of it. Is there a living legal tradition which disparages the property-talk of laymen and insists that professional talk about property be grounded instead on a special vocabulary? The answer to this question is not very difficult—every modestly sophisticated lawyer is, I think, well acquainted with the technical property-talk discussed in the following pages. While I have not run any empirical studies on the point, I should be very much surprised if any of the lawyer-readers of this book will respond to my account of professional property-talk as if it were a report from an alien legal culture.

The second subject for analysis, however, will make somewhat greater demands on the scientific imagination of the reader. The need arises because a judge's understanding of the proper limits of his own role will control his doctrinal response just as much as his perception of the substantive problem before him. Thus, even if two Scientific judges hold the same Comprehensive View, their solutions to compensation problems will differ if one is a judicial innovator while the other is an advocate of judicial restraint. Indeed, the question of the institutional competence of the judiciary has served as *the* central preoccupation of constitutional debate ever since the unhappy days—now almost half a century distant—when the Old Court did battle with the New Deal. Despite the length of the debate, however, even leading scholars and judges still use labels like "judicial activism" and "judicial restraint" without often giving a precise idea of what they mean. As a consequence, it will be necessary to break some Scientific ground and define with care a conceptual scheme which will, I hope, permit the clearer expression of familiar but vague arguments dealing with the extent to which judges may legitimately invoke the Constitution to revise the judgments of officials who are also responsible to an electoral check. We shall, in short, be developing a vocabulary adequate for dealing first with substance and second with process. On, then, to the fundamental substantive problems raised by the compensation clause, as they are seen by contemporary Legal Science.

SCIENTIFIC PROPERTY TALK

There are, I am sure, many Scientific languages that may be proposed with the aim of providing a perspicuous framework for the analysis of legal problems. Indeed, I am personally acquainted with several competing ones that differ from one another quite remarkably.[1] For present purposes, however, it will not be necessary to consider the merits of competing paradigms. For in dealing with the concept of property it is possible to detect a consensus view so pervasive that even the dimmest law student can be counted upon to parrot the ritual phrases on command. I think it fair to say that one of the main points of the first-year Property course is to disabuse entering law students of their primitive lay notions regarding ownership. They learn that only the ignorant think it meaningful to talk about owning things free and clear of further obligation. Instead of defining the relationship between a person and "his" things, property law discusses the relationships that arise *between people* with respect to things. More precisely, the law of property considers the way rights to use things may be parceled out amongst a host of competing resource users. Each resource user is conceived as holding a bundle of rights vis-à-vis other potential users; indeed in the modern American system, the ways in which user rights may be legally packaged and distributed are wondrously diverse. And it is probably never true that the law assigns to any single person the right to use any thing in absolutely *any* way he pleases. Hence, it risks serious confusion to identify any single individual as *the* owner of àny particular thing. At best, this locution may sometimes serve as a shorthand for identifying the holder of that bundle of rights which contains a range of entitlements more numerous or more valuable than the bundle held by any other person with respect to the thing in question. Yet, like all shorthands, talk about "the" property owner invites the fallacy of misplaced concreteness, of reification.[2] Once one begins to think sloppily, it is all too easy to start thinking that "the" property owner, by virtue of being "the" property owner, must *necessarily* own a *particular* bundle of rights over a thing. And this is to commit the error that separates layman from lawyer. For the fact (or is it the law?) of the matter is that property is not a thing, but a set of legal relations between persons governing the use of things.

Indeed, so far as the Scientist is concerned, it would be much better (but for the inconvenience involved in abandoning shorthand) to purge the legal language of all attempts to identify any particular person as "the" owner of a piece of property. And ordinary language too would profit from a similar purification if that could only be accomplished. At the very least, lawyers must be taught to translate with ease from shorthand to the Scientifically correct legal language. Whenever a judge says Jones rather than Smith is "the" property owner, he should be understood to mean: "in one or another resource conflict between Jones and Smith, the legal system places an entitlement in Jones's bundle of rights rather than Smith's bundle." Simply because Jones won in the battle over resource use X, it does not follow that he will win in the battle over use A. It is perfectly possible that the court will locate the right to use A in Smith's bundle rather than Jones's. Both bundles are bundles of property rights, though one may be more ample than the other. The real question for the law —Scientifically understood—is not to identify "the" rights of "the" property owner through some mysterious intuitive process but to determine in whose bundle one or another right may best be put.[3]

It follows that when the Scientific eye scans the constitutional text, it will have little difficulty interpreting the first part of the clause which commands "nor shall private property be taken. . . ." Scientifically understood, this phrase can only have an extraordinarily wide application. *Whenever* the state takes *any* user right out of Jones's bundle and puts it in *any* other bundle, private property should be understood to have been taken. For it is precisely the Scientist's main point to deny the propriety of a muddled search amongst the diverse bundles of user rights in quest of those that contain "the" rights of property. Even if Jones's bundle contains but a single user right, it is nonetheless protected against a taking by the clause. And surely others should not be disadvantaged simply because their bundles contain more user rights than does that of poor Jones. It follows that a taking has occurred whenever the law removes *any* user right formerly resident in one bundle and places it in any other. Q.E.D.

If, then, the Framers had simply let the compensation clause stand complete at the end of its sixth word, the modern Scientist would have no choice but to conclude that he was confronting one of the most resounding affirmations of the status quo ever to be uttered in the history of mankind—not a single pre-existing user right would then be subject to redistribution; government would be constitutionally limited to the role of watchman state.

But of course the clause does not end at the sixth word; instead it forbids takings only when they occur "without just compensation." And it is this caveat which permits the Scientist to escape a "literal" construction of the clause that would transform him into an implacable foe of the modern state. So long as one properly emphasizes the phrase *"just* compensation," it no longer appears that the clause may be successfully invoked by any old Jones whose user rights have been modified through law. Instead, the clause, when read as a whole, suggests that payment is constitutionally required *only when it will serve the purposes of justice*. The diverse task then becomes one of systematically working out the implications of the very abstract idea of just compensation in the wide variety of disputes in which it will come into play.

Yet this is precisely the mission of Scientific Policymaking. To put the point more generally, the constitutional text has been conceived as a mandate for the analyst to, first, impute a Comprehensive View to the legal system so as to determine the substantive principles of just compensation and, second, work out those compensation rules that will further the Comprehensive View in all litigated cases involving the taking of property rights, Scientifically understood. Thus the constitutional language serves as the foundation for a proud juridical edifice the Scientific Policymaker is apt to call the Law of Just Compensation.

And surely it is not a foundation that will seem intrinsically flawed in the eyes of a well-trained lawyer of the present day. In saying this, I do not mean to suggest that a contemporary craftsman would absolutely refuse to look at a competing set of blueprints if they were offered to him. Instead, I am making the weaker claim that we have said nothing which would arouse the suspicions of the competent lawyer, inducing him to look elsewhere in his search for solid ground for compensation doctrine. Indeed, American law has learned to live contentedly with structures based on foundations far shakier than these. So let us suspend a premature scrutiny of dark cellars to explore the upper stories of the Scientific structure. Even a cursory glance will reveal that the rooms seem livable enough; and the furniture is not unfamiliar.

The General Structure of the Takings Problem

Consider, then, the following scenario: At the beginning of the tale (Time One), observe Jones happily claiming a bundle of rights (X,Y,Z) over a particular thing that has been previously vouchsafed him by the legal system. Something has just happened, however, which has induced those in control of the state to consider again whether it best serves society's objectives to distribute property bundles in the way that has

been done in the recent past. Having considered the matter
afresh, they have rendered a negative answer: it appears that
the world will be better, given the Comprehensive View held
by the state in question, if right Z is removed from Jones's
bundle and reassigned to Smith (who may be a private citizen
or a state official). So a law is passed rearranging the bundles
in the way indicated at Time Two.

Needless to say, Jones is disappointed by this turn of events,
and comes to court at Time Three to demand his just compensation. As a result, the Policymaker is obliged to determine
the best way in which the costs involved in moving to a better
world are to be distributed among the citizenry: Should Jones
be left bearing the entire loss associated with the legal change
or should this loss be spread among some or all of his fellow
citizens?

This, it seems to me, is the general form the compensation
question assumes so long as the prevailing form of Scientific
Policymaking remains unchallenged. It will, however, help us
later if we devised a particular illustration of the general
problem that will serve to indicate more clearly the concrete
doctrinal implications of one or another form of Scientific
Policymaking. While any number of scenarios could serve this
purpose, it seems best to avoid presenting a dramatic incident
—like the virtual confiscation visited upon Sibson—to serve as
a primary illustration. To focus the issue in this way would
foster the impression that compensation law is concerned only
with extreme situations, far removed from the mainstream of
social life, when in fact we are dealing with a common problem with which everyone is familiar. Consequently, while I
shall present a hypothetical situation that suggests the character of the real cases now flooding the courts, the story I will
tell is far tamer than some that can be told.

Imagine that, at Time One, Jones is "the" owner of some
marshland who finds that his bundle of rights includes the un-
fettered right to fill in the marsh for the purpose of residential
development. Imagine further that at Time Two the legislature determines that if Jones and the other owners of marsh-

land ("the Marshans") are permitted to exercise this right, they will impair existing marine ecological systems in serious—if unquantifiable—ways. As a consequence the legislature passes a statute which redistributes property bundles, requiring the Marshans to preserve a goodly proportion of the marsh untouched as a condition for obtaining approval for development. These limitations upon the Marshans' rights serve to depress the value of their property bundle from $25,000 to $5,000 an acre. The new law, however, does not make all residential development impossible; nor does it modify any of the other user rights to be found in the Marshans' bundles.

We are now at Time Three: the disappointed Marshans seek to deflect the cost of the legal change from themselves to others by demanding compensation. The task before us is to determine the way in which a judge who thinks of himself as a Scientific Policymaker would evaluate the Marshans' claim.[4]

SPECIFICATION OF JUDICIAL ROLE

While just compensation decisions are in fact made by a wide variety of official actors, we shall be primarily concerned with the problem as it appears to judges—judges called upon to act in their priestly capacity as champions of property rights guaranteed by the Constitution. Given this special focus, it is particularly important to keep in mind that every compensation claim that comes before a judge has already been rejected by somebody else in government—indeed, many claims have been rejected many times by different officials occupying different parts of our elaborate governmental machine. It follows that before he may proceed to one or another Policymaking solution of his Scientific problem, a judge must come to terms with his peculiar position as constitutional decisionmaker of last resort: to what extent, and in what ways, is he entitled to make an independent judgment on the merits of the dispute before him? how much should he defer instead to the earlier decisions made by other officials who found the Marshans' demand for compensation to be unwarranted?

These questions, of course, go to the heart of constitutional theory. Yet, even apart from their intrinsic difficulty, it would be a mistake to attempt an answer here. For it is hardly my goal to establish any single doctrinal solution to the compensation question as the revealed truth to be recognized by all right-thinking Scientific Policymakers of the present day. Instead, I shall be trying to mark out in a relatively dispassionate way the lines of Policymaking argument that seem plausible within the existing limits of the American legal culture. Consequently, if there *is* an ongoing dispute as to the proper meaning and value of judicial restraint in constitutional adjudication, I am not interested in papering over this fact by pretending to advance a solution which will miraculously silence the contending factions. My goal is to create a Scientific vocabulary that will fairly state the institutional views of each important force in the legal culture. In this way it will be possible to express, rather than suppress, the current structure of plausible constitutional opinion when viewed from the perspective of a Scientific Policymaker. Instead of pretending that all judges understood their role in the same way, we could then speak of the way (various sorts of) *restrained* judges differed from (different kinds of) more *innovative* judges in their treatment of the compensation question—thereby fulfilling our objective of providing a sophisticated account of the range of Policymaking argument open to today's lawyers as they attempt to make sense of the Constitution.

Yet the achievement of even this modest objective will seem no easy matter to those who have spent some time with the voluminous legal literature having to do with the proprieties of the judicial role. It is a tribute, I suppose, to the adversary character of our culture that so much passion can be invested in a debate whose general outlines have been so poorly defined as the one which opposes judicial restraint to judicial innovation. While there have been a number of distinguished contributors to the discussion,[5] almost all have approached it as if they were advocates arguing before some imaginary court of last resort. Each presentation resembles a learned kind of advocate's brief, in which competing views are treated in the way that most readily justifies their easy rejection. As a consequence, while there is much that could be said about the particular opinions of particularly important judges or scholars, it is not easy to propose a more general framework in which to accommodate the existing diversity of views within the same intellectual structure.

It is true, of course, that if we limit our gaze to any concrete constitutional case, we will often find it possible to get a sense of the players even without a scorecard. Generally speaking, the "activist" is the fellow who wants to overturn the statute in the name of the Constitution, while the "restrained" judge is willing to let the legislative will be done. Nevertheless, even this rule-of-thumb is hardly an unerring guide to judicial behavior—it is easy to think of cases in which, quite mysteriously, roles are reversed and judges whose conceptions of judicial role seem well known come out just on the side where their presence is least expected. In any event, even if this result-oriented approach were far more successful than it is in fact, it would not serve our purposes here. We are not merely interested in the fact that restrained judges intervene less frequently (and on somewhat different occasions) than their more innovative counterparts, but seek to explain *the kinds of argument* that an innovative judge will find congenial but which will be ruled out of court by his restrained brethren.

I have no doubt that, given the confused nature of the debate, it is possible to distinguish between the forms of innovative and restrained argument in a variety of ways. Indeed, when we turn to consider the Ordinary Observer in the second half of this book, I shall argue that his preconceptions will lead him to understand the distinction between judicial restraint and innovation in terms very different from—and inconsistent with—the distinction that will commend itself to the Scientific Policymaker. Nonetheless, it will be enough for present purposes to characterize the ongoing debate about judicial review in a way that clarifies the variety of plausible Scientific Policymaking approaches to compensation law. Is there something about the way we have defined the Scientific

Policymaker which will lead this ideal type to understand the main issues raised by the dispute about judicial restraint and innovation in a special sort of way?

To make some headway on this question, it is necessary to reflect a bit on the definition of a Policymaker. However they differ in other respects, all Policymakers agree that the work-product of each legal institution should be evaluated in terms of the extent to which it satisfies the requirements of the Comprehensive View the Policymaker imputes to the legal system as a whole. A Utilitarian Policymaker, for example, would criticize every decision insofar as it fails to maximize utility; a Kantian would criticize it in terms of the categorical imperative; and so forth. It follows that a Policymaker (whatever his particular Comprehensive View) would understand a perfectly functioning set of institutions in the same way:

> DEFINITION 1: *A perfectly functioning set of legal institutions* is one which *always* generates a decision that best furthers the Comprehensive View guiding the legal system.

Now imagine a judge of the Scientific Policymaking persuasion whose task is to review the output of a set of perfectly functioning legal institutions. It should be plain that he would be a paradigm of perfect restraint, since he would never have reason to upset the decisions rendered initially by other institutions.

But, of course, our world is hardly any Policymaker's utopia; all sorts of decisions are being made that seem questionable under one or another Comprehensive View. Nonetheless, it is quite easy to advance a notion of judicial role that would lead a judge to act a part no different from the perfectly restrained judge of Utopia:

> DEFINITION 2: *A perfectly restrained* judge is one who *always* reviews the challenged decision before him *as if* it had been generated by a set of perfectly functioning institutions.

This is not to say, of course, that a perfectly restrained judge necessarily would believe that our society is one which is *in fact* well ordered. He might, as a sophisticated advocate of restraint, stand ready to recognize the existence of systematic malfunctioning; nonetheless, he may justify his refusal to take the flaws into account in his decisions by contending that the correction of injustice is a proper task for the political branches rather than the antidemocratic judiciary. Hence, there need be nothing at all wrong in having the court define its role in terms of a proposition that may not only be false, but obviously so. Indeed, it is precisely the counterfactual character of the role definition which permits one to account for the classic case posed by the political activist who transforms himself into a paragon of restraint upon ascending the bench. Before taking on his judicial role, the activist thought it perfectly proper to view the world in all its manifold imperfection and so took aggressive steps to remedy its failings; it is only because he believes his judicial role compels a different, though factually inaccurate, view of the world that restraint seems the proper course.

Nonetheless, it is doubtless true that, except for a few extremists like Learned Hand,[6] it is difficult to point to influential figures who come close to believing in *perfect* judicial restraint, as we have defined the term. If we hope to capture the mainstream of restrained opinion, then, we must come up with an idea of judicial role that is not quite so unbending. To do this, I shall make use of an idea that I owe to John Rawls. In his recent book, Rawls imagines a "well-ordered society" which stands at some indeterminate point between the present sorry reality and Utopia. Such a society has not been freed of injustice; nevertheless basic social, legal, and economic institutions have been structured in a way that is consistent with the prevailing Comprehensive View. Thus, while individuals may well act improperly in a particular case, the system generally performs consistently with basic principles.[7]

This notion of a well-ordered society permits one to specify a notion of *realistic* restraint that will better answer to our purpose of describing the present state of legal culture. In contrast to the perfectly restrained judge, this more moderate judicial type merely believes that judges should decide disputes *as if* they were living in a society with well-ordered, rather than perfectly functioning, institutions. Given this less extreme definition of his role, our moderately restrained judge will have no difficulty carving out a modest place for himself in constitutional adjudication. While he is obliged, by definition, to concede the legitimacy of basic economic, social, and political institutions, he may nevertheless invoke the power of judicial review as an appropriate remedy for those occasional failings that may be expected even in a well-ordered society. It is this modest role, I think, that encompasses the beliefs of that numerous band of restrained lawyers who simply wish to deny the court's right to fashion legal doctrine for the purpose of leading society down the road to Utopia. This aspiration can, by definition, never be indulged by the judge who acts as if he were *already* in a well-ordered society. For him, there is nothing left but to do his bit in trying to undo the inevitable mistakes committed by others who are striving to implement a particular Comprehensive View—with due recognition that courts too may often err.

It is this notion of realistic restraint that will play a central role in our essay. For, once it is accepted, it does not seem difficult to define an opposing conception of judicial role, which I shall attribute to the *innovative* judge. Unlike his restrained counterpart, the innovator thinks it appropriate for a judge to take into account the fact that, in one respect or another, the world he confronts falls short of a "well-ordered society." Hence, after defining the respects in which the world falls short of the "well-ordered" ideal, he will see nothing wrong in using his judicial office to improve the existing legal state of affairs.

Having marked a general contrast between two different ideas of judicial role, only the task of refining our concepts remains before we can employ the distinction in Scientific legal discussion. Refinement is required because the existing judicial corps exhibits many different kinds of restraint, many different forms of innovation—variations on a grand theme, each with its own particular implications for compensation law. To provide a structure that will permit us to grasp these important differences, we shall break up Rawls's notion of a well-ordered society into three component parts and clearly mark the way restrained and innovative judges view each component. The first element to which we shall give special treatment involves a proposition that deals with distributive justice:

> *Proposition A.* Judges are to assume that the distribution of property rights prevailing at Time One is generally consistent with the Comprehensive View they impute to the legal system, as would be the case in a well-ordered society.

It follows from our definitions that a restrained judge will affirm Proposition A, while an innovator will deny it. We shall, however, reserve special labels that describe more precisely judges' perspectives on the distributional issue: insofar as he affirms Proposition A, a judge will be called a *conservative;* insofar as he denies it, he will be called a *reformist.*

A second basic feature of a well-ordered society deals with the operation of other governmental institutions:

> *Proposition B.* Judges are to assume that nonjudicial organs of government generally act consistently with the Comprehensive View they impute to the legal system, as would be the case in a well-ordered society.

Once again, restrained judges affirm, and innovators deny, Proposition B. More specifically, judges who are restrained along this dimension will be called *deferential,* while innovators will be called *activists.*

Finally, the third feature of a well-ordered society involves a proposition of social psychology which deals with the attitude of citizens to their government. On the one hand, society may contain large groups who deny the value of the Comprehensive View invoked by the judges and so respond with a deep sense of grievance whenever their interests are denied legal protection. On the other hand, a society may be composed of citizens who—by and large—accept the values enshrined in the Comprehensive View and generally behave like "good losers" when they lose a lawsuit. It should be clear that the second state of affairs would be characteristic of a well-ordered society:

> *Proposition C.* Judges are to assume that the litigants, as good citizens, recognize that they are living in a well-ordered society and so will accept disadvantageous official decisions without a deep sense of grievance, unless they have special reason to believe that they are involved in one of the exceptional cases in which the system has malfunctioned.

The restrained judges who accept Proposition C will be called *principled* to denote their refusal to permit the hurt feelings of "bad losers" to alter a decision they think is otherwise required under the prevailing Comprehensive View. In contrast, the innovators who deny Proposition C will be called *pragmatists*, since they think it legitimate to reject a decision they would otherwise find legally binding in order to check the disaffection of a significant social group which rejected the reigning Comprehensive View.

While I take no particular joy in this proliferation of labels, it seems to me that they are essential to a sophisticated understanding of the range of options open in the Scientific interpretation of the compensation clause. For it should be apparent that constitutional doctrine need not be modeled exclusively upon the theory of restraint or innovation. Instead, it may consist of an intricate weave of elements drawn from both models. Nor does it even seem obviously desirable for judges always to conform to one or another pure type. As a consequence, it becomes of the first importance to develop a vocabulary which can express the subtler differences that provide the meat of legal disagreement as to the proprieties of judicial role. Given the difficulty of the subject, I have no doubt that our terms are too few rather than too many. Nevertheless, they at least permit us to conceive of such things as a judge who is generally *restrained* but is at times willing to indulge in certain forms of *activist* intervention, and so forth.[8] This will suffice to permit our doctrinal sketch to proceed.

TOWARD A SCIENTIFIC LANGUAGE?

It is time to recall the two main objectives set in the present chapter. To make a Scientific approach to compensation law at all plausible, it was first necessary to display a set of specialized and technical concepts, which did not depend upon the property-talk of the untrained layman and which enabled the profession to define the basic substantive problem posed by the compensation clause. In this, at least, we achieved an easy victory. Not only does such a Scientific vocabulary exist; all modern lawyers, insofar as they are Scientists, would use the *same* vocabulary to express the nature of their legal problem. Moreover, using the standard technical language leads to a distinctive understanding of the series of high-level abstractions contained in the constitutional command. Scientifically understood, a taking of property covers a very wide range of governmental activity indeed, making it all the more imperative to achieve a clear understanding of the basic legal principles—or Comprehensive View—that define the occasions upon which justice demands compensation.

All our Scientific challenges, however, are not destined to be easy ones. When we turned from substance to process, we came upon a very different scene. Not only was a single consensus view of judicial role absent; a single technical vocabulary had not even emerged which clearly expressed the nature of the underlying professional disagreement. There was, however, one aspect of the discussion that could serve at least as a small comfort. As a result of the long, complex, and often technical debate of the past half-century, the profession has accustomed itself to the idea that it does have something special to say about issues of institutional competence—things that would not occur even to intelligent laymen who were untrained in professional ways of thinking.

The ground, in short, is ready for a Scientific foundation. This said, I have only two things to claim for the rather primitive structure I have constructed. First, I hope you are persuaded that my notions of judicial restraint and innovation (as well as their subsequent refinements) follow in a straightforward fashion from the even more basic idea of Scientific Policymaking. Thus, if you believe that I have captured something important in my explanation of Scientific Policymaking, it should not be very difficult to accept the theory of judicial role which follows from it. Second, I should like to claim that my theory of judicial role does in fact provide a fruitful way of making sense of some of the basic issues underlying the long debate about judicial review that will continue to divide the profession within the foreseeable future. The initial test of this will be the extent to which the theory of judicial role in fact illuminates the discussion of the substance of compensation law to be attempted in the next two chapters.

3 Utilitarian Adjudication

CHOOSING A COMPREHENSIVE VIEW

Only one piece of the methodological puzzle remains to be solved before our model of constitutional adjudication becomes operational. Even after we have specified a judge's understanding of (a) the proper limits of his own role and (b) the basic structure of the compensation question, we shall be unable to define his preferred doctrinal solution until we are told (c) the substantive principles contained in the Comprehensive View he has chosen to guide his constitutional decisions. And it is at this point that perhaps the deepest challenge arises for those who wish to make good on the promise of Scientific Policymaking. For it is possible to imagine any number of Comprehensive Views—Marxist, Maoist, Existentialist, Absurdist—that a judge could potentially invoke to interpret the decisive concept of "just compensation" to be found in the constitutional text. Yet in making this choice, a judge surely is not entitled to roam the range of conceivable Comprehensive Views with the aim of selecting the one that suits his personal fancy. Instead, whatever his own personal predilections, the judge's choice of a *legally* binding Comprehensive View must be limited in a very constraining fashion. Yet what are these limits? How is the judge to sift the legally admissible Comprehensive View from all the others that are in fact passionately held in the world today, not to speak of those that merely seem plausible? This is the master question for the Policymaking judge, for whom the mainstream jurisprudential debate dealing with "the rule of recognition" would command far more than academic interest.[1] Despite the importance of the question, however, I shall not try to answer it. As in my treatment of the problem of institutional competence, my aim instead is to focus upon the ideas that are in fact powerful forces in the *present* legal culture—to explore the basic tensions in our *existing* legal system through an exploration of the compensation clause of our *existing* Constitution.

Once this limited field of vision is accepted, a most remarkable scene appears in view. For the fact is that lawyers—particularly those who pride themselves upon their sophistication—are increasingly willing to talk like Policymakers. Without troubling themselves over murky jurisprudential matters, they are simply invoking one or another Comprehensive View in the ordinary course of legal debate about this or that rule or decision. Moreover, if one attends to the substance of the discussion, one finds that rather than ranging widely over the endless possibilities, American lawyers are in fact limiting themselves to the elaboration of two different, but not *that* different, themes. One is "Efficiency"—which among the competing rules will maximize something-or-another-that-sounds-like-Social-Utility? The other theme is less well developed but is becoming clearer, if only in reaction to the growing Utilitarian chorus. This stream of talk I shall call Kantian simply to suggest its general concerns, if not usually its particular phrasing.

Our analytical path follows immediately from these observations. In this chapter we shall consider the way each important kind of restrained or innovative judge will deal with the compensation question if he adopts a Utilitarian Comprehensive View. The next chapter attempts a similar analysis of the various modes of Kantian constitutional adjudication. By indulging in this drastic bifurcation I do not mean to suggest that all those writers and lawyers who may be fairly placed within one or another of these two camps in fact hold identical views on all issues. Intratribal differences are always observable, often bitter, and sometimes important. Our task here is to trace the main line of analysis, deferring the elaboration of any particular variant to those who are sufficiently interested to join in the larger enterprise.

Of Judicial Role and Comprehensive View

How, then, will a Scientific judge who wishes to maximize social utility resolve the problem set for him by the compensation clause? I wish to establish that there is no single way to answer this question within our legal culture—that the proper utilitarian solution will depend upon the particular conception of judicial restraint or innovation that the decisionmaker considers to be most appropriate.[2] Yet this basic point opens up an embarrassment of expositional possibilities. In presenting the Utilitarian picture of compensation law, shall I begin from the standpoint of the perfectly restrained judge or should I start with his perfectly innovative counterpart? Or perhaps one or another model which mixes restraint and innovation provides the best entry point.

As a general matter, there is absolutely nothing to be said for giving expository priority to one or another of these approaches. Nevertheless, for the purposes of construing the compensation clause, I have found it most enlightening to begin with the purely restrained judicial type. While such a starting point would be most unrevealing for the interpretation of other basic constitutional texts, there is a sense in which just compensation law is of peculiar importance to judges who approach their task with the assumption that the distribution of property is basically just, as it would be in a "well-ordered" society. For it is these conservative judges who will find most attractive the symbolic affirmation of the status quo ante involved in compensating those injured by a legislatively inspired march to a better tomorrow. Since conservatism regarding the distribution of income is one of the principal aspects of judicial restraint—as I have defined the term—it will serve clarity to begin with the perfectly restrained judge and establish the importance of institutional role by showing how large doctrinal consequences may follow from even rather modest changes in this "pure" role specification. After considering the compensation principles that would be favored by a paragon of restraint who was (a) deferential, (b) conservative, and (c) principled, we shall introduce at first a single innovative element into the role characterization by dealing next with the judge who—while remaining both conservative and principled—adopted a variety of more activist stances. It is only at this point that we shall ring the doctrinal changes that follow upon embracing reformist rather than conservative principles, finally to consider the importance of the distinction between principled and pragmatic judges. By injecting innovative elements into the analysis in this sequential fashion, it will prove possible to sketch the rather complicated pattern of intermediate positions open to a judge with utilitarian opinions—a task all the more important since I suspect that the weight of constitutional opinion on judicial role has its center of gravity at neither of the polar extremes.

THE RESTRAINED INTERPRETATION OF THE CLAUSE

Two lines of argument would suggest themselves to the realistically restrained Scientific judge trying to make sense out of the compensation clause. We shall call the first argument the Appeal to General Uncertainty, because it is based on the fact that when any institution makes any decision which increases the level of uncertainty, this imposes costs upon all those citizens who already found their general social environment too risky. Apprised of the fact that property rights have been redistributed in cases like that of the Marshans, these risk-averse citizens will respond by investing extra resources in adaptive behavior that would have otherwise been spent obtaining positive utilities. While the size of these costs is (at least in principle) an empirical question, certain basic distinctions should be kept in mind by a judge wishing to assess the magnitude of uncertainty costs in a particular class of cases.[3]

Generally speaking, risk-averse individuals are faced with three options when apprised of the risk that future governmental regulation may make it more expensive to engage in a given activity.[4] First, they may seek to insulate themselves against the extra risk by insuring in the private market;

second, they may insulate themselves by reducing the amount they participate in the risky activity; third, they may simply bear the risk and continue as before. Now as a person becomes increasingly risk-averse, he will find it increasingly attractive to respond by selecting one of the first two strategies. It follows that, as these strategies become more expensive to implement, the Appeal to General Uncertainty becomes increasingly important. At the extreme, if it is especially difficult for people to insure against the risk or escape it by shifting resources into less risky alternatives, just compensation by the government becomes the only remaining way to save the risk-averse from accepting costs they might be willing to pay a good deal to avoid.[5]

Of course, our Utilitarian world may be inhabited not only by risk-averse citizens but by some risk-takers as well. And these people can be expected to welcome the fact that the world has become riskier and to reduce the resources they would otherwise expend in search of additional gambles not otherwise proffered in the normal course of life. While it is always an empirical question whether these cost savings are greater or less than those incurred by the risk-averse, it will often be true that the interests of the risk-averse will dominate in a sound felicific calculus.

Unfortunately, this fact, without more, will not permit litigants to argue that the Comprehensive View adopted by the Utilitarian judge requires their compensation. While there are costs involved in raising the level of uncertainty, there are also costs in reducing it by requiring governmental compensation: notably the costs involved in processing both deserving and undeserving lawsuits through the legal system to a successful conclusion.[6] Thus, the success of an Appeal to General Uncertainty turns on whether the total "uncertainty costs" (U) are greater or less than the "process costs" (P) involved in eliminating the uncertainty.[7] While, as we have suggested, there is absolutely no guarantee that $U > P$ most of the time, it is nevertheless possible to isolate the occasions when the appeal is entitled to particular weight by a restrained Utilitarian judge. Thus, if the claimant's problem seems to be one in which process costs are *exceptionally* low, or uncertainty costs *exceptionally* high, the judge should recognize that the appeal is relatively more likely to be grounded on sound Utilitarian reasoning. Of course it is always possible that, even when uncertainty costs are exceptionally high, process costs could be higher. (Similarly, when process costs are low, uncertainty costs could be even lower.) Nevertheless, a strikingly high U or low P should at least suggest the wisdom of a more searching and sympathetic scrutiny if the judge is properly to perform his restrained mission of searching out hidden lodes of Utility which have escaped the attention of a well-ordered set of political institutions.[8]

The Appeal to General Uncertainty does not by its own terms discriminate between risk-creating actions undertaken by the government and those undertaken by other institutions. Regardless of the source of the risky action, good felicific accounting may suggest that state compensation will maximize overall utility.[9] But a second set of policy guidelines may be generated if the restrained judge narrows his focus so as to concentrate upon the more particular failures of decision-making even in a "well-ordered" Utilitarian state. For it should be recalled that, under Proposition B, it remains possible that the Marshans' case represents one of those exceptional situations in which the political branches have made a mistake in their felicific calculation. And when this occurs, a special loss will be suffered as a result of the property redistribution at Time Two that is quite different from that contemplated by the Appeal to General Uncertainty. For under Proposition C the citizens of the well-ordered polity may be expected to endure restrictive legislation without complaint only if they believe that it is in fact justified on Utilitarian grounds. If, however, the Marshans believe that theirs is the exceptional case in which the felicific calculus has gone awry, they will suffer a special form of disutility as a result of the redistribution of property rights—the outrage and demoralization of good citizens who believe themselves victims of unprincipled behavior. Indeed, outrage of this kind may spread far beyond the small Marshan circle to many others who learn of the Marshans' plight. While the resulting disaffection may not manifest itself in any of the immediate and palpable ways in which risk-averse individuals respond to general uncertainty, it is of obvious concern to the restrained Utilitarian judge, who is in principle equally mindful of concealed psychological affronts as he is of more obvious forms of distress; and who is, moreover, alive to the long-run disutility attendant upon citizen disaffection with the state's decisionmaking processes.

Having isolated a second form of disutility, which we shall call Citizen Disaffection, that may result from a redistribution of property bundles, the question remains whether the compensation clause has a role in an overall policy designed to reduce disaffection to its optimal level. To make the matter complicated, it is only necessary to recognize that even good citizens may be mistaken in their criticisms of the state's cost-benefit analysis. Thus, even if the court believes the Marshans' attack on the legislative cost-benefit analysis to be wrong on the merits, it does not follow that a principled Utilitarian judge will invariably discount the Appeal to Disaffection. Right or wrong, the Marshans may still *feel* disaffected—and if the sum of uncertainty and disaffection costs is greater than the process costs involved in administering a compensation scheme,[10] the Marshans should be paid even though the court believes them wrong on the merits. Moreover, even a deferential judge may properly fear that the costs of disaffection will fail to receive their full weight by decisionmakers operating within a well-ordered framework. It takes exceptional compassion and insight for a decisionmaker to come to terms fully with the fact that others honestly and in good faith believe that his decision is just plain wrong. If there ever is a case for relying on a disinterested third party to make an independent assessment of a special kind of cost, it is this one.

This is not to say, however, that the judge's view of the merits of the Marshans' claim is altogether irrelevant to an assessment of the weight to be given to Citizen Disaffection.

If the felicific merits of the statute seem quite clear to the judge, he will consider it unlikely that the Marshans will have reasonable doubts as to the good Utilitarian foundation for the property redistribution. And so long as this is true, a principled judge will be confident that the Marshans, as good citizens, will not become unduly disaffected by an adverse decision of their compensation claim (recall Proposition C, on p. 38). Thus, the Appeal to Citizen Disaffection will seem increasingly plausible as the Utilitarian merits of the legislative calculus seem increasingly uncertain to the judge himself. At a certain point, of course, judicial doubts about the calculation will ripen into a decision entirely invalidating the challenged legislation. Since our restrained judge is deferential,[11] however, the case against the new statute may not seem to him sufficiently compelling to warrant this extreme step. Nevertheless, the court may well find the level of Citizen Disaffection with the statute of be sufficiently high to warrant compensation for the losers, even where there are rather considerable process costs involved in the attempt. Thus, the Appeal to Citizen Disaffection may be understood here as a technique by which a restrained judiciary—without committing itself to any ultimate constitutional principle—may nonetheless signal to the legislature that it is approaching the verge of constitutional propriety. Indeed, it is a way of opening a dialogue between branches of government on constitutional principle of a sort whose importance to restrained judicial theory was properly emphasized by the late Alexander Bickel. To put the point in Bickelian terms, compensation law may serve as a passive virtue—albeit of a relatively active sort.[12]

We can sum up the two different Utilitarian appeals within the framework of a single equation. The critical question, in any given class of cases,[13] is whether $P \gtrless U + D$, where $P =$ process costs, $U =$ uncertainty costs, and $D =$ the costs of citizen disaffection. If $P > U + D$, compensation should be denied; if $P < U + D$, it should be granted.[14] To put the point in terms more useful to courts, restrained Utilitarian judges should be more responsive to just compensation claims as process costs decline, as uncertainty costs increase, and as the general utility of the legislation is increasingly subject to reasonable doubt.

THE ACTIVIST INTERPRETATION OF THE CLAUSE

Thus far our sketch builds upon the pathbreaking analysis advanced by Professor Frank Michelman some time ago in the *Harvard Law Review*.[15] It is true that, in his general account of the Utilitarian's compensation calculus, Michelman does not relate his argument as clearly as he might to the restrained conception of judicial role.[16] Nor does he distinguish clearly between the Appeal to General Uncertainty and the Appeal to Citizen Disaffection.[17] On a substantive rather than methodological level, Michelman seems to emphasize far too little the importance of reasonable doubt as to the Utilitarian basis of the challenged legislation in leading a restrained judge to order compensation of those who have lost by the doubtful decision.[18] Nevertheless, I am happy to emphasize my indebtedness to Michelman's account.[19]

It is time, though, to move beyond the perfectly restrained interpretation of the clause that Michelman's approach—as reinterpreted here [20]—represents. In doing so, however, it will serve little purpose to move at once to the polar opposite represented by the "pure" judicial innovator. Such laboratory purity simply does not exist in the real world of constitutional interpretation, however much it may serve as a convenient reducing agent for the more fervent believers in judicial restraint. What is required instead is the gradual introduction of innovative elements into the restrained model, slowly moving to a conception of judicial role that is closer to the pure innovative type than it is to the pure restrained type. If we introduce these innovative elements carefully enough, it will be possible to suggest the delicate greys that in fact predominate in an accurate portrayal of the American judicial mind, Scientifically understood.

Let us begin our Scientific transformation with a critical scrutiny of the restrained judge's understanding of the operation of nonjudicial institutions, reflected in Proposition B (p. 37) in the skeletal structure of a well-ordered society.

While our restrained judge was obliged to assume that the
other parts of government generally functioned felicifically, it
is possible to generate a variety of activist positions by modifying Proposition B in one or another way. Since I shall restrict myself to the range of current professional opinion, I
will not discuss the "pure" activist who denies that judicial
deference is *ever* appropriate. Instead, I shall be dealing with
those "discriminating" activists who do not deny that they
should often show great deference to the judgments of other
branches of government, but merely wish to mark out situations in which the "normal" felicific functioning of lawmaking
institutions cannot be so readily presupposed. The principal
task then becomes the identification of those structural conditions under which the normal presumption of regularity
attaching to the conduct of nonjudicial officials should no
longer be indulged with its accustomed weight.

This discriminating form of activism is of course familiar in
modern constitutional law, where so much can be traced to the
Carolene Products footnote.[21] It fell to Professor Joseph Sax,
however, to bring the concerns of this more general movement
to the compensation problem. Thus, in the first of his two
important essays on the subject,[22] Sax urges us to recognize
that the modern welfare state seeks to discharge governmental
functions far more ambitious than those attempted by the
watchman state of classic laissez-faire theory. No longer do
officials content themselves with mediating conflicts that private parties are unable or unwilling to resolve by other means;
in addition to its "mediational" functions, the state has also
taken on tasks in which its officers are called upon to command enormous resources and large bureaucracies—functions
which may justly be called "entrepreneurial."[23]

This fact would be relevant to a Utilitarian judge of the
activist persuasion if it seemed reasonable to modify our
deferential Proposition B in the following way:

> *Proposition B₁.* An activist judge may appropriately as-
> sume that, in general, governmental enterprises involving
> large bureaucracies and vast resources tend to self-

aggrandizement. That is, they will systematically wish to pursue, and succeed in mobilizing resources for, projects that are not justified on a sober Utilitarian cost-benefit analysis.

I shall not attempt a lengthy defense of this intuitively plausible hypothesis, simply noting that modern political science does nothing to undermine it.[24] Indeed, the fact that the self-aggrandizement hypothesis does *not* seem to require complex empirical verification argues for the propriety of its use as a basic postulate of constitutional doctrine. While constitutional adjudication may sometimes require judges to evaluate complex and problematic propositions of empirical political science, it surely is far better to avoid building an impressive doctrinal edifice on so shaky a foundation.

In any event, once the self-aggrandizement hypothesis is conceded, the rest of the argument seems quite straightforward for the activist Utilitarian judge. Given the tendency of the governmental entrepreneur to discount the utilities of those it injures, a strict compensation rule will require the entrepreneur to take into account costs that will otherwise be ignored or belittled. As a result of the compensation requirement, these external costs will now represent a money drain on resources otherwise available to the agency, thereby creating internal incentives to consider them seriously in felicific calculation. Moreover, the potential ambiguities involved in an approach that seems to depend so heavily upon characterizing a governmental agency as "entrepreneurial" rather than "mediational" can generally be resolved so long as the larger purpose of the distinction is kept clearly in mind. Rather than engaging in an arbitrary exercise in stipulative definition, the distinction invites the judge to ask whether, as a person steeped in the practical operation of government, he believes the agency to be of a size and structure such as to make the self-aggrandizement hypothesis particularly plausible. If the agency passes this test, it qualifies as entrepreneurial; if not, mediational. While this test allows of doubtful cases, it seems no more vague than many administered by judges. Thus, it would seem pretty clear that the Defense Department or a Highway Department or the National Park Service would fall on the entrepreneurial side of the line; while a local zoning board would not.[25]

A second concern expressed in Sax's writings is also readily accommodated within the activist Utilitarian's concerns. Here the focus is on a class of decisions which inevitably contain a large component of arbitrariness yet which must necessarily be made if a project deemed desirable is to be accomplished at all. For example, after a city has decided to institute a system of vest-pocket parks within the town center, it must determine the particular sites that will serve this purpose. Yet competent cost-benefit analysis may reveal that any number of sites are equally desirable. Similarly, the precise location of a highway may, within broad limits, be a matter of indifference from the point of view of aggregate social utility; yet a determinate decision must be made.

In cases like these the front-line decisionmaker must inevitably make a decision that cannot be intelligently reviewed by his superiors. Yet, once unreviewable discretion is granted, will it not be abused by low-level officials? Will not each endangered property owner have every incentive to bribe the decisionmaker to burden somebody else? Given the difficulty of a probing review, will not the administrator have every incentive to sell off his decision to the highest bidder? It does not seem particularly daring for an activist judge to respond to these dangers by adopting a rule of special vigilance:

> *Proposition B_2.* In cases where a front-line decisionmaker is obliged to select from a class of similarly situated property owners a small subset who will bear the burden of a collective enterprise, it is appropriate for an activist judge to fear that corrupt or partisan factors have led the decisionmaker to burden one, rather than another, group of property owners.

Given Proposition B_2, an expanded compensation practice has two attractive properties. First, the promise of just compensation will often be enough to eliminate the incentives for bribery that would otherwise exist—if Jones will be compensated when his land is taken for a highway, there is far less reason for him to pay off the Highway Department to route the road elsewhere. Second, the payment of compensation should, at the very least, serve to reduce the serious disaffection that results when a citizen suspects (but cannot prove) that his heavy losses are due simply to corrupt or partisan official motivation. Hence, it does not seem wrong—at least for a judge with a modestly activist bent—to construct a set of doctrines to serve as "the equal protection dimension of compensation law," as Sax aptly puts it.[26]

We have, then, isolated two governmental structures in which a discriminating activist may plausibly view nonjudicial lawmakers with less than the usual deference. In the first, an agency's structure makes the risk of institutional aggrandizement so obvious that its claim to being a "well-ordered" institution seems problematic; in the second, the agency is obliged to burden one property owner rather than another when its organizational objectives do not permit it to derive a reason for choosing a unique owner as the one who will most appropriately bear the cost. This much of Sax is, I think, of incontrovertible value to any Utilitarian willing to indulge in any form of judicial activism, however discriminating.

Before turning to those elements in Sax's approach that seem a good deal more troublesome, we can consolidate our understanding of the Utilitarian approach by considering more exactly the relationship between the contributions made to compensation theory by its two leading contemporary interpreters: how precisely do Sax and Michelman—as reinterpreted here—fit together?[27] Are they at odds with each other or can their insights be reconciled? Of course, Sax's analysis requires a judge to be more activist than does Michelman's. Nonetheless, it is possible to detect a common theme; the bridge concept is, I think, the notion of Citizen Disaffection. As we have seen, the Appeal to Citizen Disaffection is ultimately grounded in the judge's perception that the Utili-

tarian justification of the challenged action is open to substantial doubt even among good Utilitarian citizens. Sax's
great achievement lies in bringing this general concern to
bear in the analysis of the concrete workings of the modern
bureaucratic state. For there can be little doubt that Citizen
Disaffection will be an inevitable by-product of the self-
aggrandizing and discretionary character of much bureaucratic
conduct. And it is at least possible that the judicious use of
compensation law will significantly reduce disaffection within
a wide variety of bureaucratic decisionmaking frameworks.
Thus, it is not at all difficult to fit Sax and Michelman into a
larger Utilitarian structure. Both may be understood to affirm
the importance of Citizen Disaffection—only Sax explicitly invites the court to adopt a discriminating form of activism
which Michelman does not require, though he does not explicitly reject it either.

The Further Reaches of the
Activist Interpretation

We are not done, however, with Professor Sax's efforts to
ring the changes on judicial activism. In a recent article in the
Yale Law Journal,[28] Sax repudiates his earlier effort to re-
orient takings law around the entrepreneurial/mediational
distinction, and instead advocates an approach which would
drastically restrict the scope of the compensation clause to
cases that fall within the "equal protection" rationale suggested by Proposition B_2. During the seven years that separate his two articles, Sax apparently confronted another
kind of breakdown in nonjudicial lawmaking that dwarfed in
significance the tendency to bureaucratic self-aggrandizement
that he had previously identified. The institutional breakdown that now most concerned him was the asserted malfunction of the legislative, rather than the administrative-bureau-
cratic, process. Sax emphasizes the difficulties a large group
encounters when it seeks to organize itself for political action,
especially when each individual group member has relatively
little at stake in the enterprise. The story is by now familiar.[29]

Despite the fact that the damage suffered by the group as a whole may be large indeed, each group member may suffer a relatively small individual loss and find it in his interest to take a free ride on the political efforts initiated by others to redress their common grievance. After all, if the others are successful in inducing a legislative redistribution of property rights, the free rider may well gain the benefits of political action without bearing any of its costs. To a self-interested economic man the prospect is delightful; and if enough people behave as the economic model indicates, the result will be that interests in which multitudes are affected will tend to be at a disadvantage in the legislative process if they are obliged to engage in a political struggle with a small number of opponents, each of whom has a great deal at stake. While their adversaries will have little difficulty organizing their political forces, the large diffuse group will carry far less weight than their interests deserve in the ideal Utilitarian calculus. It is this picture of the political process that seems to motivate Sax's new-found hostility to compensation practices. Apparently, the concern is that a compensation requirement will place yet another obstacle in the path of those groups— notably environmentalists—whose road to political efficacy is already improperly obstructed by organizational difficulties.[30]

Yet surely this is take too simple a view of the relationship between compensation law and political action. Even if the model sketched above were to constitute the whole truth about political efficacy—something which is most emphatically not the case—the result suggested still does not follow with anything like the inexorability called up in casual conversations on the subject. Indeed, it is quite easy to use this simple model to suggest the wisdom, rather than the folly, of a wide-ranging compensation practice. The counterargument proceeds by focusing upon the motives of the relatively small group of property owners whom Sax believes to have an improper organizational advantage in the political struggle: why precisely is it that they are expending their scarce resources on politics rather than using the money to buy other goods?

The answer—especially given the materialistic cast of the model—seems reasonably easy to establish. The property owners, it is fair to guess, are spending money in politics principally because they are afraid that restrictive laws will be passed *without their receiving compensation.* If they were in fact assured of obtaining compensation to cover the losses generated by restrictive legislation, they would no longer have any direct financial incentive to continue the political struggle. Thus, rather than making their task more difficult, a compensation practice could well make the environmentalists' struggle an easier one. Rather than confronting fierce resistance from a small number of well-organized property owners, they will instead do battle principally with the representatives of a diffuse group of taxpayers who would—if asked—be unwilling to pay the higher taxes required by the enactment of restrictive environmental laws which guaranteed compensation to those particularly affected. Yet this numerous band of anti-environmentalist taxpayers may well be as difficult to organize as the environmentalists themselves.

It follows that Sax has moved far too quickly from (a) the admitted free-rider difficulties of environmental groups to (b) the need for restricting the range of compensation law. The "free-rider" argument, by itself, does not provide a convincing reason to believe that the outcome of the environmentalist-*taxpayer* struggle under a pro-compensation policy will be less favorable to environmental interests than will the outcome of an environmentalist-*property owner* struggle occurring under an anti-compensation policy. Of course, the "free-ride" phenomenon is but one of many in political life, and it may well be that Sax's intuition could be vindicated in a more fully developed model that took into account ideology, political parties, and corporate-bureaucratic behavior, among other things. All I wish to suggest is that the relationship between compensation practices and political efficacy is *far* more complicated than it would seem at first glance; and that the activist case for a dramatic restriction in the scope of compensation law has yet to be made.

The Reformist Interpretation
of the Clause

Thus far, we have considered the implications of changing only a single assumption that gave shape to the jurisprudential universe inhabited by the restrained Utilitarian judge. Doubtless there remain unexamined a number of interesting activist ways of modifying the restrained judge's deference toward other institutions; [31] it has been my intention to say enough merely to suggest the main lines of the analysis. It remains to perform a similar sketch of the legal prospect afforded to the judicial innovator if he subjects Propositions A and C, describing the distributional and social psychological dimensions of the well-ordered society, to analogous modifications. Let us turn first to the restrained judge's conservative stipulation of the generally utility-maximizing character of the distribution of property rights obtaining at Time One (Proposition A, on p. 37). If the innovator wishes to reject this general endorsement of the status quo, there are several reformist positions he might adopt, each with different implications for a proper construction of the compensation clause.

The most modest kind of reformer is the judge who, while refusing to accept the conservative's view of the status quo, also refuses to commit himself to the proposition that the existing distribution is affirmatively unjust. Instead this modest reformer simply takes an agnostic position on the Utilitarian foundation of the distribution of property, and expresses complete ignorance as to the degree to which the state of affairs prevailing at Time One can be justified in terms of the prevailing Comprehensive View. Given the judge's agnosticism, it seems almost certain that he will defer on this question to the legislature's judgment.[32] Thus, if the legislature seems to be proceeding on the assumption that the general distribution of property at Time One was just, the agnostic judge has no reason to doubt the validity of this assumption, and his analysis of the compensation issue will proceed as if he were a conservative judge.

But suppose the legislature's action is proceeding on a different premise. Suppose the principal reason the law restricting the Marshans has been passed is the belief that they have been getting too much utility, and the Earthlings too little, if society is to reach an overall maximum. Once again, as an agnostic, the judge has no good reason to question this judgment any more than he has the alternative one. Only this time the legislative purpose *does* make a difference in the analysis. If the legislative action is premised on the notion that the Marshans have previously had an overly large slice of the utility pie, it would obviously defeat this judgment if the court were to decree that the Marshans be compensated for their loss. Hence, since the agnostic is unwilling to impugn the validity of the legislature's distributional judgment, compensation must be denied regardless of the preceding analysis.

It follows that the agnostic judge will be very much alive to the need for ascertaining the principal purposes motivating the challenged legislative decision. In one way or another, he must ascertain whether the statute is principally grounded in a judgment that a particular class in the population *generally* has too much utility for society's good, in which case compensation must be denied; or whether the legislature instead proceeded on the theory that while the general distributive pattern is sound, overall utility may be maximized yet further by the reallocation of a particular class of property rights, in which case the usual conservative analysis of takings law applies. In terms of our standard hypothetical case, has the legislature acted against the Marshans because they are too rich for society's good or because there is some peculiar inefficiency involved in marshfilling, quite apart from the general principles upon which property is distributed in society?

Within the context of the present legal culture, this particular question is an easy one. It is a rare legislator *in our society* who sees important questions of class justice involved in the marshfilling ordinance. (Not that it is impossible to imagine a society in which important groups of legislators understood the marshfilling issue in class terms. But ours is not at present such a society; and we are engaged in ascertaining the purposes of existing legislatures.) [33] In contrast, it is also easy to think of types of legislation in which distributive considerations are typically paramount in every legislator's mind. Tax legislation falls into this category, which is probably one powerful reason that the Scientific judge will not press the compensation question too fiercely in connection with legislation taking that form.[34] And there are doubtless many hard cases, in which the standard intractable difficulties inherent in the ascertainment of legislative purpose will arise to trouble us. I hope, however, that none of my readers will be unduly disturbed if I keep this particunlar skeleton safely cabined during the present voyage.[35]

So much for the agnostic; on to the judge who believes, for one reason or another, that he is better able to assess the overall felicity of the income distribution than is the political process. Needless to say, this mode of judicial innovation need not take the extreme form in which the judge thinks himself entitled to impose a fixed and unchanging pattern upon the income shares possessed by one or another class in the population.[36] Instead, the distributive judgment may take the form of a principle rather than an ironclad rule,[37] authorizing the judge to give at least some, though not necessarily decisive, weight to distributional factors in devising a doctrinal response. Since we are still operating within a Utilitarian framework, probably the most plausible principle would be grounded on the familiar claim that marginal utility should generally be understood to decline with increasing income.[38] Assuming this to be so, the reformist judge would skew his doctrinal response in such a way as to advantage the poor, except in those cases (whose frequency is a matter of wide disagreement) in which the material losses suffered by the rich would be so great as to offset the fact that their marginal utility is lower than the poorer beneficiaries of the program. If this approach were applied to compensation law, the result would be a systematic tendency to favor the protection of those interests typically held by poor people—residential leases and the like—while systematically slighting those forms of property—undeveloped real estate, perhaps—typically held by rich people like the Marshans.

In weighing this approach, however, even a reformist judge —committed to redistributionism in the name of the Constitution—may well take pause at the prospect of selecting the compensation clause as a principal vehicle for his endeavors. There is, I think, an almost inevitably conservative quality to compensation litigation, however much a reformer may try to write an opinion that avoids the symbolic affirmation of the status quo ante involved in compensating property owners aggrieved by the concededly legitimate exercise of public power. Consequently, rather than seeking to fashion the compensation clause self-consciously to his purposes, it may better serve the reformer's larger program to limit drastically the occasions upon which *any* kind of compensation claim will be vindicated—thereby indicating to the general population that undue reliance on the existing distribution of property relationships is not a part of the long-run, utility-maximizing solution to society's welfare problem. This is, of course, the most extreme reformist solution to the problem of interpretation, and one which is not likely to be publicly embraced by many judges who manage to gain appointment under either Democratic or Republican administrations.

Pragmatic Interpretations of the Clause

We turn finally to social psychology. Under Proposition C, our restrained judge indulged the principled assumption that his fellow citizens were all good Utilitarians who would not grieve much over their loss once they were convinced that the redistribution was soundly justified by Utilitarian principles. What are the consequences that follow if the judge takes it upon himself to fashion doctrine in a pragmatic fashion, explicitly taking into account the fact that substantial numbers of his fellow citizens do not necessarily evaluate social conflict in the way good Utilitarians should?

I shall argue that the doctrinal implications of such a move toward pragmatism would be significant indeed. One of the major concerns we have traced in the Utilitarian approach is the fear lest good citizens be demoralized when they see that their rights are compromised in ways not clearly justified on utility maximizing grounds. Yet this concern would seem misplaced if the bulk of the citizenry were *not* good Utilitarians, since it is difficult to believe that these non-Utilitarians would be greatly demoralized upon learning that the state had been untrue to its own invalid principles. Thus, as the number of non-Utilitarians in the population increases, it seems likely that pragmatic judges would take the Appeal to Citizen Disaffection, and related doctrines, less seriously than before.

Indeed, the pragmatist might well be tempted to go further. If a significant number of citizens held a particular non-Utilitarian creed, it is likely they would feel particularly intense dissatisfaction on occasions when good Utilitarians would feel no similar disaffection—and vice versa. Thus, the pragmatic judge may be tempted to compensate citizens for disaffections they ought *not* to feel if they had been good Utilitarians, so long as the costs of doing so were not greater than the disutility saved. Imagine, for example, that a large fundamentalist sect, which rejected Utilitarianism as evil, would become exceedingly disaffected if church property were subjected to restrictive regulations, however justified this would be on other felicific grounds. If disaffection would be reduced by compensation, the pragmatic judge might well be tempted to require payment even in circumstances in which it would otherwise be unjustified. Or, to take a case that is central, imagine that a large group of people committed the error that separates untrained laymen from Scientific lawyers and mistakenly thought they owned things rather than mere bundles of rights. If this group became especially disaffected when their claims of ownership were undercut by state regulation, the pragmatic judge might be sympathetic to their complaint, even though compensation would not be justified under any of the other rubrics of Utilitarian doctrine.

It would seem, however, that even a judge committed to

other modes of innovative analysis would be mindful of the
deep institutional difficulties involved in *constitutionally* requiring compensation to reduce forms of disaffection felt only
by those holding anti-Utilitarian views. After all, the legislature has, by hypothesis, already considered whether overall
utility will be served by granting compensation for the affront
to anti-Utilitarian sensibilities. By deciding against payment,
it may have found the special pain suffered by anti-Utilitarians
outweighed by the pain of good Utilitarians who would be
distressed at the prospect of the Marshans obtaining money
simply because they (or others) have failed to think about the
issue in a way that clearly revealed the overall balance of
social utility. Moreover, quite apart from the affront to good
Utilitarians, the legislature could well conclude that denying
compensation would serve therapeutic purposes, inducing the
anti-Utilitarians to reconsider the character of beliefs which,
by hypothesis, do not serve the general felicific good. Finally,
the legislature may have reasoned that the legal recognition of
a right to be compensated on grounds that are proper only on
one or another non-Utilitarian ideology would, on a symbolic
level, be generally interpreted as a declaration that Utilitarianism was no longer the Comprehensive View that governed the adjustment of legal relations in a good society.

This enumeration of grounds for restraint should suffice to
chill even an ardent innovative heart—so long as it beats
within the breast of a judge who wholeheartedly approaches
the task of adjudication as a Scientific Policymaker committed
to the Utilitarian Comprehensive View. To put the institutional point broadly, if politicians are good at anything, they
are good at tempering the rigors of the prevailing Comprehensive View so as to accommodate the hurt feelings of those
who fail (or refuse) to think like Scientific Utilitarians when
approaching the business of resolving social conflict. And if
even politicians do not find the claims of pragmatism sufficient
to outweigh the demands of principle, why should judges be
so inclined? Removed as they are from day-to-day politics,

surely they are in a poor position to introduce pragmatic factors into the case when the politicians themselves have seen no need to do so.

This is not to say, however, that judges should never consider pragmatic arguments relevant in constitutional adjudication. Often enough, the legislature itself will pass a statute that cannot be justified on grounds of Utilitarian principle but must be based entirely on pragmatic considerations. And in such a case, courts may well have to judge whether the pragmatic arguments are sufficiently weighty to warrant upholding the unprincipled action. Consider, for example, the problem that would arise if the legislature pragmatically granted payment to the Marshans even though this could not be justified on principled utility-maximizing grounds. If this decision is challenged in court (by a taxpayer, let us say) the relevance of pragmatic argument to the ultimate constitutional judgment is far easier to appreciate. Since the legislation cannot by hypothesis be justified by an appeal to the utility-maximizing principle, the decisive issue would be whether the court should defer to the legislature's decision that pragmatic factors were sufficiently persuasive to uphold the grant of compensation anyway. And with this the issue, it is easy to imagine an activist judge inquiring quite closely into the validity of the legislature's pragmatic judgment before he would assent to its constitutionality.

Nonetheless, this more appropriate kind of pragmatic inquiry need not detain us here. For we are not concerned, in this book at least, with the interesting range of issues that are presented by a wrongful legislative *grant* of compensation. Instead, we mean only to explore the existing body of constitutional compensation doctrine, which concerns itself exclusively with the wrongful legislative *denial* of payment. Given this focus, judges will only have occasion to consider pragmatic arguments that the political branches have already found unpersuasive. It follows that a judge who is willing to grant even the most limited deference to political institutions will find pragmatism a peculiarly uncongenial virtue in his effort to understand just compensation law from a Utilitarian point of view.

A UTILITARIAN VIEW OF EXISTING DOCTRINE

We are now in a position to describe the basic legal trends that would be discernible in a regime in which judges understood themselves as Scientific Policymakers committed to the implementation of a Utilitarian Comprehensive View. Eschewing all talk about the intrinsic rights of a property owner, the courts would self-consciously explore the "real issue," understood as the identification of the social group which can bear the burden entailed by the new legislative decision with the smallest loss in overall utility. Judicial discussion of the ease of insurance, the costs of disaffection, and the costs of settlement would abound. Similarly, the degree to which one or another form of administrative agency could abuse the Utilitarian calculus would be a matter earnestly considered, especially by activists, as would the relationship of just compensation law to the overall distribution of property rights. In contrast, even those who were generally innovative would be quite wary about rewarding those who suffer from forms of disaffection that would not be indulged by good Scientific Utilitarians; more particularly, there would be little judicial inclination to second-guess a legislative decision to deny compensation to those benighted souls who insist on payment simply because they thought they "owned" the thing subjected to one or another form of regulation or control.

Having attempted a thumbnail sketch of the plausible modalities of utilitarian doctrine, it is time to recall the ultimate objectives of the exercise. The first of these has, I hope, already been accomplished. My aim has been to establish Scientific Utilitarianism as a cultural reality of prime importance in American law today. I have sought to convince you by providing a concrete example of the Scientific Utilitarian's method in action—from a statement of the substantive problem, to a specification of judicial role, to the derivation of basic doctrinal solutions. By examining, perhaps too laboriously, each piece of the methodological puzzle, my intention was not to shock, or even so much as ruffle, the professional sensibilities of my lawyer-readers, but merely to organize and clarify kinds of arguments with whose general character they were already perfectly familiar. For only in this way is it possible to establish Scientific Utilitarianism as a *conventional method of modern legal argument which may be used as a matter of course by well-trained professionals* rather than as an interesting rite practiced in some exotic legal culture. Similarly, now that each piece of the puzzle is in place, the larger pattern revealed should not seem startling, especially to those who are acquainted with the evolving pattern of doctrinal discussion in a wide range of legal areas, from common law subjects, like torts [39] and property,[40] to the more modern fields of antitrust,[41] taxation,[42] and industrial regulation.[43]

But I do not wish to leave the case for the *legal* relevance of Scientific Utilitarianism entirely at the mercy of my readers' lawyerly intuitions. There are somewhat harder facts that also make the point in the context of our concrete constitutional problem. It is a fact that Michelman and Sax have both written important commentaries from a Scientific Utilitarian's point of view. It is also a fact that these commentaries have spawned others,[44] and are perceived as a beacon of light in an otherwise desperate darkness. Not surprisingly, these academic writings are already being considered seriously by courts as they struggle with the legal consequences of the environmental revolution.[45] And there is every reason to think that judicial reliance on academic doctrine will increase as the legislative challenge to traditional private property rights increases in its breadth and intensity.[46]

Yet, in saying all this, I mean only to mark the path toward the second main objective motivating our search in the labyrinth. For my aim in developing the Utilitarian Policymaker's approach to the compensation clause is hardly to convince anyone that it represents the only path to Legal Truth that may be traveled by a competent lawyer of the present day. While Michelman and Sax have prepared the way for a powerful formulation of legal doctrine, it does not follow that the present corps of judges have already taken up the banner of Scientific Utilitarianism as their own. Indeed, my main aim is to convince you of a very different truth. While Scientific Policymaking is undoubtedly the most dynamic tendency in the law today, it has not yet transformed all legal doctrine in its own image. Though signs of discontent are visible everywhere, I intend to argue that compensation law has yet to make a decisive break with deeply entrenched Observing ways. Indeed, it is this fact which makes the conflict between Ordinary Observing and Scientific Policymaking a central professional problem for the present generation.

Now, in the second half of the book, I shall try to establish this claim about existing law in a systematic way.[47] It is possible, however, to gain a good deal of insight simply by comparing the conventional treatment of a standard case with the analysis suggested by the present chapter. Consider, then, the way a conventional judge would appraise the Marshans' law suit. By a conventional judge I mean someone who is content to ground his decision on the bedrock of conventional legal wisdom,[48] without pausing to inspect the signs of doctrinal erosion that mar the landscape. For such a judge the first relevant point is that the government has in no way denied the Marshans' title to their property or taken possession of their land.[49] Having satisfied himself that there is no taking so far as title or possession is concerned, the judge would next turn to consider the extent to which the land's market value had diminished as a result of the regulation: if the property had been rendered virtually worthless, the judge would, at the very least, profess concern;[50] but if the price remained considerable, he would tolerate a very appreciable drop in market value—like the eighty percent loss suffered by the Marshans—without upsetting the statute.[51] Even if the land's value had plummeted to the desolate region near absolute zero, however, the Marshans' success would not be at all certain. For their claim will then be tested one final time when the judge undertakes to determine whether marsh-filling constitutes a "noxious use" or whether, instead, such a use is sufficiently innocent as to justify compensation.[52] Typically, this final decision will be rendered without any analysis whatever, and when something is attempted it will be so obscure as to quite baffle the Scientific spirit.[53] Nevertheless, with the pronouncement on the noxious or innocent character of the use, the analysis will come to an end. While the chances of the Marshans clearing this final hurdle are not bad,[54] it is very likely that they will find themselves disqualified from recovery at an earlier stage, since their land remains quite valuable even after the regulation has been put into force.[55]

Putting the likely outcome to one side for a moment, I think it fair to say that this very common form of analysis would deeply distress the Scientific Utilitarian. It is not so much that the three-stage approach—title or possession; diminution of value; noxious or innocent use—is so very simple-minded. Indeed, simplicity is a great virtue for the Scientific mind. It is rather that the categories have so little to do with the "real issues" as a Utilitarian would understand them.[56] Considering, first, the Marshans' Appeal to Citizen Disaffection, a good Utilitarian judge would doubtless wish to understand the extent to which the marshland statute could be supported by sound felicific calculation. If, as will often be the case, he learns that the ecological regulation is based upon the flimsiest technical analysis,[57] this should count as a reason for giving considerable weight to the disaffection suffered by the Marshans. For it should be recalled that these property owners will, as good citizens, suffer their loss without a sense of grievance only if they have reason to believe that the new regulation is in fact justified by a net increase in the general utility. Turning next to general uncertainty, the Marshan's case would seem less compelling: while it is true that an insurance market against anti-fill regulations does not exist, land speculation is an activity that generally attracts risk-taking types; and the risk of costly ecological regulation is one of which any sensible

speculator will be cognizant at the time he is considering the
wisdom of investment.[58] Turning to more innovative lines of
inquiry, the activist judge will most likely give little weight
to the "equal protection" dimension of takings law—at least
if the ordinance applies to all undeveloped marshland within
the jurisdiction.[59] In contrast, he would give far more weight
to the kind of governmental agency which promulgated the
ordinance. If, for example, the lawmaker were a state park
agency entitled to impose special land-use regulations upon
surrounding land-owners,[60] the court could well express fears
of institutional self-aggrandizement that Sax seeks to capture
in his entrepreneur/mediator distinction; similar fears could
plausibly be expressed if the lawmaker were the federal Environmental Protection Agency or the Army Corps of Engineers. Finally, depending upon his larger distributional
views, the reformist judge may wish to weigh the interests of
the typically rich land-speculator as less significant than those
of the typically poorer Earthlings whose interests in good
water and flood control the ordinance is intended to assure; [61]
or, more dramatically, the judge's convictions as to the larger
injustice of the distribution may be of such a character that he
will wish to limit the class of successful plaintiffs drastically,
reserving compensation only to those whose interests seem very
compelling when measured by the other terms in the judicial
calculus.

Having considered those factors in the preceding enumeration he believes to be consistent with his judicial role, the
competent Utilitarian judge will finally turn to the costs of
processing compensation claims from those who stand in
situations similar to the Marshans.[62] While the expected settlement costs would not be trivial, it seems fair to say that they
would not bulk so large as to preclude all thought of an
affirmative response, especially if the Appeal to Citizen Disaffection and the Appeal to Institutional Self-Aggrandizement
were found to have considerable weight. In short, what to the
conventional judge seemed a rather easy case would appear
quite difficult to many (if not all!) of the judges who took a
view of law that was both Scientific and Utilitarian.

The most important point to recognize, however, is not the possible difference in outcome but the extraordinary difference in the *kind of analysis* that would be attempted by the Utilitarian judge as he sought to devise the appropriate legal response. This is *not* to assert that the conventional categories are entirely devoid of Utilitarian sense. For example, as Professor Michelman has suggested, the importance given to title and possession in the conventional law can be understood to reflect a Utilitarian concern with isolating situations in which settlement costs will not be prohibitively high.[63] Nonetheless, even after a good faith effort is made to emphasize the Utilitarian aspect of present doctrine,[64] it would seem that over the centuries judges have managed to capture only a few stray elements of the full Utilitarian calculus within their conceptual net. In short, if it is appropriate to view the problem of just compensation from a Scientific Utilitarian point of view, it would seem that the law requires a rather fundamental overhaul and not merely a bit of tinkering here and there. The conceptual redesign would not be so revolutionary, however, as to be beyond the traditional capacity of courts to accomplish. The basic concepts—the Appeal to General Uncertainty, to Citizen Disaffection, to Institutional Self-Aggrandizement, to the "Equal Protection" dimension, and so forth—seem neither peculiarly recondite nor foreign to the central concerns of our legal system. I have little doubt that the basic lines of the doctrinal reorientation could be effected by two or three good opinions from the Supreme Court—though the work of elaboration would, of course, take a couple of generations.

Moving from method to substance, the likely—if not certain [65]—outcome of such a juridical reorientation would be a very considerable expansion in the scope of constitutionally mandated compensation practices, as our consideration of the Marshans' case itself suggests. It should be clear, moreover, that we are dealing here with a doctrinal pattern that has a far broader range of application than cases having to do with the environment or any other single substantive issue, however important it may be. To choose but a single example, the recipients of social security, welfare, and other forms of governmental largesse would benefit mightily if compensation law concerned itself less with questions of title and more with uncertainty, disaffection, and equal protection.[66] This is not to say that even a Utilitarian court bent upon expanding the range of the clause in many directions would never feel called upon to cut back on the protection offered under the older doctrine. Once again, the principal, if not the only, problem would be raised by the present per se rule insisting upon compensation when the claimant is deprived of title or possession of the thing in dispute. At a certain point in the judicial evolution of the new Utilitarian doctrine, it would be natural to consider whether this rigid rule is still justified within the context of a more supple and discriminating system. Such a question remains for the next generation, however, provided the present one takes the course marked out here.

And it is this question which is of central concern to us. Not that I wish to present an advocate's brief on behalf of Utility in particular or Scientific Policymaking in general. Instead, our intention here is to attempt a relatively dispassionate canvass of the basic options that the present legal culture permits the profession to take seriously. While Scientific Utilitarianism is one such option, it is not the only one. And so we shall in succeeding chapters consider two other perspectives on legal analysis that, I think, permit one to envision plausible alternative courses for future doctrinal development. Under the first of these scenarios, "Kantian" judges are imagined to accept the basic premises of Scientific Policymaking but reject the Utilitarian's insistence that all law be fashioned to maximize Social Utility. Under the second scenario, judges are understood to reject the propriety of Scientific Policymaking as such, and to view the compensation clause from the radically different perspective of the Ordinary Observer. On, then, to the Kantian judge.

4 Kantian Adjudication

After a generation and more of near silence, professional philosophy has come alive with political theory. While the new theorists make atonal music if they are heard together, it is nevertheless possible to detect a common theme—or perhaps anti-theme—which is highly relevant to our purposes. Whoever one reads—be it Rawls or Nozick, Wolff or Walzer, Freed or Dworkin [1]—there seems a remarkable agreement that Utilitarianism is deeply misconceived.[2] What is more, this otherwise diverse group has a common understanding of the principal cause of the Benthamite doctrine's failure. Utilitarianism, it is said, fails to take individualism seriously when it insists that the sum of social satisfactions be maximized regardless of its distribution among persons. In one way or another, the critics of Utilitarianism insist that individuals are entitled to certain rights simply because they are autonomous beings worthy of respect—rights which cannot be overridden simply by an appeal to general Utility. It is at this point that the common theme transforms itself into a modern atonal chorus, as each writer attempts to state affirmatively the concept of social order that in his view best captures the proper notion of autonomy and respect for the rights of individual persons. When approached at this level, the writers offer a wide range of choice, from anarchy [3] to democratic socialism [4] with suitable intermediate positions available for the fencesitters. For present purposes, however, I think it more appropriate to emphasize the common critique of Utilitarianism rather than the diversity of response that has followed upon the general recognition that Bentham is dead.[5]

With some hesitation, I shall associate this developing line of non-Utilitarian political thought with the name of Immanuel Kant. This has the advantage of suggesting the possibility that there may be more at stake here than a few books written by some clever men who have captured the public's ear for a passing moment. It has the disadvantage, however, of risking a misrepresentation of the chapter's basic ambition. For what follows is most definitely not an exegetical attempt to apply Kant's particular philosophy to the takings problem. As constitutional lawyers, we are no more interested in the details of Kant's particular theories in this chapter than we were concerned with an interpretation of Bentham's writings in the last. Instead, Kant serves merely as a symbol of a fundamental principle that attains one of its deepest statements in the categorical imperative: the idea that Policymakers are not to conceive of their fellow citizens as merely means to the larger end of maximizing social utility, but are instead to treat them as ends in themselves.[6] While the vagueness of this Principle of Exploitation is of course notorious, I shall argue that, within the domain of just compensation law, it will serve with some success as the source of judicially manageable standards.

To see this, consider the way in which a restrained Kantian judge would deal with a legislative and administrative process that operated in a way a Utilitarian would consider well-ordered. That is, imagine the judge could properly assume that the legislative decision taking some property rights from the Marshans' bundle was one that could generally be presumed to be well-grounded in a sound felicific calculus. Even after the judge had been assured, for example, that the Marshans had lost a hundred thousand utiles [7] while the rest of society had gained a million, there would remain an issue open for him that would not at all trouble his utilitarian counterpart. For the judge, as a Kantian, is not merely interested in maximizing social utility; he is primarily concerned with assuring a social order in which no individual is used merely as a means to the satisfaction of another's ends.[8] Yet is this not precisely the plight of the Marshans in our hypothetical situation? Are they not being called upon to sacrifice some of their rights simply because others would find it terribly convenient for them to do so? If this is not serving merely as a means for the satisfaction of another's ends, it is hard to imagine any legislative action which would fall under this description.

Indeed, the mere fact that the Earthlings, as in the case hypothesized, have profited enormously by the legislative reassignment of property rights only makes the Kantian's case for compensation seem more, not less, compelling. For in such a case, it may be quite possible [9] to force the Earthlings to share some of their gains with the Marshans so that *nobody* is made any worse off at Time Three than at Time One. By placing the losers in at least as good a position as they were at Time One, it has been made clear that the Marshans are not conceived merely as means to the greater satisfaction of social utility; instead they are being treated as ends in themselves who need not be required to sacrifice their interests merely to satisfy others' convenience.

The contrast with the restrained Utilitarian judge on this point could not be more fundamental. As we have seen, the restrained Utilitarian would give little or no weight to the Appeal to Citizen Disaffection in cases like the present one, in which the societal benefit-cost ratio is overwhelmingly favorable.[10] Yet it is precisely here that the Kantian judge would have relatively little difficulty in requiring the state to force the community at large to share some of the gains generated by the property redistribution with the hapless Marshans. But we can be more precise than this. The *easy* case for the Kantian judge is one in which the costs of administering a compensation practice (process costs) are not so large that they eat up the entire net benefit generated by the redistribution. For example, if the Marshans' loss were placed at a hundred thousand dollars, while the Earthlings gained a million, compensation would be required if process costs amounted to less than $900,000. For in these easy cases it would be possible to make all other members of society better off without making the Marshans worse off, and hence to remain

unambiguously consistent with the Kantian dictum.[11] Or to
put the point in terms of a formula, compensation is required
when $P < B - C$, where P is process cost, B is project benefit,
and C is other project costs.[12]

In contrast, this formula would seem far too generous to
the Marshans in a restrained Utilitarian jurisprudence. The
judge here would be willing to tolerate high process costs if
and only if the costs of failing to compensate, borne principally by the Marshans, would be even higher. Or, in terms of
the formula developed previously, compensation would be due
only if $P < U + D$, where U is uncertainty cost and D the
costs of citizen disaffection.[13] Thus, in the case hypothesized,
is would not be enough for the Utilitarian judge to learn that
process costs (P) were less than the net benefits generated by
the landfill statute $(B - C)$. For it remains quite possible that
$U + D$ is less than P. And if this turns out to be the case,
compensation will be refused despite the fact that the
Marshans have been made worse off as a result of a social decision requiring them to sacrifice their preexisting rights so as
to further others' utility. Or, to put the point in terms of
plausible judicial guidelines, the restrained Utilitarian judge
will be especially predisposed toward compensation if he observed that process costs were *particularly low;* for the Kantian,
however, the easy case would be one in which process costs
were *not so high* as to make it impossible to compensate the
Marshans without making the Earthlings worse off than they
were at Time One.

This difference in the decisive formula merely dramatizes
the deeper philosophical difference that we have already noted:
the Utilitarian counts the costs suffered by uncompensated
Marshans, and others threatened by similar redistributions, as
if they were no different from any other costs suffered by anyone else in society; hence he is willing to take actions to reduce these costs only to the extent that doing so will not
impose greater costs on others. In contrast, the restrained
Kantian judge views the Marshans as having a *special* claim on

the state's concern by virtue of its prior decision marking them out as appropriate means for the greater utility of others. From this point of view, the state has a special obligation to assure the Marshans that they are not viewed as means but as ends; and the fulfillment of this obligation takes precedence over others' desire to keep as much as possible of the gains generated by the redistribution of property rights.[14]

It is not every case, however, that can be handled in such a summary fashion by the Kantian judge. Up to the present point we have been dealing with those cases in which process costs do not exceed the net benefits generated by the property reassignment. It should be plain, however, that many cases will arise where process costs *will* exceed net benefits and we have yet to consider the way in which the Kantian would resolve these cases.

So far as the restrained Utilitarian is concerned, these cases raise no important analytical problems of any novelty. Here, as elsewhere, compensation will be granted if, and only if, the sum of uncertainty and disaffection costs is higher than process costs. So far as the Kantian is concerned, however, these cases present a new and more difficult problem. Because of relatively high process costs it is impossible for the judge to require the beneficiaries of the land-filling ordinance to share some of the gains of the property reassignment with the Marshans so that *nobody* will be worse off at Time Three than they were at Time One. For if others are required to pay both the costs of compensation and the costs of process, they will find themselves worse off than they were at Time One; while, if the Marshans remain uncompensated, they obviously will be worse off at Time Three than they were previously. Hence, in this case, the Kantian's simple Principle of Exploitation seems incapable of generating a unique solution; [15] either one side or the other will be called upon to sacrifice its interests as a result of legal change.[16] Since the principle does not permit the Kantian judge to say that one outcome is superior to the other, it follows that, as a restrained judge, he will defer to

the legislative judgment on the matter. To sum up, the restrained Kantian's approach to compensation will be in some
respects more, and in some respects less, demanding than that
of his Utilitarian counterpart. When there is reason to believe
that $P < B - C$, the Kantian will *always* insist upon compensation while the Utilitarian will only sometimes do so; in
contrast, when $P > B - C$, the Kantian will *never* insist upon
compensation, while the Utilitarian sometimes will.

There is, however, nothing writ in the stars which decrees
that a judge select a single objective to which he expresses
exclusive fidelity.[17] Indeed, if the question were addressed at
this level, I should imagine that the typical contemporary judge
would report that he was concerned *both* with maximizing
overall utility *and* with the elimination of legal structures in
which one citizen is treated as merely a means for the gratifi-
cation of another. Given these dual concerns, he could well
prefer an approach to takings law which borrowed elements
from both of our pure models. Here the judge would first
apply the Kantian test to determine whether it was possible to
transform the situation into one in which nobody was made
worse off by the property reassignment occurring at Time
Two. If, however, such a solution was made impossible by
virtue of relatively high process costs, the restrained judge
would put on his Utilitarian spectacles and consider whether
the costs of disaffection and uncertainty were greater than the
process costs. Put more generally, the eclectic Kantian-
Utilitarian may invoke a lexicographic approach of the sort
increasingly familiar in talk about social evaluation. While
giving first priority to his Kantian principle of non-exploitation
where it can be unambiguously applied, he will be willing to
invoke Utilitarian criteria where his first priority principle
does not lead to a unique outcome.[18] Although I myself suspect that this eclectic Kantian-Utilitarian approach will appeal
to many,[19] my discussion will continue on the supposition that
our Kantian judge is a purist, since it seems easy enough for
the reader to combine the two approaches on his own if he so
chooses.

THE KANTIAN TENDENCY TOWARD ACTIVISM

In order to highlight the contrast between Kantian and Utilitarian approaches to compensation law, the previous discussion considered the way a restrained Kantian judge would evaluate legislation generated by a political process which the *Utilitarian* would deem to be "well-ordered," in the sense we have defined the term. While this comparison permitted us to isolate some basic differences, it may be properly suggested that this clarification was purchased at the cost of playing fast and loose with the concept of judicial restraint, at least as we have defined it. For recall that, within our framework, the restrained judge was defined as an official who acts *as if* the social and political universe generally conforms to the Comprehensive View that he thinks properly expresses the objectives of the legal system within which he operates.[20] Thus, it would appear that if our Kantian judge truly conformed to the definition of judicial restraint, he would *not* address legislation as if it were the product of a well-ordered *Utilitarian* process, but as if it emerged from a well-ordered *Kantian* process in which the issue of fairness, as well as utility, had already been resolved by legislators in a fashion that was generally—though not unfailingly—consistent with the preferred Comprehensive View.

Taken by itself, this more careful specification of the notion of Kantian restraint does not require a complicated reformulation of the analysis. Our restrained judge will still inquire whether it is possible to compensate the Marshans at Time Three without generating process costs that will make the Earthlings worse off than they were at Time One—only now he will give the legislature the benefit of the doubt in cases open to reasonable dispute. If we reflect more broadly upon the restrained Kantian's notion of the political process, however, it is possible to add a second contrast to the one already drawn between the Utilitarian and Kantian varieties of restraint. I should like to suggest that not only will the restrained Kantian's decisive doctrinal formula differ from his Utilitarian counterpart but that the entire idea of judicial deference will seem less plausible to the Kantian than it will to the Utilitarian. In short, a Kantian judge will, ceteris paribus, tend to be more activist than he would have been if he had accepted a Utilitarian Comprehensive View.

To see why, consider the stringent demands the Kantian places upon a political process before it will qualify as "well-ordered" and so entitled to deference. For him, it is not enough to assert that the American political system provides a good framework for the collective search for the largest possible utility pie. Instead, he will insist that individual rights be protected even when this inconveniences large groups in the population. Hence, the Kantian will remain unimpressed when he learns that the American political structure sometimes provides even rather small groups with ample means to protect their vital interests against a more numerous coalition whose goals are less intensely held. While a Utilitarian may be quite pleased with the intricate trade-offs between numbers and intensity sometimes achieved in American politics, the Kantian will demand far more. While protecting minorities against apathetic majorities is fine as far as it goes, the Kantian will insist that a "well-ordered" political system must also generally assure the protection of individual rights even when large coalitions *do* intensely wish to abridge them. Since it is obviously more difficult to assert that American political reality satisfies this stringent condition, it follows that Kantians will have a harder time finding that American politics is well-ordered than will their Utilitarian brethren.

We have, then, reached an important, albeit intermediary, stage in the argument. For if you are convinced that Kantians are less likely to believe that American politics is in fact well ordered, only one final problem must be resolved before one may permissibly conclude that Kantians will, ceteris paribus, find deference less attractive as a judicial attitude than will their Utilitarian counterparts. The nature of the difficulty may be perceived once one recalls that to qualify as deferential, it is not necessary for a judge to assert that the political process is *in fact* well-ordered, but only to affirm the weaker proposition that judges are bound by their office to view the political branches *as if* they conformed to the well-ordered ideal. Indeed, I have already emphasized that many advocates of deference are quite willing to concede the counter-factual character of their role premise. Nonetheless, this important point need not stand in the way of the more modest suggestion I am making here. For I do not argue that deference is an impossible (or even a very difficult) position for the Kantian judge to accept. I only assert that the burden of persuasion seems *relatively* heavier for the Kantian than the Utilitarian. And to make this claim all I need argue is that, other things being equal, a judge will prefer to define his role in a way that does not require him to assume the truth of a proposition which is almost certainly false. So long as the propriety of this rather inoffensive judicial preference for truth is conceded, the Kantian tendency toward activism may be readily established. This is not to say that American politics should be considered "well-ordered" even when judged by the Utilitarian's more modest test, only to say that the claim made by the deferential Utilitarian is less obviously false than the one that must be advanced by his deferential Kantian counterpart—placing a weightier burden of justification upon the latter to defend the propriety of his general judicial stance.[21]

Having located the general place of activism in Kantian jurisprudence, it remains to consider the particular forms of intervention that will commend themselves to those who find that a strict rule of deference cannot be justified. Here, I think, there is a great deal of similarity between the Kantian and Utilitarian doctrinal conclusions. Thus, just as Sax was concerned to check institutional self-aggrandizement at the expense of good cost-benefit analysis, so too would the activist Kantian be concerned lest a particular interest group, in control of a self-aggrandizing bureaucracy, use its power to exploit others' rights as a means to their own ends.[22] Similarly, the Kantian would be concerned to develop the "equal protection" dimension of takings law to cushion the impact of official decisions that mark out one property holder, rather than another who seems similarly situated, to serve as the exclusive means to a social end that benefits others.[23]

Yet, however much the Kantian may look to Sax for suggestive leads, the fact is that Sax quite explicitly sought only to develop activist doctrine from a Utilitarian point of view. It remains an open question, then, whether new and distinctive forms of intervention may be generated by scholars and judges if they come to think of themselves self-consciously as Scientific Kantians of the activist persuasion. Since Kantian themes have only just begun to touch compensation law,[24] it seems especially wise here to refrain from mistaking our present ignorance for the final Scientific truth on the matter. This said, it will not hurt to summarize our tentative conclusion: while Kantians will find it easier to adopt an activist stance than will Utilitarians, those who embrace activism will focus their concerns on much the same issues as those marked out by Utilitarian doctrine.

REFORMISM

Thus far, we have introduced only a single innovative variable into our model of judicial restraint. To put the point in pictures, we have been concerned up to the present only with the shift from a purely restrained judge (Table 2) to one whose general position is that a strict rule of deference cannot be justified (Table 3).

TABLE 2

Proposition A [25]	Conservative
Proposition B	Deferential
Proposition C	Principled

TABLE 3

Proposition A	Conservative
Proposition B	*Activist*
Proposition C	Principled

Yet even the most summary sketch must take a more comprehensive view, and assess the extent to which all three role
variables interact to transform the shape of Kantian doctrine.
To discharge this task, we next consider the conservative
dimension of the model: in which doctrinal directions will a
judge move once he challenges the restrained assumption upholding the distribution of property rights at Time One?

In a general way, the options open to the reformist Kantian
parallel those that confront the Utilitarian judge.[26] Thus, he
may declare himself an agnostic and defer to the legislature
if he understands its enactment to be grounded on a belief
that the Marshans have—on Kantian principles—too large a
share of the pie. Or he may go further in his rejection of the
status quo and declare it justified for judges to impose their
larger conception of social justice on the political branches.
As in the case of the Utilitarian, this kind of innovation need
not take the form of imposing a complete or detailed distributive blueprint upon society. Instead the judge may simply content himself with selecting out certain salient, if limited, principles for testing the validity of the legislative judgment.

Unlike the Utilitarian, however, the Kantian judge has a
special problem in addressing the issue of social justice even
in limited terms. While the Utilitarian may take recourse to a
relatively well-developed theory dealing with distributive justice (whose problematic elements are at least understood, if
not resolved), the Kantian notoriously has had great difficulty
even defining the general way in which he would evaluate the
justice of an overall distribution of property rights, as distinguished from particular governmental actions burdening
some at the expense of others. From this point of view, the
publication of Rawls's book on justice is a matter of some importance—for as Rawls himself recognizes, it may readily be
understood as an effort to reformulate Kantian concerns so
that they may be more readily applied to an evaluation of the
basic structure of society.[27] This is not to say that a single book
can make for a constitutional revolution, especially one that
contains as many problematic elements as does Rawls's construction. Nevertheless, a reformist Kantian may be expected

to take heart from Rawls's effort as an indication of an increasing willingness among philosophers to do the hard conceptual work necessary before the vague Kantian notion can be made a touchstone for comprehensive legal analysis. At present, however, it seems fair to say that a Kantian theory of distributive justice is even less well worked out, and less widely held, than its Utilitarian counterpart; hence it would appear that, ceteris paribus, a judge would have greater difficulty pursuing this innovative line if he were a pure Kantian than if he were a pure Utilitarian.[28]

This result contrasts sharply with the one reached only a moment ago in our consideration of Kantian activism. There we concluded that activism would seem more attractive to the Kantian,[29] while here reformism seems a relatively less attractive option. These seemingly disparate conclusions may peacefully coexist without internal contradiction because each depends upon a different factual claim that I have advanced concerning the legal culture of the present day. Thus, the relative strength of Kantian *activism* is based on my claim that the generality of modern lawyers (a) will in fact have little doubt that American politics falls far short of the Kantian's notion of a well-ordered process, and (b) will only reluctantly assert that Kantian judges should base their role on an assumption about political life that is not only false, but obviously so. In contrast, the relative weakness of Kantian *reformism* rests on my claim that the generality of lawyers are (a) at present rather unfamiliar with Kantian arguments for redistribution and so (b) will only reluctantly use such arguments to justify reformism as a matter of constitutional principle.

It is, then, quite easy to resolve the apparent tension in Kantian role theory—so long as one accepts the accuracy of my factual assertions about the diverse dominant tendencies in today's legal culture. Apart from the pleasure of dissolving a paradox, however, there is a larger lesson to be learned from all this. And that is the importance of resolute sophistication when dealing with role theory. It is simply not true, as is sometimes hinted,[30] that Kantian judges will systematically take individual rights more seriously than will their Utilitarian colleagues—at least if the willingness to extend constitutional protection to individuals is taken as an adequate indicator of seriousness. For as soon as the theory of judicial role is taken explicitly into account, the picture that emerges is far more complex than a simple slogan will allow—with Kantian judges sometimes more, but sometimes less, innovative in their doctrinal responses.

PRAGMATISM

We turn, finally, to consider the extent to which a Kantian innovator will reject principled adjudication on behalf of a more pragmatic adaptation to the views of non-Kantians in the community. It would appear here that a Kantian judge would have even less reason to depart from principle than would his Utilitarian counterpart. The easy case for the Kantian would be one in which the Earthlings believed that they were intrinsically superior to the Marshans and so became terribly resentful upon learning that the Marshans were to be granted compensation for their sacrifice. From a Kantian point of view, it is precisely the law's highest duty to deny that some citizens exist for the mere convenience of others. Since such a denial will inevitably anger those who declare themselves intrinsically superior, deferring to their resentment is tantamount to abandoning the ultimate aims of the legal system.

The harder case for the Kantian judge would arise if the Marshans adopted a broader conception of the concept of exploitation than the judge thought justified, and so were terribly disaffected as a result of the judicial denial of compensation. While there is something more to be said for giving weight to this kind of disaffection, it appears to me that the grounds for judicial restraint—enumerated in our parallel treatment of the activist Utilitarian [31]—counsel that such factors should be taken into account only on the rarest occasions.

Conclusion

In sketching both Utilitarian and Kantian approaches to the compensation clause I do not wish to pretend to have done more than I set out to accomplish. I have not tried to explicate, let alone defend, the master concepts that lie at the core of the different Comprehensive Views we have explored. Thus, I have made no attempt to be precise about the variety of conceptions of utility that may plausibly be invoked in Utilitarian theories; nor have I considered the difficulties a Utilitarian confronts as he attempts to sum up the utilities experienced by different people at different times in order to arrive at a social total.[32] Similarly, I have dealt with the Kantian notion of treating a person as an end rather than merely as a means far too casually to satisfy myself, let alone someone of a more exacting disposition. It should be recalled, however, that we are not attempting an exercise in pure philosophy but are instead trying to illuminate the relationship between general philosophical perspectives and particular legal doctrine. If some clarity concerning this interrelationship can be purchased only at the cost of some ambiguity as to the precise contours of the basic philosophical concepts, it is a price worth paying. Otherwise, we would be obliged to launch into a philosophical excursus which would rapidly overwhelm the peculiarly legal aspect of this inquiry. Moreover, in speaking of Utilitarianism and Kantianism, I am not invoking concepts that are utterly foreign to the legal culture. Those sympathetic to the concerns expressed by talk of utility and/or exploitation will not permit the admitted difficulties in interpreting the master concepts to serve as an excuse for eliminating the use of such terms from legal analysis. Instead, they will take the hopeful view that the ambiguities revealed in legal analysis will serve as a prod to the further development of the philosophical foundations of the Comprehensive View in question. In contrast, those hostile to one or another view will doubtless exploit their current conceptual imprecision as an important technique by which to discredit the use of a particular mode of Policymaking in legal analysis. The present essay, however, does not seek to convince anyone to adopt one or another of the Comprehensive Views under consideration but proceeds on the premise that they are sufficiently attractive to be considered seriously by anyone who wishes to analyze American law in the spirit of a Scientific Policymaker.

So much for modesty. As an affirmative exercise in legal scholarship I hope to have accomplished two things beyond establishing that the two Comprehensive Views *do* have determinate implications in just compensation litigation which depend in part upon the degree and kind of judicial innovation or restraint that is deemed appropriate. First, I have tried to establish that it makes a difference which Comprehensive View one adopts—that the two Policymaking forms differ from one another in very important, if not earth-shattering, ways.[33] If one had to focus on a single difference, I suppose the most striking is the restrained Kantian's insistence upon compensation in *all* cases in which process costs are less than the net benefits generated by the property redistribution. In this respect, the Kantian's jurisprudence is far more powerful than is the Utilitarian's. In other respects, however, the Utilitarian will strike out more aggressively on behalf of compensation— notably in those cases in which $P > B - C$. Finally, if the judge is willing to mix a Kantian-Utilitarian brew, the resulting compensation clause may be far stronger, or far weaker, than either of the unadulterated products, depending once again upon the varieties of innovation that the eclectic judge is willing to admit into his conception of judicial propriety.

The second main point concerns the relationship between Kantian Policymaking and the shape of existing legal doctrine. Here, as with Utilitarianism, the important conclusion is a negative one: Kantian Policymaking does not greatly illuminate existing doctrine. Like their Utilitarian counterparts, Kantian judges would be asking themselves different questions from those implicit in the case law. A conscientious Kantian could hardly stop his analysis of the Marshans' case with the recognition that title and possession have not been impugned, nor market value utterly destroyed. For him, at least one of the critical issues lies elsewhere—whether the net benefits generated by the redistribution are greater than the process costs. Moreover, the innovative Kantian will, like his Utilitarian counterpart, be concerned with the varieties of institutional breakdown and distributive injustice that serve to set the stage for the particular dispute in question. It would be more tiresome than instructive, however, to make these points in great detail, since they parallel those presented in our earlier discussion of the activist Utilitarian's treatment of the Marshans' claim. Similarly, it seems reasonable to expect that a Kantian judiciary (like a Utilitarian one) would tend to expand very considerably the contexts in which compensation would be constitutionally compelled—though the conventional per se rule, requiring compensation whenever the claimant was deprived of title or ousted from possession, would undergo increasingly critical scrutiny as Kantian jurisprudence developed.

In short, even those who find Scientific Policymaking to be an obviously desirable framework for the compensation law of the future must recognize that neither Utilitarian nor Kantian Comprehensive Views capture the animating principles of the law of the present. Several things could follow from this insight. First, one may conclude that to make sense of present doctrine one must adopt some third Comprehensive View radically different from that espoused by a Utilitarian or a Kantian. On its face, however, this seems a dubious undertaking, since I do not think it can be plausibly maintained that there *are* other Comprehensive Views with sufficient currency in American legal circles to make it reasonable to expect that the judges have been drawing their basic concepts from them. If, however, this first path seems unpromising, it is always possible to draw a second conclusion from our investigation and to adopt the legal nihilist position that the judges are talking about things which in fact make no sense whatever. This is of course a real possibility, and represents one's ultimate fallback position. It is, moreover, a position full of consequence for the course of future doctrinal development. For I take it as a desideratum of our constitutional law that its structure be something more than a jumble of legal technicalities, rooted in nothing remotely approximating basic principle. Thus, if the real choice for the future course of adjudication is between a legalistic jumble or some form of Scientific Policymaking, this would be the strongest kind of argument for choosing Scientific Policymaking. From this standpoint, the deep and unresolved question in interpreting the compensation clause is the proper identification of the Comprehensive View—Utilitarian, Kantian, mixed Utilitarian-Kantian, or something else entirely—that ought to be adopted as the key to the interpretation of the ambiguous constitutional text. In short, if the nihilist view were correct, the question would not be whether the present ramshackle judicial structure is worth saving—since it has no foundation, it should be abandoned with all deliberate speed—but the precise character of the blueprints which promise a habitable structure for the future.

Unfortunately for those who require a clear sense of legal direction, this nihilist view represents a fundamental misreading of the present state of the law. Rather than merely expressing intellectual chaos, the present case law *can* be understood as a coherent whole, so long as one is prepared to think about law in a way that challenges the very premises of Scientific Policymaking itself. This alternative form of legal thought—which we hope to structure through the idea of the Ordinary Observer—lacks the clarity, self-consciousness, and dynamism of its rival. Nonetheless, it is a central legal reality whose hold upon the legal mind is based upon centuries of common law tradition. The profession is not, in short, obliged to choose between Scientific Policymaking and simple chaos. However we decide to view compensation law, it will be necessary to deny, as we affirm, a basic part of our present legal culture.

5 Ordinary Adjudication

As we approach the task of rendering Ordinary Observing an operational legal method within the normal repertoire of practicing lawyers, it is wise to reflect on the analogous problems faced in sketching the Scientific Policymaking side of the present legal culture. To establish Scientific Policymaking as a form of thought important to the contemporary legal profession, it was not enough to offer an abstract definition of its distinguishing characteristics. In addition, it was necessary to show that the *existing* legal culture contained a rich store of ideas that could be exploited by a judge who chose to think like a Scientific Policymaker. To be more precise, we needed to establish (a) the existence of a form of Scientific property talk that was very familiar in legal circles; (b) the possibility of developing a plausible Scientific vocabulary dealing with the proprieties of judicial role which seemed capable of expressing the professional concerns of constitutional law; and (c) the existence of normative theories— Utilitarianism and Kantianism—that had a sufficient hold on the present legal culture to be taken seriously as candidates for the position of Comprehensive View in our existing legal system. Without this attempt to clothe the Scientific Policymaker with contemporary Scientific vocabularies and Comprehensive Views, the notion of Scientific adjudication would have remained a speculative fantasy of no interest to practicing constitutional lawyers.

Similarly, before we can make the view of the Ordinary Observer professionally significant, we must move beyond definition to the cultural realities that permit it to become an operational method of legal reasoning. In one respect at least, the task is precisely analogous to the one attempted on behalf of Scientific Policymaking. Just like his counterpart, the Ordinary Observer will require a theory of judicial role to inform him of the extent to which he should restrain himself and defer to the actions of others instead of innovatively employing the analytic tools at his command. At this point, however, the effort to render Ordinary adjudication a significant legal reality must depart from the paths taken in the preceding chapters. Given our definition of the Ordinary Observer, it will not do to point to a technical language and a Comprehensive View that will give our ideal type contemporary relevance. For it is precisely the defining characteristic of our model that he looks on legal language not as a set of technical concepts but as a form of ordinary language; and that he refuses to resolve legal disputes by invoking a Comprehensive View, but instead selects the rule that seems best to support dominant institutional expectations. Thus, to make out Ordinary Observing as a plausible perspective from which to interpret the compensation clause, it will be necessary to consider the basic premises informing its rejection of Scientific Policymaking: Why would a good Ordinary Observer of American society reject the Policymaker's claim that proper legal analysis should begin by positing a dominant Comprehensive View for the legal system? How would an Ordinary lawyer go about grounding legal concepts on the talk of untrained laymen? How would an Observing judge go about determining which expectations were "dominant" in society and hence entitled to the support of the legal order?

My aim in raising these questions now is not, alas, to answer them decisively. Indeed, even to attempt an authoritative answer would falsify the very picture of the present legal culture that I wish to sketch. For my main thesis is that while both Scientific Policymaking and Ordinary Observing seem *plausible* to contemporary lawyers, neither seems sufficiently convincing at present to permit the decisive rejection of the other from the legitimate canon of juridical argument. Hence, it is the purpose of my general remarks to point to those basic features of American social life which make Ordinary Observing an attractive, yet a deeply problematic, method of legal analysis.

Once we have located the general method in the haze of ultimate doubt which is our legal culture, the second half of the chapter will try to demonstrate that the methods of Ordinary Observing—whatever their ultimate validity—can in fact focus a shaft of bright light upon the practical professional problems posed by the compensation clause. This more concrete analysis begins by showing how the structure of Ordinary property-talk in modern America differs fundamentally from the Scientific concept familiar in the professional talk of lawyers. It will then prove possible to move closer to our goal by sketching the outlines of an Ordinary Observer's interpretation of the compensation clause, as well as a theory of judicial restraint and innovation, that diverge quite profoundly from the understandings of the judge who thinks like a Scientific Policymaker.

THE MODERN AMERICAN MIND: ITS BASIC LEGAL STRUCTURE

I shall begin by explaining why a professionally untrained person's understanding of his relationship to social institutions will diverge fundamentally from that adopted by the Scientific Policymaker. To do this, it is necessary to recall once more the basic intellectual move that marked a person as a Policymaker. To qualify, one *must learn to think of the legal system as if it were organized around a self-consistent set of abstract principles that comprise the system's Comprehensive View*. It is central to my thesis that this kind of highly abstract thinking does not spontaneously arise in the heads of all people everywhere. Indeed, as soon as it is recognized that this form of thought must be *learned* before it can be assimilated, it seems clear that the untrained layman in modern society has neither the time, inclination, nor training to determine for himself the extent to which the existing rules of the legal system actually do make sense in terms of any determinate Comprehensive View.[1]

Instead, the typical American understands his relation to the legal system in terms that are very similar to those by which he understands his relation to the economic system. As he looks out at the marketplace, he observes frequent—and sometimes considerable—fluctuations in the market prices of those objects and opportunities that he wishes to acquire. The price of gas is a quarter today, a dollar tomorrow; the price of bubble-gum is a nickel today, six cents tomorrow; all as a result of forces beyond the individual's control. And precisely because market prices *are* beyond his control, the layman generally does not have any reason to spend much time thinking about whether the price-setting mechanism, considered as a whole, makes sense in terms of a self-consistent set of principles called economic theory. To master such theory as we have is hard professional work—and, unless one intends to become a professional economist, the practical utility of the training will be dwarfed by its very considerable costs in terms of time, money, and lost opportunity. It is possible, of course, that a layman may occasionally encounter a problem that, even to him, seems to suggest the practical utility of economic science—perhaps he is a businessman for whom it is worth a great deal to know the future course of oil prices. Even here, however, it will probably not pay the layman to devote the time and effort necessary to master economic theory himself. Instead, if he is a man of great faith, he will pay someone who claims to be a specialist to make the projections for him. Although the specialist will, of course, *claim* that the price system can be understood in terms of a set of self-consistent principles, the layman will still be quite unable to undertake an independent evaluation of this claim. Indeed, even after the Scientist's predictions of the future are tested by time, the layman will still be incapable of evaluating the Scientist's claim. If the economist's prediction turns out right, it could have been luck and common sense that turned the trick; if it is wrong, whoever said that contemporary science was perfect?

Now, I should like to argue that the layman has an analogous relationship to the legal system. Just as market prices constantly change for reasons over which the typical citizen has no control, so too legal rules are constantly changing in ways that he is powerless to guide. Today he can buy leaded gasoline; tomorrow he cannot; today he can buy sugar-rich bubble-gum; tomorrow, only sugar-free. To use the language of neoclassical economists, just as the average consumer is a "price-taker," so too the average citizen is a "law-taker." Yet, as in the case of price changes, the typical layman generally has better ways to spend his time than to determine whether all these legal changes are related to one another by means of a determinate Comprehensive View that can be said to be characteristic of the legal system. Of course, on certain occasions laymen may think it wise to employ someone who knows about such things. But even after the accuracy of the expert's predictions is tested by events, the layman will be quite unable to make an intelligent judgment as to whether the system of rules can best be thought of as organized around a Comprehensive View.

In saying this I do not wish to become a latter-day adherent of Holmes's bad man theory of law.[2] My claim is *not* that laymen are bad people who deny that the law has any moral content, much less that lawyers ought to think about the law in this way. Instead, my claim is that laymen are ignorant rather than malign. Given their ignorance, they may of course have a blind faith that the legal experts with whom they interact really know what they are doing in terms of a Comprehensive View. Or they may assert that a lawyer's successes (when they occur) are to be attributed entirely to luck and horse sense. In either case, however, the layman's opinion is based on ignorance, nothing more. What is more, the typical American entertains few pretensions to knowledge on this score: not only does he not know whether legal rules are patterned around a determinate Comprehensive View, but he knows that he does not know. Even if he is unhappy with the professional opinion he receives from his lawyer, it is only the fool who will continue trusting his own unprofessional opinion as to the legality of his conduct. At best, a layman—if he is rich enough—will pay a second professional in the hope of receiving an opinion more to his liking. But even if this expedient generates a statement of the law more favorable to his interests, the layman's need to offset one professional judgment with another itself indicates his recognition that he is in no position to judge for himself the extent to which the legal rules affecting him may be evaluated in terms of a Comprehensive View.

It follows, then, that one of the defining elements of the perspective we have assigned to our ideal Observer is deeply rooted in the structure of American life.[3] For it is precisely the Observer's unwillingness to *begin* his analysis by assuming that rules should be assessed in terms of a Comprehensive View that sets the Observer apart from the Policymaker. Since untrained folk make no such assumption, it is perfectly consistent with the Observer's basic premises for him to do the same, despite the disdain of his Policymaking competitors.

THE AFFIRMATIVE MISSION OF ORDINARY OBSERVING

In one sense, all this simply says that the division of labor characteristic of modern society has created the possibility that ordinary people will think about their social world in terms that differ fundamentally from those in which specialists sometimes view social phenomena. As a proposition in the sociology of knowledge this is, of course, not news.[4] As a proposition in legal theory, however, its significance has not been fully appreciated. For what we have suggested is that Ordinary Observing can be understood as an effort *to reject* the possibility of a specialized discourse that the division of labor has permitted the legal class.

It is one thing, however, to reject the premises of Scientific Policymaking; quite another to generate a different juridical method that will withstand the strains of a modern differentiated society. To put the point in terms of our definitions, there is far more to our concept of an Ordinary Observer than the negative point that legal rules need not necessarily be

evaluated in terms of a Comprehensive View. More affirmatively, an Ordinary Observer is committed to the notion that
law should support dominant social expectations as these are
expressed in ordinary language. Yet it is arguable that the
conditions of modern society render this affirmative objective
impossible to conceive, let alone achieve. To see the difficulty,
consider first the claim—central to Ordinary analysis—that it
is possible to base modern law on *ordinary* language. Before
this claim can make sense, one must believe that it is possible
to identify a single way of talking among the laity as the one
that shall be considered Ordinary for legal analysis. Yet how is
this to be done?

It is possible to imagine a society in which this question
would cause no great anxiety. In this society, call it Uniformity, *each* layman not only speaks something-that-passess-for-
English but uses precisely *the same* English sentences to express himself in each and every one of the many life situations
of interest to the law.[5] In such a world, all an Ordinary lawyer
need do to discover the truth about Ordinary language is to
consider, introspectively, how he would express himself about
the subject in his own daily conversation. In contrast, it is
equally possible to imagine a society, call it Babel, in which it
would be absurd for a lawyer to assume that his own daily conversation was typical of the generality of untrained laymen.
Here, unless the legal culture wished to declare itself captured
by a small fraction of the population, lawyers would have no
choice but to devise a scientific legal language whose clear
definitions could be translated into the diversity of tongues in
common use. It should be clear, I suppose, that contemporary
American society is somewhere between these two extremes.
The futility of basing law upon *the* Ordinary language is not
so apparent as it would be in Babel. Yet, we are far from Uniformity. In a well-developed jurisprudence, then, the Ordinary
analyst would have a lot to say about the difference between
dialect and standard English, and how the lawyer is to respond
when he finds that standard English itself is capable of wide
variation.

While the existence of linguistic diversity poses very serious theoretical problems for Ordinary analysis, even these do not represent the heaviest burden that must be borne by those who wish to vindicate the methods of Ordinary Observation in American law. Our ideal type is not only devoted to the use of Ordinary language; he is—as an Observer—committed to selecting those rules which ordinary analysis reveals to best support the expectations generated by *dominant* social institutions. Yet it should be plain that this aspect of the Observer's enterprise presupposes some basic facts about social life that are far from obviously true of American society. To begin with the least controversial notion, I shall not pause to dispute the idea—fundamental to sociology—that people often expect each other to interact in terms of institutionalized behavioral norms defining socially appropriate conduct. This simple notion, however, is not enough to support the entire weight of the Observer's method. By definition, an Observer is not content to isolate one or another pattern of institutionalized expectation; he is searching instead for the single pattern of practice that may be called *the* dominant one in a given social system. And this, of course, is a far more controversial endeavor. In a complex society like America, it is only to be expected that different people of different classes with different cultures will expect different things from the same interactional context. Indeed, it is precisely where interactional expectations diverge that intractable disputes are most likely to arise, driving the participants to the courts in a last effort to resolve their dispute.

It follows that it will not be enough for an Observing judge to believe—in a fuzzy way—that it is possible to identify certain institutionalized expectations as "dominant" within a given society. Instead he will often be confronted with disputes in which *both* sides invoke subtly different conceptions of social practice—differences which predictably redound to their partisan advantage in the case at bar. At this point, of course, the Observing judge will be obliged to sift social interaction in a very refined way if he is to determine which social pattern merits the privileged juridical status of dominant social norm and which will be downgraded as a mere variant of, or downright deviation from, the norm. To put the point more generally, a fully developed Observing jurisprudence must specify with precision the criteria by which a judge is to recognize a particular interactional norm as one that has been generated by "the" dominant set of institutions, rather than some other set. And how is this to be done?

The problem is precisely parallel to our statement, in Chapter 3, of the master question for Policymaking jurisprudence.[6] There the Policymaker was confronted with the fact that there are any number of Comprehensive Views held by any number of different people; yet, as a decisionmaker, he was obliged in the end to identify a single view as the one with definitive *legal* authority. Here it is the Observer who must face the fact that the social world is a big, big place; yet once again the requisites of legal decision demand that a complex social web be reduced to a single line. As in my treatment of Policymaking, however, I am not interested here in attempting a deep jurisprudential answer to the Observer's master question.[7] Instead, after glimpsing the depth and obscurity of the abyss, I mean to tiptoe around it in a lawyerly fashion by noting that practical men of affairs have long since resigned themselves to using methods which they do not fully understand. It is enough for lawyers that a method seem plausible, rather than that it be warranted as foolproof. Indeed, if the legal profession were more demanding, it would have no choice but to dissolve posthaste—for there is absolutely no chance that the conceptual foundations of either Policymaking or Observing will become transparent overnight.

Our task here is not to resolve ultimate issues but to convince the profession that the ascent to theory is a practical necessity. To do this, it must first be shown that Ordinary Observing permits the lawyer to view the established rules of compensation law as something more than the hopeless scramble perceived by his Scientific Policymaking colleague. It is only after the practical reality of the analytic conflict has been established beyond reasonable doubt that an invitation to further theoretical inquiry, in the concluding chapter, can appear as something more than an academic exercise.

ORDINARY PROPERTY TALK

Let us, then, take the Ordinary Observer seriously and trace the way he would go about defining the problem in interpretation posed by the compensation clause. Unlike his Scientific rival, our new ideal type will not spurn the mass of property-talk and practice indulged in by the untrained multitude. Nor will he be deterred by the fact that if one presses on at once to an excessively detailed level of Observation, it will become apparent that all Americans do not talk, think, and act about private property in precisely the same way. Instead of losing himself in a Babel of detail, the Observer will instead move to a somewhat higher level of abstraction to describe the larger Uniformities that for him provide the key to property-talk.

The place to begin is with platitude. Private property *is* a fundamental institution of American life. A foreigner who knew nothing about private property would have the greatest difficulty conducting the most trivial transactions with the natives—even if he resembled the typical American in all other respects. As soon as this is conceded, the Observer can be provided with a relatively clear question which can serve to direct his inquiry: What must a foreigner be taught about property before he can hope to avoid calling attention to himself as a strange and alien being? Or, to put the point closer to home, most of us are obliged as parents to solve a similar problem as we undertake to teach our children to survive successfully in the larger society that awaits them. Just as the Observer could ask himself how he might ease the path of the entirely ignorant foreigner, so he might consider the things a child must (and does) learn about property on pain of being labeled a deviant by the dominant institutions of American society.

Consider, then, the life of a perfectly socialized middle-class child [8] whom we shall call Layman. From a very early point, young Layman has been taught to distinguish between things that are his and things that are not his. If something belongs to him, others are under a prima facie obligation to ask his permission before using it; they are justified in using his things without obtaining Layman's permission only if they have some especially compelling reason for this extraordinary action. In contrast, Layman may properly use his things in a large number of ways without asking anybody's permission. Even Layman, however, cannot use his things in absolutely any way he wants; instead he is taught to refrain from actions that, as a well-socialized child, he should know are unduly harmful to others.

Now, in saying all this, I mean merely to provide a highly abstract account of the conceptual framework into which a middle-class child is socialized before he may claim to know what is involved in asserting that a particular thing (say, a bicycle) is his. These general principles are taught and internalized in the way that is normal for such things—through precept and example, within the family, the school, the peer group, on television. And the sanctions that are imposed for deviant behavior are also quite familiar—physical abuse, temporary withdrawal of affection, stigmatization by one's peers, the symbolic defeat of the bad guys on television, and so forth.[9]

Within this general framework there are doubtless many subtle differences in the pattern of claim and counterclaim that coexist within a group as large and heterogeneous as "middle-class" America. My abstract account is not intended to deny these differences, but rather to give them structure. Thus, while I would anticipate different subcultures to hold disparate ideas of what constitutes an "exceptional" circumstance that justifies somebody else (Johnny) in using Layman's bicycle without his permission, I would not expect a great deal of dispute on the point that there must be *something* exceptional about the situation to justify the use of the bike. Otherwise the bike was not Layman's in the first place but belonged, at best, to both Johnny and Layman. Similarly, I would expect widespread differences among subgroups as to what precisely it is that a "well-socialized" child should know is unduly harmful to others and hence wrong to do with his thing. Nonetheless, I would not expect disagreement on the proposition that Layman, by virtue of the fact that it is *his* bike, may properly do many more things with it than Johnny, who merely covets it: if the notion of "harm" were so expansive as to limit Layman to very much the same uses of the bike that were open to Johnny, I should be happy to concede that my abstract account had been shown to be inapplicable to the property talk and practice of the particular subgroup under study. To put the point in terms of a useful distinction recently advanced by Ronald Dworkin: while the various socialization groups in middle-class America seem to me to have a common *abstract* concept of what it means for a thing to belong to Layman, they may well have different *concrete* conceptions of property ownership.[10] At bottom, I am making an *empirical* claim here that could in principle be disproved by a social anthropologist.

It is central, however, to the Ordinary Observer's method that he does not require the services of an anthropologist before he believes himself entitled to give legal status to the Ordinary Observations we have made thus far about dominant property practices. Instead, as a successful lawyer in American society, the Observer believes himself sufficiently familiar with the customs of the natives to judge my account without the need for further independent authority. I shall not, therefore, attempt to *prove* that my account—when taken at its proper level of abstraction—is true. Instead, the analysis only requires an appeal to the intuitions of my (presumably) well-socialized colleagues in the law—and an invitation to make these undoubted intuitions the basis of legal doctrine.

To sum up: while the Scientist rebels at the thought that a single person can be properly identified as *the* owner of a thing, the Ordinary Observer takes a very different view. A particular thing is *Layman's* thing when: (a) Layman may, without negative social sanction, use the thing in lots more

ways than others can; and (b) others need a specially compelling reason if they hope to escape the negative social sanctions
that are normally visited upon those who use another's things
without receiving his permission.[11] As we shall see, this account of the Ordinary concept of property ownership suffers
from many kinds of ambiguity that are generally irrelevant in
everyday use, but which come to the surface at the times of
crisis with which the law has to deal. Nevertheless, we have
said enough to permit us to provide a general account of the
takings problem to parallel the one provided earlier for the
Scientific Policymaker.[12]

The General Structure of the Takings Problem

Consider the following scenario: At Time One, observe
some particular thing that Layman would say was *his* thing.
During this period, Layman uses his thing in lots of different
ways—or at least thinks he can if he wants to. Similarly,
Layman's associates generally refrain from using his thing
without his permission, except in special circumstances. And
if somebody takes his thing unjustifiably, Layman can always
go to the police or a lawyer who will profess concern and try
to do something about it.

During this time, changes are doubtless occurring in both
the legal and economic systems that affect the value of Layman's thing and the uses to which it may be put. Nonetheless,
throughout the period none of Layman's ordinary associates
would ever deny that the thing was Layman's thing, rather
than somebody else's. At Time Two, however, it appears that
some lawmaking institution has made a new decision (for reasons which Layman may or may not understand) of a fundamentally different kind, at least so far as Layman is concerned.
As a result of this new legal decision, Layman *can no longer
call the thing his own* and have that claim recognized in ordinary discourse. Instead of belonging to Layman, it either has
been destroyed or belongs to somebody else—generally, but
not necessarily some state official—whose permission must generally be obtained before the thing may legitimately be used.[13]

It is this assault upon his accustomed way of understanding his relationship to the economic and social world that brings Layman into court to complain at Time Three. According to him, the state has taken his property *in the only sense he understands the term.* At Time One the thing was Layman's thing; at Time Two it is no longer Layman's thing, but belongs to somebody else. What could be simpler and more straightforward? And it is this obvious point which will be of the first importance to a judge bent on interpreting the compensation clause from the perspective of the Ordinary Observer. To translate Layman's grievance into a legal question for judicial inquiry: As a result of action taken at Time Two, *is it fair to say that the state has taken one of Layman's things away from him?* If the answer to this question is in the affirmative, a prima facie case of a constitutional "taking" has been established; if not, not. By putting the question (and answering it) in this simple-seeming way, the judge has begun the task of transforming the constitutional text into a mandate for the Ordinary Observer's approach to law.

It would be a serious misrepresentation, however, to suggest that this initial inquiry will exhaust the Observer's inquiry into the compensation clause. For it should be recalled that the (middle-class American) Layman does not believe that, simply because something is his, he is thereby justified in doing *whatever* he wants with it. Rather, from earliest childhood, he has been taught that while he can use his things in lots of different ways, he is not justified in using them in some ways that, as a well-socialized person, he ought to recognize as unduly harmful to others. Imagine, for example, that young Layman has a bike which he constantly rides over the neighbor's flowerbeds. When told to desist from his actions, Layman becomes perverse and defiantly asserts that it is his bike and he will deflower as many marigolds as he pleases. If, in response, his parents take his bike away from Layman until he promises not to harm the interests of others, the parental taking assumes a very different aspect from one which is not so justified. Indeed, it is precisely by the imposition of such sanctions as these that the child eventually becomes a successfully socialized adult who recognizes that, simply because something is his, he is not justified in using it in ways that he ought to recognize as unduly harmful to others. Hence, if the courts were looking at the compensation clause from the vantage point of an Ordinary Observer, one would *not* expect them to grant the aggrieved plaintiff compensation as soon as it was determined that, as a result of the legal change, it no longer could be fairly said to be Layman's thing. This finding would only serve to establish a prima facie case [14] that compensation was required. For it remains possible that Layman had been using his property in a way that *he ought, as a well-socialized individual, to recognize as unduly harmful to others*. And if the government did no more than prevent Layman from continuing such a use, it should be permitted to defend its action as justified within the Ordinary meaning of the takings clause. Now, of course, interpreting the concept of "undue harm" will give the courts a great deal of trouble, since the cases coming to litigation will reveal ambiguities in Ordinary conversation that do not often come to the surface in the ebb and flow of daily life. Nonetheless, if the judge is committed to the Ordinary Observer's point of view, he will have no choice but to resolve these difficulties as best he is able. All this leads us to two simple-seeming questions that will engage the attention of the Ordinary judge:

1. Has the state taken one of Layman's things away from him?

2. If a taking has occurred, can it be justified on the ground that it was necessary to stop Layman from engaging in conduct he ought, as a well-socialized adult, to have recognized as unduly harmful to others?

It should be clear enough that these questions mark out a path very different from the one taken by the Scientific Policymaker as he searches for the answer to his version of the takings problem by elaborating the Comprehensive View he understands to prevail in the legal system. Nonetheless, it is central to my argument that the lawyer who seeks to choose one path over another will find in the present legal culture no argument that self-evidently serves as an authoritative signpost pointing in the direction of Legal Truth. In particular, neither side can point to the language of the Constitution itself as decisively indicating that one or the other approach has superior textual support. Indeed, the present problem serves as an excellent example of the failure of literalism as a technique of constitutional interpretation. On the one hand, we have already seen that the Scientific Policymaker has little difficulty reading the Constitution so as to legitimate his mission: "nor shall private property [i.e., any legal right to use a thing held by a private person] be taken [no serious interpretative difficulty here] . . . without just compensation [i.e., payment is due to the extent deemed just under the prevailing Comprehensive View]." The Ordinary Observer, however, will choose to read the same words with a significantly different understanding: "nor shall private property [i.e., any thing that Layman would call his own] be taken [unless it is necessary to prevent Layman from using his thing in a way he should recognize as unduly harmful] without just compensation [i.e., payment should be sufficient to permit Layman to buy a thing as good as the one he lost]."

It is, I think, quite pointless to decide which of these readings qualifies as the Constitution's "plain meaning." Both are elaborations of the text; neither is a complete fabrication; each is, in short, an *interpretation,* whose ultimate validity depends upon the value of the form of legal culture which gives the interpretation meaning. It is for this reason that a lawyer who seeks to interpret the Constitution cannot stop short of a confrontation with the conflict in the legal culture we are seeking to elaborate.

SPECIFICATION OF JUDICIAL ROLE

First Principles of Role Theory

Having outlined the basic framework within which an Ordinary judge will understand and attempt to resolve the

takings problem, only one final element must be considered
before our model of Ordinary adjudication can become fully
operational. I refer, of course, to the way an Ordinary judge
will understand the limits of his office when he is called upon
to exercise the power of constitutional review. More particularly, we must compare the way an Ordinary Observer will
understand the nature of judicial restraint and innovation
with the way a Scientific Policymaker will deal with these
same concepts.[15]

We begin by asking why an Ordinary Observer will find his
rival's role theory deeply misconceived. The problem arises
because the Scientific Policymaker's distinction between judicial restraint and innovation only makes sense in terms of
his larger concern with linking the analysis of legal rules to a
broader Comprehesive View. Thus, a *restrained* Policymaker
is a judge who is willing to assume that the world-outside-
his-courtroom is "well-ordered" in terms of the legal system's
Comprehensive View; while the *innovative* Policymaker thinks
it proper for a judge to notice the world's imperfections and
use his judicial power to lead society closer to a "well-ordered"
condition, as defined by the Comprehensive View imputed to
the legal system. Unfortunately, however, since the Ordinary
Observer thinks it a mistake to impute *any* Comprehensive
View to the legal system, he can hardly embrace a distinction
which presupposes that such a move must be made by any
self-respecting judge. The Ordinary Observer's task, then, is to
express the meaning of judicial role in terms of the idea that
a primary task of adjudication is to grasp and explicate the
conceptual structure of Layman's social reality, rather than
some Comprehensive View said to constitute the ultimate objective of the legal order.

To do this, it is necessary to reflect a bit upon the nature
of the relationship between the Observing judge and the well-
socialized Layman, whose talk and action constitute the prime
object of judicial interest. As we have seen, the modern day
Layman looks at the legal system as if he were a "law-taker"—
no more capable of changing legal rules by his own actions

than he is of changing market prices. Yet this is precisely the respect in which a judge may be understood to differ from his fellow citizens. Especially when he addresses a constitutional question, he has it in his power to act as a *law-maker*, unchecked by many of the restraints that bind the ordinary *law-taker*. It follows that before a judge can approach the constitutional text as an Ordinary Observer, he must embrace a very distinctive notion which will occupy a central role in his understanding of the judicial function:

> *First Principle of the Ordinary Observer's Judicial Role:* While the judge has it in his power to act like a *law-maker*, he should not use this power to further his own personal predilections but should instead think about each lawsuit as if he were a *law-taker*.

Needless to say, all Policymaking judges would reject such a notion. To them, it represents nothing less than an act of judicial self-mystification—a perverse refusal to recognize a judge's obligation to use his power to further the highest ideals established by the legal system. Yet what follows would seem even more disturbing. Not only does the Ordinary judge commit intellectual suicide in the name of self-restraint, but he proposes—in the name of constitutional interpretation—to invalidate legislation which may be based upon a perfectly sound Comprehensive View simply because it is inconsistent with the Layman's understanding of his existing relationship to society. So far as the Policymaker is concerned, this is to assert that, for constitutional purposes, concrete expectations whose only legitimacy lies in their brute existence may contain a higher truth than a piece of coherent and appropriate Scientific legislation that can be justified under the best Comprehensive View a legal system might possibly have. In short, the Observer's first principle has—in the Policymaker's eyes— wrongly transformed the Constitution into a document that shields the status quo from normal legislative change without anyone asking whether existing socially based expectations make some larger normative sense.

This is not to say that the Policymaker is blind to the concerns that led the Observer to place such striking limitations upon the judicial office. Like his counterpart, the Policymaker is also concerned with the possibility that judges will use their lawmaking powers simply to impose their idiosyncratic notions of the public good upon the parties to the dispute. Only to him the disease is capable of a more sophisticated cure, which does not require the judge to accept the superficialities of the law-taker as the acme of legal thought:

> *First Principle of the Scientific Policymaker's Judicial Role:* While the judge has it in his power to act as a *law-maker,* he should not use this power to further his personal predilections, but instead should think about each lawsuit *as if he were an agent of the state charged with implementing the public good as it is defined in the legal system's Comprehensive View.*

To the Ordinary Observer, however, this "sophisticated" solution to the problem of judicial subjectivity is no solution at all. According to this ideal type, once the Scientific Policymaker has liberated himself from the concrete thinking of ordinary members of the community, he will have no place to go but to his own idiosyncratic notions of the public good. True, Policymaking judges may delude themselves into thinking that the Comprehensive View they impute to the legal system represents the will of the people as it is expressed in the Constitution and other fundamental legislation. But this, to the Observer, simply represents yet another manifestation of the *hubris* that led the Policymaker originally to assert that judges are entitled to reshape the law in abstract terms that have only a problematic relationship to the existing structure of social life as expressed in ordinary language.

The Structure of Ordinary Role Theory

I have said enough, I hope, to locate the Ordinary theory of judicial role in the larger debate, dealing with the nature and object of legal language, to which we shall ultimately turn.

For present purposes, however, it will be necessary to move beyond first principles if we are to develop a sensitive understanding of the range of choice open to an Ordinary Observer as he approaches the takings clause. Even after a judge has embraced the Observer's first principle of role, he must resolve a host of (logically) secondary issues before he can apply his chosen methodology to the case before him. Most important, he will be obliged to consider whether he should read the takings clause in a *restrained* or an *innovative* way. These terms are, of course, the same as those used earlier to describe the Scientific Policymaker's basic problem in role definition. Yet, though the words may be the same, they will have a very different meaning when read in the light of different first principles. Thus, a "realistically" [16] restrained Observing judge will, like his Policymaking counterpart, recognize that even a "well-ordered" governmental scheme will malfunction in particular cases. Unlike the Policymaker, however, he will not use this insight to justify constitutional intervention when the challenged legislation constitutes a blatant departure from his understanding of the legal system's Comprehensive View. Instead, the restrained Observer will intervene in the name of the compensation clause when the legislative action plainly fails to correspond to the dominant pattern of institutionalized expectation. Similarly, the Observer's definition of judicial innovation will undergo an analogous transformation. Instead of innovating in areas where legal rules systematically fall short of the dominant Comprehensive View, the innovative Observer will conceive himself entitled to scrutinize with special care official action in areas which seem to him to be peculiarly insensitive to socially dominant mores.

It should be plain, moreover, that a sophisticated Observing judge need not respond to every role question as would a single-minded paragon of restraint or innovation. Instead, just as in our treatment of Policymaking adjudication, it should be possible to identify different issue clusters which could be profitably grouped together so as to reveal the outlines of the shaded and refined discourse of which the Observer's legal culture is capable. Thus, we may define [17] a *deferential* judge as one who takes a restrained attitude to the decisions of the political branches, while an *activist* is willing to assert that one or another nonjudicial institution should not be so readily trusted to generate rules that are consistent with prevailing social norms. Similarly, a *conservative* judge is one who considers the distribution of property rights prevailing at Time One to be generally consistent with dominant socially based expectations, while a *reformist* will point to contexts in which he is unwilling to indulge this assumption.[18] And an analogous transformation can be made in the distinction between principled and pragmatic judges that we developed in the Policymaking context.[19]

Once armed with these categories, it would be quite rewarding to explore systematically the way in which one or another change in the Observer's role definition will alter the pattern of prevailing doctrinal responses. The resulting substantive analysis would resemble in form, if not in content, the discussion presented in Chapters 3 and 4, in which the plausible modes of Policymaking doctrine were viewed against the background of restrained and innovative role theory. To make an analogous effort on behalf of Observing doctrine, however, would transform an exploratory essay into a rather weighty tome. Moreover, a full-scale effort to ring the changes on Observing role theory is not nearly so central to our more general thesis as was the analogous attempt made on behalf of Scientific Policymaking. After all, in the first half of the book, we were out to show that *no* plausible form of Scientific Policymaking existed which gave solid support to conventional takings law. While proving a negative is always impossible, it seemed reasonable to explore a wide variety of plausible Policymaking approaches in order to render our thesis even moderately convincing. But the thesis now under scrutiny is (at least from a logical point of view) far less demanding. Rather than proving a negative, we wish here to establish the affirmative existence of a form of Ordinary Observing which *does* make sense of existing doctrinal categories. To accomplish this mission it is not necessary to explore a wide range of doctrinal dead-ends, but only to elaborate those judicial approaches which do successfully enlighten received doctrine.

This narrow objective establishes the entire purpose of the lengthy Chapter 6. I shall argue there that the established legal rules of the present day can best be interpreted as the work of a corps of Ordinary Observers who understood their judicial function in a rather *restrained* fashion. To be more precise about the notion of restraint implicit in existing law, we need only locate the prevailing judicial role in the three-dimensional space that we have labored to construct. First, and most simply, the decisions proceed from an entirely *principled* cast of mind, without even the slightest hint of an effort to take pragmatic account of those whose expectations deviate from the well-socialized norm. Second, the courts seem to have accepted only the mildest form of *reformism* to temper their generally *conservative* assumptions dealing with the existing distribution of property. More precisely, the position taken on the distributional issue is one we have previously characterized as *agnostic*.[20] That is, today's judges are *reformist* only insofar as they will not challenge an official action on takings grounds if it is plainly motivated by redistributive concerns—thus tax legislation is generally immune from serious scrutiny.[21] If, however, the challenged legislation is not motivated by an obvious redistributionist objective, the courts proceed to analyze the takings problem on *conservative* premises, assuming that the distribution of property is consistent with dominant social mores unless the political branches have indicated otherwise. Finally, the judges do not customarily engage in exceedingly *activist* efforts which require them to argue that they are notably superior to other institutions when it comes to elaborating the Ordinary conception of property that lies at the heart of the takings clause. Hence, unless the challenged action quite plainly undercuts Observable expectations, the judiciary will stay its hand and uphold the judgment reached by the political branches. It is on this dimension, however, that the greatest amount of practical disagreement exists. While extremely activist adventures are everywhere avoided, it nevertheless seems plain that some courts are less deferential than others.[22]

In short, my aim is to establish existing law as the work of principled, agnostic, and at least moderately deferential Ordinary Observers. Since even this limited insight is no longer clear to the profession, it seems important to develop it with care: for it is only by understanding the bases of our present law that we can responsibly decide whether it is worth preserving against the challenge of Scientific Policymaking. If Ordinary Observing survives the present struggle, however, it will be important to keep in mind that the present doctrine represents but one of the possible outcomes that may be generated within the larger Observing theory of judicial role.

MIXING POLICYMAKING AND OBSERVING MODES OF ADJUDICATION

Before setting out to prove our thesis, it is best to note an oversimplification in its formulation which could potentially destroy the value of the entire enterprise. Up to now we have been dealing in ideal types, talking as if a body of legal doctrine expressed the concerns *either* of Scientific Policymaking *or* Ordinary Observing, but not both. However necessary this technique may be to achieve a clearer view of the legal culture, it should be plain that there is no reason to expect the existing legal universe to be so neatly organized. Indeed, if our present legal culture is as confused as I say it is, one should expect it to contain a rich variety of exotic doctrinal notions that draw simultaneously from both sides of the living tradition. Hence, it would be very rewarding to attempt a kind of analytic chemistry upon the various compounds to be found in constitutional law (and law more generally). It may be that one or another unstable compound accounts for some of the deeper obscurities in our law; it may also be possible to locate compounds that seem to yield a result that appears more satisfactory than any of the "pure" solutions, suggesting in concrete terms the possibility of deriving more abstract principles for synthesizing the two seemingly conflicting legal styles. Guided by these discoveries, we may come to mix our modalities in a more deliberate way. Perhaps lawyers generally attracted to Scientific Policymaking might learn to mark out certain doctrinal areas as appropriate for Ordinary Observation; and vice versa. Even if such a stable and thoughtful synthesis should fail to develop, we would at least be in a better position to understand the direction(s) in which (various parts of) our law is (are) evolving.

In the present investigation of judicial doctrine, however, we have to do with a rather pure type, whose study will not be greatly aided by the development of a complex theory of mixed modalities. Indeed, I think the mention of a single, probably quite common, eclectic strategy will serve our purposes here. The eclectic approach I have in mind begins from the premises of Ordinary Observation: the principal task is the explication of the layman's ordinary patterns of discourse and expectation. In the course of the effort, however, it becomes clear to the judge that the peculiar situation he confronts forces to the surface ambiguities in ordinary language that ordinary folk are almost never forced to face in the common run of life. As a consequence, concepts that are harmoniously employed in ordinary communication seem to suggest disparate ways of understanding the decisive characteristics of the dispute at bar. At this point, the committed Ordinary Observer may press on with his method, asking himself what *the* ordinary person would say, even though he recognizes his appeal to *the* structure of ordinary concepts has become little more than a legal fiction. It is quite possible, however, that even a judge generally committed to Ordinary adjudication may refuse to go quite this far in his acceptance of its first principle of judicial restraint. Instead, recognizing that the life experience the judiciary is called upon to evaluate is sometimes far removed from the common run of things, the eclectic judge will invoke a principle or policy drawn from some Comprehensive View to resolve his decisionmaking problem. Scientific Policymaking is thus called upon to remedy the admittedly incomplete and imprecise conceptual apparatus of the Ordinary Observer. Nonetheless, the judge I have in mind would never think of according Scientific Policymaking more than a supplemental role. It is only in contexts in which Ordinary concepts may not be deployed in a coherent fashion—where it may be fairly doubted that ordinary language *has* a structure—that the Scientific Policymaker is permitted to intervene.

This is, of course, rather a humble role to be accorded the Scientific Policymaker. So far as he is concerned, it is as if Newton or Einstein were invoked only to explain the movements of celestial bodies (or perhaps the flight of an airplane) but not the fall of an apple. Nonetheless, it is more than the pure Ordinary Observer would concede. It is therefore relevant for our own immediate concerns, since it is possible to catch glimpses of this view in some of the more recent opinions that form the subject of our investigation.[23] Whether these scattered opinions mark the foundations for a stable compromise, however, is far too early to judge. They may instead be the first sign of a sweeping Scientific wave or merely a ripple in the Ordinary tide.

6 Layman's Things

Needless to say, the best way to prove my thesis would be to point to a large number of opinions in which judges self-consciously declared themselves to be Ordinary Observers of a moderately restrained kind,[1] ordering compensation whenever it seemed fair to say that the state (a) had taken one of Layman's things away from him (b) without showing that the taking was necessary to prevent Layman from using his thing in a way that he ought to have recognized as unduly harmful to others. Unfortunately, the run of opinions, taken as a whole, does not suggest a judiciary self-confident in the possession of a basic methodology, however simple. Indeed, the judges seem anxiously aware of the absence of an organizing conception of the takings clause. There is much talk of judging the merits of each case in a particularistic fashion and a great reluctance to limit future freedom of action by making clear the precise factors that are decisive in the instant dispute. Indeed, when judges do intervene on behalf of compensation, they are often distressingly candid in confessing that they are motivated by nothing more than a vague sense of the importance of drawing a line somewhere.[2]

Perhaps it is the Scientific Policymaker in me that rebels at all this. Perhaps the very absence of self-conscious reflection is the mark of a judiciary bent on protecting the perceptions of the ordinary layman. This is not to say that Ordinary Observing is *necessarily* obscurantist; [3] only that it values doctrinal system-building less than its Scientific Policymaking counterpart. However this may be, there are, I think, additional reason that help account for the absence of reasoned justification for existing doctrine.

Most important is the Supreme Court's general treatment of

economic issues since the constitutional revolution of the
1930s. While the takings clause was never consigned to the
dust bin with economic due process [4] and freedom of contract,[5] there was nevertheless an understandable reluctance to
move too deeply into takings theory. As we have pointed out,[6]
the clause is—on any interpretation—something of a reaffirma-
tion of the economic status quo; and it could readily be
suspected that taking the clause too seriously would lead a
conscientious judge to unearth premises that deeply challenged the New Court's determination to coexist peacefully
with the New Deal. Indeed, the only really major Supreme
Court pronouncement has been the *Hope Natural Gas* case [7]—
in which Justice Douglas undercut the constitutional foundation for aggressive judicial review of public utility regulation.
Along with the Old Court's decision in *Euclid v. Ambler,*[8] it
could then be taken as settled that takings doctrine would not
be invoked as a source of principle deeply hostile to the activist welfare state. So long as this principle of peaceful coexistence was not challenged in a way that was too obvious,
the Supreme Court has been content to permit inferior judges
—who are generally far more solicitous of property rights—
to fight a rearguard battle in their defense. Within this general
context, it is not surprising that the lower courts have not
thought themselves called upon to indulge in ambitious efforts
at doctrinal statement and justification. Similarly, in those
relatively few cases in which certiorari has been granted, the
Supreme Court has been peculiarly free of its general tempta-
tion to write opinions that assay constitutional foundations in
the course of refashioning basic doctrine.[9] Even if the general
constitutional situation were more hospitable to judicial statement of the grounds for takings doctrine, however, there is a
final factor that would deter its clear expression. For reasons
that will concern us later,[10] there has been, I think, a gradual
yet discernible increase in the Scientific Policymaking character of our legal culture, to the point where express reliance
upon Ordinary concepts sometimes seems of questionable propriety. To any modern lawyer, there is an irreducible crudity

about a decision that justifies compensation on the ground that the plaintiff has been deprived of some thing that formerly was "his." If there is anything a lawyer remembers from his legal education, it is that laymen are deeply confused in their property talk; that the law of property concerns itself with bundles of user-rights, not with the awkward idea that things "belong to" particular people. Hence, if a judge is thinking about property in a thoroughly non-Scientific way, he may find it easier to say that he is making highly individualistic judgments on the merits of each case, rather than to be clear about what it is he *is* doing.

I shall not attempt to prove my thesis, then, by turning the common lawyer's trick of relying upon some judicial dicta that can, with a bit of straining, be invoked in its support. Instead I hope to show that the Ordinary Observer's perspective orders the existing set of judicial holdings in a fashion far more perspicuous than does any Scientific Policymaking approach we have considered. I shall argue that the surface categories of legal doctrine can best be understood as the product of a deeper judicial struggle with the fundamental categories of Ordinary adjudication.[11] To do this successfully, it is not only necessary to show that the cases the Ordinary Observer finds easy are treated as bedrock certainties by the judges, but also to establish that the situations which expose the ambiguities of the Ordinary Observer's conceptual apparatus are precisely those that are presently considered to be the "hard cases" of takings law. I shall not, however, go further than this and seek to instruct the judges concerning the "correct" way to resolve their "hard cases." For it is precisely my point that the hard cases will remain hard *however they are decided* because the problems they raise cannot be satisfactorily resolved within the structure of Ordinary adjudication. Indeed, it will become apparent that the only way to make these cases easy is to learn to think like a Scientific Policymaker.[12] In short, rather than organizing the discussion around some "leading cases," we shall proceed by examining the doctrinal certainties and ambiguities generated as an Ordinary judge seeks to determine whether (a) one of Layman's things (b) has been taken (c) by the state (d) without Ordinary justification; and will find that they are a mirror of the current law's perplexities.

LAYMAN'S THINGS

Social Property and Legal Property

For the legal Scientist, the cardinal sin is to discriminate among property-bundles and declare that some contain the essential rights of property while others do not.[13] While the Scientist recognizes that some bundles contain more rights than others, all are equally property-bundles. To provide a convincing account of legal principles from the Ordinary Observer's point of view, however, it will be necessary to make a distinction that will disturb these deeply ingrained Scientific sensibilities. For given the Ordinary Observer's premises, it makes good sense to discriminate between two types of rights bundle and to think of one set as realizing the "true nature" of property far more completely than the other.

To see why, we must begin with the observable facts of ordinary life. Every day, Layman is obliged to make countless decisions as to whether one thing or another belongs to him or somebody else. Yet it is a rare thing indeed for him to find it profitable to obtain carefully considered legal advice before making this decision. Indeed, most of the time Layman negotiates his way through the complex web of property relationships that structures his social universe without even perceiving a need for expert guidance. But if Layman usually does not perceive the need of a lawyer's advice before saying that something is his, upon what precisely does he ground his claim?

He bases it on the fact that his right to control the use of his thing is generally recognized in his everyday dealings with other well-socialized individuals. That is, others will ask his permission to use his thing before doing so; similarly, they will not interfere with many of the ways he can make use of his thing.[14] I should emphasize that I am speaking here of the way in which *well-socialized* people deal with Layman's things. Obviously criminals and other no-goods or incompetents may take or use Layman's thing without permission. But the important point here is that Layman is confident that well-socialized folk (among whom he is numbered) consider these people to be no-good or incompetent and he needs no lawyer to tell him that the police are there to stop their depredations.

None of this is to deny that *some* of the time Layman will himself perceive the need to consult a lawyer before he can knowledgeably claim some thing as his. On rare occasions, for example, another well-socialized person will make a claim of right to one of Layman's things. It will then be necessary for both to consult lawyers (and perhaps judges) to determine who has the better claim. Similarly, the rights that Layman possesses over a thing may be of such a kind that they cannot be evidenced by a reference to existing patterns of social restraint and practice. We shall deal more closely with the nature of these interests shortly. For now, it is important to see that in conducting his daily life, Layman will make a fundamental distinction between his *social property* and his *legal property*. As to social property, Layman will claim to be in a position to point to existing social practices which any well-socialized person should recognize as marking a thing out as *Layman's* thing. If, however, Layman does not believe himself justified in claiming something as his without appealing to the opinion of a legal specialist, then I shall say he has only legal, but not social, property, in the thing in question.[15]

This distinction between social property and legal property will be of the first importance in the Ordinary Observer's interpretation of the takings clause. For if the Observing judge's principal objective is to protect Layman's understanding of his relationship to his things, this concern will apply with its full force only with regard to social property. It is only here that Layman can come into court at Time Three protesting about a government decision to take something away from him that he *knew* was his at Time One. In contrast, Layman must recognize that his claim upon legal property is far more tenuous—since only a lawyer could tell him whether it was his in the first place.[16] This is not to say that an Observing judge will always deny compensation when it is legal, rather than social, property that is taken. It is simply to assert that, within his chosen analytic framework, cases involving social property will seem far easier to the Observer than will cases involving legal property.

Testing the Hypothesis

Having marked a distinction that would seem of the first importance to an *ideal* Ordinary Observer, I should like to propose that *existing* law marks out a similar bright line between social property and legal property. While I shall discuss later the complexities that arise in the treatment of legal property by Ordinary judges,[17] it is possible to see how the basic distinction operates by considering a few easy cases upon whose doctrinal solutions all lawyers can be expected to agree. Imagine, for example, that you are the owner of a hundred-acre farm, worth $10,000 an acre, which is the victim of two simultaneous governmental depredations, each of which generates a $10,000 diminution in the value of your investment. On one and the same unhappy day, you receive word that the Highway Department has selected a thin strip of land along your border for road construction and that the Air Force has marked out a traffic lane two miles overhead for the purposes of military transport. In neither case does the governmental activity cause a massive disruption in farm life; in both cases, the monetary loss suffered on total investment is relatively small. Nevertheless, every competent lawyer would say that under present law the Highway Department must pay $10,000 for its road, while the Air Force need not make good on the $10,000 loss caused by its traffic lane. Why?

The answer becomes clear when one reflects upon the extent to which Layman can gain recognition of his property rights from nonlegal actors before the governmental action takes place. So far as the thin strip of land is concerned, Layman will typically have no difficulty persuading his peers that the thing was his social property at Time One. This can be done by pointing to the fact (usually undisputed) [18] that during Time One, Layman's neighbors would not think it proper to use the thin strip without first obtaining Layman's permission. Moreover, if on occasion some no-good did trespass on the land, even he would generally recognize that he was doing something considered wrong by the well-socialized members of the community. In contrast, consider Layman's difficulties if he tried to establish an analogous claim with regard to "his" strip of airspace during Time One:

> *Fair Minded Friend:* It's certainly a big place you have here.
>
> *Layman:* Yup. As far as the eye can see—it's all mine.
>
> *Friend:* Just how much of this place *is* yours anyway?
>
> *Layman:* Well, so far as the land is concerned—from here to here (pointing to the map). And I own all the airspace up to here (pointing again). That's mine too.
>
> *Friend:* How is this last claim of yours any different from your saying that the moon is yours? Are you using it in any way different from the way I am?
>
> *Layman:* Not right now.
>
> *Friend:* What do you mean by that? Are you planning something?
>
> *Layman:* No. But if I did I could use it without anybody having the right to complain.
>
> *Friend:* But that's just the question at issue. And what I'm looking for are some facts in our existing social world which substantiate your claim. How do others treat this thing you say is yours? Do they ask your permission before they use it?
>
> *Layman:* But nobody *is* using it.
>
> *Friend:* That's not quite right. Isn't industry, for example, using it for waste disposal purposes?
>
> *Layman:* Oh, them. . . . Well, I think I'll just let them use it . . . just as a favor, you might say.
>
> *Friend:* Are you quite sure that you're letting them use

your thing as a favor to them? Aren't you afraid that
they would refuse to recognize the airspace as yours
if you pressed your claim?

Layman: Well, if they rejected my claim, they would be
nothing better than common thieves.

Friend: That's what you say. But the people who run big
business are not generally presumed to be antisocial
in our society. Perhaps they merely think your claim
to the airspace is not in fact a good one.

Layman: Well, they're wrong on that.

Friend: But I'm still waiting for you to point out to me
some features of social practice which give social support to your subjective certainties. After all, just wanting something is not enough to support a claim of
ownership in our society.

Layman: Perhaps your doubts will be resolved once you
look at this piece of paper. My lawyer says it entitles
me to claim the airspace. He says: *"Cujus est solum
ejus est usque ad coelum."* How about that?

Friend: Well, I think this mumbo-jumbo is something
best left to lawyers. While your lawyer may be perfectly right on the matter, you have not come up with
anything that makes it plain *to me* that the airspace
is yours. In order to do that, you must point out an
existing pattern of social practice in which ordinary
folk respect your claim to the thing by refraining from
using it without obtaining your permission except in
extraordinary circumstances.

The fact that modern judges have found it hard to devise
rules governing compensation for the taking of airspace is,
then, not terribly surprising under an Ordinary interpretation
of the takings clause. In saying this I do not mean to suggest
that legal property will *never* be afforded protection by Ordinary judges—as we shall see later, the entire problem will
give them immense difficulty.[19] Instead, I maintain the more
modest thesis that the protection of legal property interests

under present law seems a far more problematic matter than the protection of social property. Hence, it is not surprising to find comparable cases—like the ones involving the Highway Department and the Air Force we have just hypothesized—in which the owner of social property is granted compensation *as a matter of course,* while the holder of legal property may well be left out in the cold.[20]

Legal property, of course, encompasses much more than air-rights, and it is important to obtain a rough sense of the sweep of the concept. It seems relatively easy to extend our air-rights hypothetical case to other spatial domains which are inhospitable to ordinary human interaction. For example, we shall later consider the way in which the Supreme Court labored with a problem posed by the decision of a coal company to sell a homeowner rights to the surface while reserving to itself the right to mine subsurface minerals at some future time. Whatever else can be said about this problem,[21] it would seem reasonably clear that, until the time the coal company began actual mining operations, its rights in the land were only legal, not social. That is, until mining commenced,[22] the company could point to no observable pattern of interaction and restraint that would indicate to a fair-minded Layman that the subjacent coal belonged to the company rather than to somebody else. It is true that a search of the legal records would reveal a piece of paper reserving certain rights to the company—but this is sufficient only to establish legal property, not social property.

It is possible, I think, to generalize this talk about air and mineral rights further, provided one is willing to suffer the embarrassment of reasoning from the absurdly crude fact that people, in general, conduct their lives on the earth's surface or things attached to it. As a consequence, when well-socialized members of mankind refrain from using a surface-based thing that Layman claims belongs to him, it seems reasonable for the non-lawyer to infer that the thing is actually Layman's thing. For if it were *not* Layman's thing, at least one of the many socialized people in the environment would have taken it without asking. In contrast, so far as things not proximate to the earth's surface are concerned, the non-lawyer will require something more than the fact that others are *not* using the thing before he will accept Layman's claim that the thing belongs to him. Here the non-lawyer will insist that Layman exercise some obvious form of dominion over the thing he claims is his before he can qualify as holding social, as opposed to merely legal, property in the thing. Thus, if Layman had built a two-mile-high skyscraper on his hundred acre lot, there would have been no difficulty in his satisfying his fair-minded friend that the air-space was his; similarly, if he had actively engaged in the practice of charging firms for the use they made of the air-column, Layman would have converted his legal right into a social right. The same is true of a person who claims the subsurface; as soon as the coal company began actually to mine its claim, there would be a set of practices evidencing rightful dominion over a distinct thing under the surface. But until a set of social practices comes into existence evidencing control over the subsurface as a distinct thing, the coal company must recognize that a legally untrained Layman would have no reasonable way of assessing the validity of its claim of ownership without hiring a legal specialist.[23]

Needless to say, the fact that Laymen are ready to credit surface-based claims more readily than others is for the Scientific Policymaker just one fact among many, whose importance is to be judged by consulting the implications of the Comprehensive View he has imputed to the legal system. The idea that the intellectual limitations of legal ignoramuses should be given legal importance in their own right—independent of *any* Comprehensive View—is, however, the last thing that would seem to him reasonable. For in Scientific terms, the Layman seems to be blindly insisting that property bundles containing surface-based rights are "truer" property bundles than all the others. And that is dangerous obscurantism.

It is even more dangerous when a second intellectual deficiency of the Layman comes sharply into focus. For it appears that he is more willing to grant the privileged status of social property to a claimant who is capable of exercising dominion over a surface-connected thing *at the very moment in time* he is claiming the thing as his. Thus, a person who has only a future interest in a thing—no matter how ample it will be on fruition—may very easily find himself in the position of the holder of legal rather than social rights, capable of evidencing his claim to a thing only by invoking a specialist opinion.[24] No matter how crude this focus upon contemporaneous life on the planet's surface may seem to the Scientist, however, it makes perfectly good sense from the Layman's point of view. For the Layman just happens to be living right now on the surface of the earth, and what he most pressingly needs are some simple criteria that (a) will permit him to identify those things that he may presently use to achieve his present purposes, and (b) the people he must contact if he is to obtain permission to use things that are not his. For these purposes, the distinction between social property and legal property makes very good sense indeed. And since the idea of social property is of such central importance in everyday life, it will serve to define the focus of takings law, so long as it is dominated by the concerns of Ordinary Observers.

LAYMAN'S THING HAS BEEN TAKEN

Transfer of Rightful Possession

Let us limit our attention for a time to social property— Layman's things—and count the ways in which Layman's things can be taken from him. I shall begin by contrasting two hypothetical cases whose correct doctrinal solution I think any competent lawyer will find easy; in the first case, no compensation will be awarded under present law; in the second, compensation will be granted as a matter of course. Despite the fact that these cases are easy under existing law, they do not seem easy under any of the modes of Scientific adjudication we have considered; in contrast, when viewed from the perspective of a moderately restrained Ordinary judge, existing doctrine is not only predictable but inevitable. In short, it is only by adopting an Ordinary interpretation of the takings clause that one can explain why these easy cases— in which the correct solution is not open to endless argument and anxious indecision—are easy.

Consider, then, the Layman family, proud in their possession of two Cadillac cars and the other accoutrements of the good life. Layman's present standard of living, it appears, is being threatened by a new crisis in Arab-American relations which has forced the American government to choose between two drastic gas conservation measures, each of which will make automotive travel far more costly than at present. Under the first statute, the maximum speed limit on all highways will be lowered to twenty-five miles an hour, a limit designed to cut gasoline consumption by half. Under the second statute, the government will leave the speed limit intact but take possession of half the nation's automobiles and ship them to Montana for the duration of the crisis—once again cutting fuel consumption by half. For present purposes, I am not interested in whether there are better ways to fulfill the energy objective than the two I have hypothesized. My only aim here is to determine how Layman's claim for compensation will be treated under the alternative scenarios. To make the comparison more striking, imagine that the monetary loss suffered by Layman under both statutes is precisely the same. Assume that, as a result of the speed-limit statute, each of Layman's Cadillacs depreciates in value from $5000 to $3000, leaving him $4000 poorer overall. Similarly, under the car seizure statute, Layman is left with one car whose value increases from $5000 to $6000 as a result of the legislated automobile scarcity, once again leaving Layman $4000 poorer at Time Three than he was at Time One. Nonetheless, despite the equal monetary loss, Layman will obtain compensation in the car-seizure case,[25] but will be required to bear the loss in the speed-limit case. Not only will these seemingly similar cases be treated differently, but neither will strike the contemporary lawyer as raising a difficult legal issue under established doctrine. In the car seizure case, the government has taken possession of Layman's car—an act that traditionally carries with it the requirement that compensation be paid.[26] In the speed-limit case, the government will be said by courts to have merely passed a regulation which has caused Layman a 40 percent loss —an amount that will be considered far too little to warrant compensation.[27]

As we have seen, it is easy for the Scientific Policymaker to look on this doctrinal effort as grossly oversimplified at best. On the one hand, recall that both Utilitarian and Kantian judges will have great difficulty accepting the present per se rule requiring compensation whenever a property owner is ousted from title or possession [28]—hence the car-shipment statute will not so clearly seem to require compensation. On the other hand, Scientific Policymakers will not stop their inquiry into the speed-limit statute as soon as they learn that Layman's Cadillacs have only declined in value by 40 percent, since many other factors will be considered relevant as well.[29] Hence the speed-limit statute will not so clearly seem to escape the compensation requirement. This said, I am not terribly interested in predicting how one or another Policymaking judge would actually decide these two cases; this will depend greatly both on the particular Comprehensive View and the particular conception of judicial role that prevails within the legal system. For present purposes it is enough to note, first, that the correct result in either case is *not* obvious under many plausible forms of Scientific Policymaking, and, second, that it is even less obvious that a clear-thinking Policymaking judge will grant recovery in one case and deny it in the other, rather than treating the two cases in the same way.

Nevertheless, drawing a sharp distinction between the two cases seems ridiculously easy to those who attempt an Ordinary Observer's interpretation of the takings clause. In the car-shipment case, it seems clear that as a result of the government's action at Time Two, one of Layman's Cadillacs is no longer Layman's thing at Time Three, but instead belongs to some government bureaucrat out there in Montana. Hence, a prima facie case of a taking has been made out. The only question left open is whether a well-socialized Layman ought to recognize that driving two Cadillacs during the fuel crisis is unacceptably harmful to others. In contrast, despite Layman's displeasure at the $4000 loss he has suffered under the speed-limit law, he would be exceedingly puzzled if somebody thought it proper to assert: "As a result of the statute, this Cadillac isn't *your* Cadillac anymore." As a matter of ordinary language, this is quite plainly false. *Despite the fact that the thing is worth a good deal less, it is just as much Layman's thing as it was before:* others still have a prima facie obligation to ask his permission to use the cars, while he can still use his Cadillacs in lots of ways that others can't. Since, despite the speed law, both Cadillacs remain Layman's things at Time Three, it follows that an Ordinary judge would find that the plaintiff has not even made out a good prima facie case for compensation.[30] The two cases not only fall out in opposite categories, but they fall out just as they do in the received doctrine of the present day. Indeed, even the law's doctrinal labels are here suggestive of their Ordinary origin—the car-seizure situation being the classic legal case of a "taking," while the speed-limit statute serves as the classic case of a noncompensable "regulation." [31]

In saying this, I would not wish you to think that the Ordinary Observer pictures his problem as if it contained nothing but crude and simple lines while his Scientific counterpart paints only gray on gray. Instead, the roles can be reversed, with the Ordinary jurist calling for the exercise of delicate judgment and the Scientist wondering what the complex analysis is all about. To illustrate this, let us consider a different aspect of the problem raised by my hypothetical car-seizure statute. Assume for the moment that the Scientific Policymaker, for reasons that seem sufficient to him, joins with his Ordinary colleague in concluding that Layman is entitled to compensation. Having cleared the initial hurdle without an upset, it remains for both our worthies to determine the dollar amount owing to Layman that will justly compensate him for his loss. This issue is problematic when it is recalled that, as a result of the car-seizure statute, the market value of the Cadillac remaining in private hands has increased in value from five thousand dollars to six. Hence, while the market value of the Cadillac taken by the government was five thousand dollars at Time One, the *net* impact on Layman's wealth as a result of the statutory redistribution of property bundles is only four thousand dollars. How much, then, should Layman receive in just compensation—five thousand or four?

Despite their differences on other matters, all Scientific Policymakers will think the answer to this question easy and obvious. Putting administrative costs to one side for the moment, Scientists would assert that the correct sum of money due is four thousand dollars. For them, the fact that one bundle of rights, labeled Cadillac No. 1, suffered a $5000 loss does not count as a reason for ignoring the fact that a second bundle of rights, labeled Cadillac No. 2, has gained in value as a result of the very same legislative redistribution. For the Scientist will recall that these two "bundles" are treated as separate packages, rather than one larger package, merely for reasons of technical analytic convenience which ought not be considered normatively important in their own right. Hence, no good reason can be given for refusing to treat the two bundles as one when this will generate a result more consistent with the Comprehensive View. And this, it would seem, is precisely the case here—for nothing we have said suggests that any Utilitarian or Kantian judge would claim that Layman has a constitutional right to be *better* off at Time Three than he was at Time One. Yet is this not precisely what will happen if Layman receives more than four thousand dollars?

To ask the Scientific question is to answer it, which is, of course, the very essence of an "easy" case. Indeed, the only factor that could conceivably make the issue difficult is the added administrative cost involved in making the extra factual finding as to the extent to which Cadillac No. 2—still in Layman's possession—has increased in value. If the extra cost of fact-finding exceeded a thousand dollars, for example, most Utilitarian judges would have little difficulty in concluding that the extra factual precision was not worth the trouble.[32] The extent to which a Scientific judge will search beyond the bundle labeled Cadillac No. 1 in his calculation of net impact is, however, a question of administrative convenience only, whose answer may well differ if the litigant is Hertz Rent-A-Car rather than a single middle-class Layman. At best, then, it may be *prudent* to give Layman five thousand dollars and be done with the matter, making him the beneficiary of the fact that determining facts is a costly business. In situations in which this consideration is unimportant, Layman will receive only four thousand dollars and not a penny more.

In contrast, the Ordinary judge will suspect that Layman is entitled to five thousand dollars on grounds of basic principle. According to him, Layman has qualified for compensation not because he has suffered some general diminution in the value of his asset portfolio *but because one of his things has been taken.* Since that thing was worth five thousand dollars, this is what should be paid without further inquiry into the recent fluctuations in other parts of Layman's portfolio. After all, that inquiry might reveal that some of Layman's other things have also diminished in value as a result of government action, yet these losses would *not* ordinarily be compensable unless they involved a taking of a distinct thing. And if other government-induced losses are ignored in the compensation calculus, the existence of government-induced gains that have accrued in other parts of the portfolio should also be deemed irrelevant. For it would seem quite unfair to look beyond Cadillac No. 1 only to find the gains but not the losses. As a consequence, the Ordinary judge will tend to limit very narrowly the range of inquiry concerning the degree to which a government taking has generated benefits in other parts of the petitioner's portfolio. It is only if the government has taken a part of one of Layman's things (for example, by taking half of Layman's land for a highway, thereby making the other half more valuable) that the Ordinary judge can see some sense in netting the losses by the gains. It is revealing, then, that the present case-law conforms to the pattern predicted of the Ordinary judge, in which the thoroughly un-Scientific notion of a "partial taking" occupies a prominent place.[33]

We are now in a position to discern larger patterns emerging from our treatment of separate issues. In the car-seizure case, for example, a typical American judge would have no difficulty finding that Layman's Cadillac has been subjected to a taking under the Constitution; then he would go on to award Layman five thousand dollars for his loss, though here he might be troubled by the analogy of the "partial" takings cases, under which the loss suffered on one part of a single parcel of land may be offset by the gains accruing to another portion of the parcel. While this pattern is readily explicable in terms of Ordinary Observing, it is quite puzzling from a Scientific Policymaking point of view. Both the judge's confidence as to the *need* for compensation and his perplexity as to the *measure* of compensation seem misplaced. As to the need for compensation, some Policymakers will conclude that compensation ought not be paid at all, and many will think that if compensation is to be paid in the car-seizure case, it should also be paid in the speed-limit case. As to the measure of compensation, all will think Layman is entitled to no more than $4000 provided that the change in the price of his remaining car is a fact that may be easily ascertained in a relatively accurate way. We are confronted, then, with a difference in approach that is important not only here and there but seems to command attention everywhere.

The Destruction of a Thing

Up to now we have been dealing with two of the simplest and most fundamental categories invoked in the Ordinary Observer's interpretation of the takings clause. In one group can be placed all those cases—like the one involved under the car-seizure statute—in which it seems plain as a matter of Ordinary language that Layman's Cadillac has been taken from him and now belongs to a third party, who is usually—

but not always—some state official.[34] In the second group can
be placed all those cases—like the one involved under the
speed-limit statute—in which, though Layman's thing has diminished in value, it is still fair to say that it remains Layman's Cadillac, and nobody else's, at Time Three. Cases of the
first type will seem to Ordinary judges to constitute prima
facie instances of governmental taking; situations of the second
type will be derogated as involving nothing more than a
"mere" regulation for which compensation is not required.

Unfortunately, however, the case-law has thrown up countless instances that defy classification in terms of our two simple
categories. The problem is that the car-seizure scenario represents only one of the ways in which Layman's things can be
taken from him by the activist state. In cases of this first type,
not only does the state (a) deprive Layman of his thing, but it
also (b) gives the thing to someone else who thenceforth exercises social property rights in it. Yet a moment's thought indicates that condition (b) is not necessary before Layman may
properly complain that the state has taken something from
him. Imagine, for example, that the state, in order to limit
energy demand, simply orders each two-car family to destroy
one of its automobiles posthaste. In such a case there could
be no doubt that standard English permits Layman to assert
that the state has *taken* his Cadillac from him, even though it
has not *given* the Cadillac to anybody else. And if a Layman
can properly use language in this way, it follows that an Ordinary Observer will recognize a prima facie taking not only
when Layman's thing has been *transferred* to a third party but
when it has been utterly *destroyed* by the state as well.

Once again, the distinctive character of this second class of
Ordinary takings—in which Layman's thing has been destroyed—can best be brought out by a comparison of cases that
seem quite similar to each other from the Scientific point of
view. Consider, for example, the relative position of two property owners—Layman and Speculator—who happen to own
some land in the same part of town. Layman's land is occupied by a Hamburger Heaven which, unhappily, is a very

marginal operation. Indeed, if Layman were obliged to raze
his store to the ground and resell the land for residential
purposes, his total loss would be only $10,000. In contrast,
Speculator's site, bordering on nearby Highway One, is ideally
situated for a fast-order eatery; indeed, the Hamburger
Heaven folks have recently offered him $100,000 for his lot
while it is worth only $50,000 as a place for houses. Despite
the good offer, however, Speculator has decided to bide his
time and wait for the even better deal he is sure will come.
Unfortunately for both our characters, the town has just
marked out their area as a purely residential zone, in which
all forms of commercial enterprise are forbidden. As a consequence Layman loses $10,000; Speculator at least $50,000; and
both sue for compensation under the takings clause.

It should be clear by now that a Scientific judge would approach these two law-suits acutely aware of their similarities. So
far as he is concerned, the town has taken the same right out
of both the property-bundle held by Layman and the bundle
held by Speculator. Moreover, the money loss suffered by
Speculator as a result of the property redistribution is five
times that suffered by Layman. Hence, it would seem that—
other things being equal—Speculator's claim to consideration
under the compensation clause is entitled to greater attention.
Of course, other things may not be equal. Perhaps the process
costs involved in accurately measuring Layman's loss are
somewhat lower than in Speculator's case. Perhaps operators of
hamburger joints are more risk-averse than land speculators,
thereby permitting Layman to advance a weightier Appeal to
General Uncertainty on his own behalf. Nevertheless, it is
far from obvious that these differences will convince all Scientific Policymakers to treat the two cases differently, paying
Layman $10,000, while denying Speculator his $50,000.[35]

Yet this is precisely the law of the United States today.[36] Indeed, not only is the law perfectly clear in its different treatment of Speculator and Layman, but judges consistently reach
these disparate results without any of the agonizing which
normally accompanies the perception of a peculiarly difficult

problem. Once again, it is the ease with which the judges come to seemingly un-Scientific results that constitutes the deeper mystery which lies at the heart of contemporary takings law.

The puzzle can be readily resolved, however, as soon as the problem is viewed from the perspective of the Ordinary Observer. So far as he is concerned, it is easy to see that Layman has been deprived of one of his things as a result of the town's new zoning law. At Time One, Layman had a Hamburger Heaven; at Time Three, Layman's store is no more; and so a prima facie case of takings has been established. In contrast, the town's new regulation has not deprived Speculator of any of the things that formerly belonged to him. Thus, if a non-lawyer had asked Speculator to describe what he owned at Time One in ordinary language, Speculator would doubtless have replied: "That patch of land over there belongs to me." [37] And despite the town's new enactment, it is still appropriate for Speculator to say the same thing about his land at Time Three. While doubtless Speculator is no longer able to use his thing in as many ways as he could before, we have already noted that (in modern America at least) nobody thinks that one is entitled to use his things in any way he pleases.[38] Instead, it will suffice if Speculator can use his land in lots of ways that others can only undertake with his permission. There is, of course, much imprecision in a formula invoking the right to do a *lot* of things with one's thing, and we shall soon be obliged to investigate this formula further.[39] For present purposes, however, it should be clear that depriving Speculator of the right to build things like a Hamburger Heaven will still typically permit him to develop "his" land in any number of different ways. To put the point in terms that can be found in countless judicial opinions, what the town has done is "merely" to deprive Speculator of one of the possible uses to which the land may be put.[40] Or, in my terms, it remains fair to say that the regulation has not deprived Speculator of *his* land or any of the other things that belonged to him at Time One. While Layman has established a prima facie case of a taking, Speculator is merely complaining about a regulation that has deprived him of one of the many ways in which he can use his thing.[41]

Lest one think that the distinction between Layman and Speculator is "really" rooted in some deep judicial antipathy to land speculators, it will be wise to ring one final change on our Hamburger Heaven scenario. This time imagine that Speculator sells his land to Proprietor who in turn builds a Hamburger Heaven that does a thriving business with the teeming throng traveling on neighboring U.S. 1. After some time passes, however, the state opens a new interstate, reducing the flood of traffic on the old highway to a trickle. While Proprietor finds it possible to stay in business under the new conditions, he has suffered a $100,000 loss as a result of the state action. Nonetheless, the same American judge who is so solicitous over Layman's loss of $10,000 will deny Proprietor any compensation for his $100,000 injury.[42] The reason for Layman's recovery is not, then, to be found in some petty bourgeois prejudice for the small Proprietor, as opposed to the land Speculator. Rather it is based on the judicial perception that the challenged state action has deprived Layman of his Hamburger Heaven while the new road has not taken Proprietor's Heaven away from him.[43]

It is true, of course, that the road did divert many of Proprietor's customers away from his Hamburger Heaven. His former customers, however, were never Proprietor's things in the sense that he could use them in lots of ways without their consent, while others were obligated to obtain his permission before using them. Instead the travelers merely represented *an opportunity* from which he might profit, not one of the things he might use. It was, for example, perfectly plain to Proprietor (if he were even moderately well socialized) that he could not force passing motorists to stop at his stand; nor could he stop other hamburger joints from horning in on his customers. Since Proprietor could not convince a fellow Layman that the customers were *his things* during Time One, he cannot claim that one of his things has been taken from him at Time Two. As in Speculator's case, the new state action has deprived Proprietor of some of the profitable ways he could use his Hamburger Heaven; it has not, however, destroyed the thing itself in such a way that it could no longer be said to belong to Proprietor. And it is this fact of Ordinary language which is decisive.

It is important to emphasize how deeply unintelligible all this is to the Scientific Policymaker. Let us decompose Layman's bundle of rights into two smaller packages—one (marked "realty") dealing with the raw land on which his Hamburger Heaven is perched; the other (marked "fixtures") dealing with Heaven itself. So far as the package marked realty is concerned, Layman's bundle is identical to that held by Speculator at Time One. So far as the bundle marked fixtures is concerned, Layman is in the same position as Proprietor. Yet Layman wins and the other two lose, even though the dollar value of Layman's loss is smaller than *either* of the others. Moreover, this result is not reached by the courts after some complicated chain of policy-reasoning, but in a series of opinions that bear the marks of very little reasoning of any kind.[44] Why? So far as any Scientist is concerned, the answer must be that the judges have attended so little to takings law of late that they have failed to confront even the most glaring incongruities. The Ordinary Observer, in contrast, will advance a far different answer—the cases have provoked so little serious reasoning because their proper disposition seems so easy and obvious that any elaborate argument is superfluous.

It is, of course, the present thesis that there is a sense in which both sides are correct in their assessment of the existing legal situation. On the one hand, there can be no doubt that the Layman-Speculator-Proprietor problems *are* easy from the Ordinary Observing point of view and so unlikely to provoke prolonged and elaborate justification. On the other hand, as a result of our long neglect of the foundations of takings law, as well as the gradual increase in the Scientific character of the legal culture, these "easy" cases—and the unreasoned judicial responses they usually engender—begin to trouble the modern legal sensibility. Instead of taking the lack of judicial argumentation to suggest the presence of bedrock certainties, the

(Scientific) suspicion arises that the lines drawn by the Layman-Speculator-Proprietor trilogy are based on nothing more than arbitrary fiat—whose true character can be readily unmasked by the most elementary Scientific analysis.

It is not, however, the main point of this chapter to assess the power of the Scientific Policymaking challenge to the Ordinary Observing ideas that have for so long reigned supreme in Anglo-American law. Instead, my aim is to reconstruct sympathetically a form of thought which is no longer as accessible to us as it once was (and as it may once more become). Hence, it will pay to reflect one last time on what precisely it is that Layman—and not Speculator or Proprietor—has lost as a result of the town's new zoning law. After all, even at Time Three, it remains possible to point to a particular object that remains Layman's land, and particular objects that formerly constituted Layman's hamburger joint. Indeed, it may be possible to point to *every* physical object that formerly constituted Hamburger Heaven and say each still belongs to Layman. So what sort of thing is it that Layman has lost when the state closed down his Hamburger Heaven?

The answer, from the Ordinary Observer's point of view, does not seem too difficult. In engaging in property-talk with one another, ordinary people usually are not interested in enumerating a catalogue of physical objects that may or may not be theirs. Instead, Ordinary property talk is important because it provides a conceptual framework in which Laymen may understand the patterns of their legitimate social interaction and so conduct their lives in a socially respectable way. Hence it is critically important, both to Layman and his peers, whether or not Layman's land and Layman's hot plates add up, socially, to Layman's Hamburger Heaven. If they do, Layman (or his delegate) will be immersed in a complex pattern of interaction that would be entirely absent from his social universe if all he owned were some land, some hot plates, and other restaurant equipment. Thus, by transforming a functioning Hamburger Heaven into an assortment of random objects, the state has deprived Layman of an important way in which he understands himself and his relationship to his

world. When the state expels Layman from his Hamburger
Heaven, then, it would be peculiarly obtuse for an Observing
judge to deny compensation on the grounds that *all physical
objects* remain Layman's things, even if he can, at modest cost,
rebuild his very same Heaven on a new square of earth after
selling his old parcel. For the ultimate objective of the Ordinary Observer's interpretation of the Constitution is precisely to protect expectations of the well-socialized citizens who
relate to their world in the ordinary way. And it is this relationship which is at risk when the judge observes that Layman's Hamburger Heaven has been destroyed by state action.
Layman's things are social property, not merely packages of
legal rights existing solely for the convenience of the legal
analyst.

In saying this, I do not mean to suggest that if the state
leaves Hamburger Heaven intact as an operating enterprise
and merely takes one of the Heavenly hot plates, it should be
free from the burden of compensation under the Ordinary interpretation of the takings clause. Even though it is almost
certainly true that Layman's larger relationship to his world
is not dependent upon his continuing control over one hot
plate, it remains true that the state has deprived him of one
of his things, and this should be enough to establish a prima
facie case of a taking.[45] My point here is that Ordinary judges
(as revealed by their actual decisions) respect all the levels of
generality upon which laymen understand and describe their
relationships to things, and are prepared to intervene on behalf of *all* of Layman's things, whether they be relatively hard
and solid objects, like a hot plate, or some artifact whose social
identity as a thing is determined more by the distinctive way
in which a variety of hard and solid objects are socially patterned, like Hamburger Heaven.

Rendering a Thing Useless

Extending the class of prima facie takings to include cases
in which one of Layman's things has been destroyed does not,
I think, place any significant strain upon an Ordinary inter-

pretation of the takings clause. Just as it makes perfect ordinary sense to say that *Layman's thing has been taken from
him* when his car is shipped to Montana, so too an Ordinary
English speaker can say that same thing with the same con-
viction to describe the consequences of a state decision that
destroys Hamburger Heaven. A more difficult problem arises,
however, as soon as one presses onward to consider whether
our recently expanded class of prima facie takings cases still
remains too narrow: Is it possible for an Ordinary judge to
conclude that the state has taken one of Layman's things, even
though it has neither transferred nor destroyed it? [46]

I think so. To see why, let us return to Layman's Cadillacs
and consider a third device by which the American government might wish to attain energy independence from hostile
foreign powers. Imagine that a bright policy analyst discovers
that the cost of shipping half of America's cars to Montana is
astronomical, as is the cost of policing a twenty-five-mile-an-
hour speed limit. Consequently, he proposes that Congress pass
a law requiring two-car families like Layman's to keep one of
their cars permanently parked in the garage for the duration
of the crisis. Assume, moreover, that the analyst has the foresight to forbid Layman from selling his immobilized Cadillac
to anybody else, thereby assuring that the car will not slip its
way back unnoticed into the transportation stock. As a consequence of this new statute, Layman will, by hypothesis, suffer some familiar grievances: although the value of his remaining Cadillac has increased from $5000 to $6000, this
thousand dollar increment is not sufficient to offset completely
the $5000 loss he has suffered on his other car. And so, once
again, the Ordinary judge is obliged to determine whether the
new statute has so changed Layman's social relationship to the
car that it is no longer fair to say that it remains *Layman's*
Cadillac.

It should be plain that this question will seem a good deal
more difficult to the Ordinary judge than the cases of prima
facie taking we have previously discussed. When Layman's
Cadillac was shipped to Montana or simply destroyed, there

could be no doubt that the Ordinary sentence, "Layman's car has been taken from him," could be appropriately applied in common speech. In the case of compulsory garaging, however, it still makes *some* Ordinary sense to say that the Cadillac remains Layman's thing at Time Three. There it would be, all right, clogging up Layman's garage rather than anyone else's— generating tax liabilities and maybe even damage suits for him if it is an attractive nuisance. Moreover, if Layman tried to unload his white elephant in the black market, one could readily imagine a policeman discovering the crime with the exclamation: "Hey buddy, what are you doing driving that car! That's not your car. It's *Layman's* Cadillac!"

Yet while it sometimes makes Ordinary sense to identify the car as Layman's thing there is something very Pickwickian involved in the property talk at issue here. To put the problem dramatically, consider the following Ordinary scenario:

> *Friend:* Layman, I should like to make you a gift of this beautiful new Cadillac.
>
> *Layman:* Wonderful! What a beautiful machine! Thank you very much!
>
> *Friend:* It's nothing really.
>
> *Layman:* You're too kind. Now I wonder what I shall do with this fantastic gift.
>
> *Friend:* Hold it. The Cadillac is yours so long as you keep it in your garage. No other use is permitted to you.
>
> *Layman:* Is this some sort of joke? Why would I want to keep a useless car in my garage?
>
> *Friend:* But aren't you pleased that the car is yours for-ever more?
>
> *Layman:* If that's what you mean by ownership, I want no part of it.

In ordinary life, of course, this conversation would end with Layman refusing the "gift" of the car, retaining his Ordinary conception of ownership intact. Under the compulsory garaging statute, however, the Layman is given no such choice. Like it or not, he has been saddled with the car. Hence, the problem for the Ordinary Observer: On the one hand, there remain contexts in which it makes perfectly good sense to identify the car as Layman's Cadillac even after the compulsory garaging statute has been enacted; on the other hand, there is an Ordinary sense in which it is nothing but a bad joke to say that the Cadillac remains Layman's thing at Time Three. We are, then, confronted with a "hard case" from the Ordinary point of view, since its consideration forces to the surface ambiguities in Ordinary talk which are generally irrelevant to the conduct of everyday life. Despite the difficulty, however, an Ordinary judge cannot remain forever in a state of perplexity. The constitutional text makes the decisive question whether Layman's thing has been "taken." And so the Ordinary judge must choose in the end between the divergent implications of Ordinary talk as he tries to make sense of a constitutional text and apply its command to the case before him.

It is at this point that the Ordinary theory of judicial role becomes of the first importance. A deferential judge will adopt a relatively "strict" construction of the text, restricting his conception of a prima facie taking to the easy cases which would plainly be called takings in ordinary life. For him, the decisive fact is that before Layman ever came to court, officials in the political branches considered his plea for relief and rejected it as unmeritorious. As a deferential judge, he will not upset this presumptively well-ordered judgment unless its lack of congruence with Ordinary talk and expectation is plain.

In contrast, an activist judge will not trust the political branches to elaborate unaided the dominant structure of institutionalized expectation even in hard cases. Instead, he will—to one degree or another—scrutinize the divergent tendencies of Ordinary usage in the hope of observing more sensitively the subtler patterns of social expectation which (he assumes) the linguistic tensions reveal. For him, the Pickwickian sense in which the car remains Layman's thing serves as a signal that there is something deeply wrong with the compulsory garaging statute. The problem is that, as a result of the compulsory garaging statute, it seems likely that Layman will *never* be advantaged by the attribution to him of a property relationship to "his" car; instead, *Layman's special relationship to the car threatens to serve exclusively as a reason for imposing burdens upon him which he would otherwise have avoided.*[47] Yet it is not for the sake of assuming extra burdens that property-talk is of such importance in Layman's effort to construct an intelligible relationship between himself and his social reality. While the ordinary person understands that certain liabilities may follow if he claims something as his, the principal point of property talk is to permit Layman to identify some things in his environment that he may exploit *to his advantage* without incurring adverse social sanction. It is for this reason that a person who says "From now on, this car is yours so long as you don't use it in any way that you find useful," exhibits either a bad sense of humor or a complete ignorance of the point of property-talk in American society. This conceded, it follows that the state has undercut Layman's expectations regarding "his" thing no less surely by passing the garaging statute than it would have if it had simply destroyed the car or shipped it to Montana. To put the point in a more legalistic way: once the judge is willing to indulge the activist premise that judges are sometimes institutionally competent to sift the fine grain of ordinary usage, he can with little difficulty construe the constitutional text that insists on a "taking" to embrace "hard" cases in which the state renders a thing useless by declaring these situations analogous to "easy" cases of transfer or destruction.[48]

While this argument by analogy will not, I think, seem dubious for those even slightly inclined toward activism, I have thus far couched the argument in terms that require a very problematic finding of fact from the activist Ordinary judge. Before a judge could find that the state has taken Layman's thing by rendering it useless, it would seem that he must confront the disquieting fact that many things can be exceedingly valuable to one particular Layman, yet worse than useless to another, depending upon their particular goals in life. Even so far as the Cadillac is concerned, it is barely conceivable that a particular Layman will find the car a thing of such beauty that it will seem worthwhile (to him) to keep it as a kind of free-standing sculpture; or perhaps even an immobilized Cadillac will still serve as a valuable status symbol; or perhaps Layman's children will find it an admirable playhouse; or. . . . And while the Ordinary judge might find these remaining potential uses sufficiently rare or trivial to warrant the construction of a per se rule requiring the compensation of all Laymen faced with the "compulsory-garaging" statute, it is easy to imagine cases in which this kind of rough justice will seem very rough indeed.[49] Thus, to evaluate the merit of this third "harder" category of takings cases, the Ordinary judge must sometimes undertake a forbidding inquiry into the subjective tastes and values of the particular Layman whose things have arguably become useless.

Fortunately, however, it should prove possible in almost all cases to devise a satisfactory solution without undertaking such a problematic judicial enterprise. For unlike our hypothetical compulsory-garaging statute, the law does not usually deprive Laymen of the right to sell their things on the marketplace. And when alienability is permitted, judges will generally be able to determine whether a thing has been rendered useless simply by looking at the price it fetches on the market. If the market price remains substantial, this means that someone, somewhere, finds Layman's thing to have positive value. Thus if Layman does not happen to find the thing *intrinsically* valuable, he will still see a point in claiming it as his for its *resale* value. In contrast, if the market value of the thing approaches zero,[50] then there is good reason to believe that Layman would think it merely a bad joke for him to be told that, despite the new statute, the thing remains his. For it is precisely Layman's point that he will simply abandon his claim to the thing, and no longer treat it as his own, if it remains burdened by its new restrictions.

Having come this far in our theoretical argument, it is possible to understand a number of peculiar features of present-day legal doctrine that otherwise are deeply puzzling. For example, in assessing compensation claims for property that has neither been transferred or destroyed by state action, modern judges are only interested in the *percentage* by which a thing's market value has declined between Time One and Time Three, rather than the *dollar amount* of the loss that has been suffered.[51] Thus, if a thing's value drops by a thousand dollars from $1010 to $10, all but the most deferential judges will concede that a prima facie taking has occurred and anxiously consider whether the taking can be justified; in contrast, if a thing's value diminishes from $100 million to $90 million, even the most activist judge will dismiss the takings claim as frivolous.[52] Indeed, despite the fact that judges speak in terms of the *percentage* of diminution in value, it seems that only when the *absolute value* of Layman's thing approaches zero can one be at all confident that judges will be satisfied that a prima facie taking has occurred.[53] As Michelman puts it, "the [diminution of value] test poses not nearly so loose a question of degree; it does not ask "how much" but rather (like the physical-occupation test) it asks 'whether or not'; whether or not the measure in question can easily be seen to have practically deprived the claimant of some distinctly perceived, sharply crystallized, investment-backed expectation." [54] To put the point in terms of the 80 percent loss suffered by our unhappy Marshans, their case would seem more promising to the professional eye if instead of their land declining from $25,000 to $5,000, their marsh had originally been valued at $250 an acre and then depreciated to $50. This of course is precisely what one would expect from judges who are attempting to ascertain whether it seems only a bad joke to assure Layman that the thing remains his own despite the new governmental regulation.[55]

Apart from rendering intelligible the general drift of cases in which a taking is found on the basis of a severe diminution of market value, an Ordinary Observing approach makes intelligible that aspect of the formula that has most troubled thoughtful observers.[56] Several writers have noted the puzzling fact that in assessing the degree of financial loss, the judges never consider the extent to which the claimant's *entire* port-folio has suffered a diminution of value, but only seek to deter-mine the extent to which the price of the *particular thing* sub-ject to regulation has plummeted toward zero. Yet if, by in-voking the diminution of value formula, the courts were trying to isolate crudely those who have most suffered from legislative redistributions, this form of myopia could hardly be justified. For it predictably leads to a system under which many people suffering relatively small losses in total wealth recover while many suffering large losses go entirely ignored. Layman may recover $5000 when his car is immobilized but may be without a remedy when his house plummets in value from $75,000 to $25,000 as a result of the enactment of some "mere" regulation. It is, I think, far from obvious that such disparate outcomes could be defended in any way that a Scientific judge of the Kantian variety would think persuasive.[57] And so far as a Utilitarian judge is concerned, Michelman has provided us with a telling account of the difficulty of justifying the pre-vailing judicial concentration on the extent to which the par-ticular thing, rather than the entire portfolio, has diminished in value:

> The worth of this kind of analysis in a utilitarian compen-sation scheme depends on a number of assumptions which, while not void of plausibility, are surely debatable. The assumptions are (1) that one thinks of himself not just as owning a total amount of wealth or income, but also as owning several discrete "things" whose destinies he con-trols; (2) that deprivation of one of these mentally circum-scribed things is an event attended by pain of a specially acute or demoralizing kind, as compared with what one ex-periences in response to the different kind of event con-sisting of a general decline in one's net worth; and (3) that

events of the specially painful kind can usually be identified by compensation tribunals with relative ease.

Of the three propositions, the second surely is the most
suspect. The first seems self-evident, and the third seems
probably true.[58]

As soon as one shifts from the Scientific to the Ordinary
theory of judging,[59] however, the legal scene is quite transformed and a dark cloud of suspicion no longer surrounds the
law's traditional concentration on the *thing's* diminution in
value.[60] In contrast to his Scientific Utilitarian counterpart, an
Ordinary Observer is not required to indulge Michelman's
second, "suspect" assumption that the "deprivation of one of
these mentally circumscribed things is an event attended by
pain of a specially acute or demoralizing kind." Instead, without pretending to any effort at felicific calculation, it is enough
for the Ordinary judge to reason from Michelman's first, "self-
evident" assumption that the ordinary person "thinks of himself not just as owning a total amount of wealth or income but
also as owning several discrete 'things.' " For if this is a "self
evident" fact about the structure of Ordinary lay thought, the
Ordinary judge, as a matter of basic principle, will find no
difficulty in incorporating it into legal analysis—indeed, to do
so will seem to him the very essence of judicial principle. Since
the typical Layman thinks of himself as owning things, the
Ordinary judge can readily accept a "diminution of value" test
which indicates whether particular *things* have been rendered
useless without perceiving the need to consider whether aggregate *personal* wealth has suffered an extreme decline. Unfortunately, while Michelman is obviously searching for the
key which will unlock the deeper meaning of existing doctrinal
categories, he can never quite overcome his fascination with
the Scientific approach, especially its Utilitarian variety,[61] to
bring himself to contemplate the possibility that courts may be
understanding their mission in a way that deeply challenges
the premises of his own analysis. As a consequence, Michelman's doctrinal discussion takes the form of an earnest attempt

to weave a Scientifically respectable cloak for otherwise shabby judicial doctrine. The fact that Michelman himself recognizes the cloak to be awkward and ill-fitting is, of course, a very high tribute to his scholarly integrity. Even more important, it is a revealing indication of the increasing reluctance of sophisticated American legal scholars to take Ordinary Observing seriously. For surely it is surprising that a scholar of the first rank—who manifests no desire to reform existing judicial doctrine [62]— nevertheless devotes himself to an elaborate Scientific analysis without noting the existence of an alternative legal analytic that will provide far more compelling support for the juridical status quo.[63] Why would a leading scholar disdain a comfortable and close-fitting garment for one so awkward and ill-fitting? Is it simply a matter of chance that *neither* leading courts *nor* modern commentators are capable of providing a convincing elaboration of the premises that seem nevertheless to structure constitutional doctrine? Or is it a sign that Ordinary Observing is losing its hold upon the American legal mind?

I shall fumble with these large questions in the concluding chapter. Since I do not pretend to answer them even there, I am happy to invite the reader to think about them on his own while we go about the business of completing a sketch of the Ordinary interpretation of the takings clause.

LAYMAN'S THING HAS BEEN TAKEN BY THE STATE

Thus far we have merely enumerated the three basic ways in which one of Layman's things may be taken from him—the thing may be transferred to a third party; it may be destroyed; it may be rendered useless. But even if Layman is deprived of his things in one of these ways, he may nevertheless fail to make out a prima facie case of a taking. The fact that a thing is taken constitutes a necessary, but not a sufficient, condition for recovery. To see this, let us return to Layman and his Cadillacs. This time imagine that, despite the American government's efforts, the Arab oil cartel gets even tougher with the West, raising the price of gasoline to ten dollars a gallon.

As a consequence, neither Layman nor anybody else is interested in operating a gas-guzzling Cadillac. What was once Layman's Cadillac has suddenly become only a piece of junk—to be sold to a scrap dealer for recycling.[64] Nevertheless, I take it that no lawyer would think the United States government has a constitutional obligation to pay for his loss, despite the fact that Layman's Cadillac has been rendered useless as a result of the change in relative prices.[65] It is not enough that one of Layman's things be taken; it is necessary that it be taken in a way in which the state's involvement is judged significant. To put the point in the conventional legal way, there can be little doubt that the takings clause—like so much else in the Constitution—is understood to constrain only state action and not analogous conduct attempted by private parties.[66]

It should be emphasized, moreover, that the Ordinary Observer's conception of state action will be quite different from that which will impress a Scientific Policymaker. From the latter's point of view it is apparent that officials of the modern state act to control the marketplace in manifold ways—weaving a web of taxes, subsidies, regulations so complex as to challenge the understanding of the most acute analyst. The Ordinary Observer, in contrast, will be impressed by the fact that the typical middle-class Layman is quite unwilling to spend the enormous time and effort required to master the complex state-market relationship that obtains in contemporary society and apply this understanding to the evaluation of state responsibility for particular events in his environment. As a consequence, the Layman's understanding of the extent of state involvement will be shaped by a set of cultural cues that appear on the surface of ordinary life. For example, Layman has been taught to associate changes in prices with the economic system while changes in laws are associated with the state. Thus, if the *price* of gas increases, Layman will not attempt to move beyond the surface of things to determine whether the increase is to be attributed to the Arab cartel, a presidential decision to increase tariffs, or a multitude of other factors. Instead, he will invoke the simple rule of thumb that price changes are typically generated by market forces for which the state does not assume particular responsibility. In contrast, if gas is allocated through ration-books or explicit bureaucratic order, the state has been implicated in the decision in a way Layman can readily recognize. It follows that if the judge wishes to apply the state action doctrine in a way consistent with Ordinary Observing, he will refuse to apply the takings clause to a multitude of situations in which the state's guiding hand is invisible to the Layman's eye, limiting the clause to those contexts in which official power assumes a form that ordinary people have been taught to recognize as characteristic of state involvement.

From the point of view of the Scientific Policymaker, of course, such a dramatic limitation of the clause's scope is indefensible. So far as he is concerned, there are a variety of market and nonmarket ways of effectuating a Comprehensive View [67] and no a priori reason to believe that the justice of compensation should be fundamentally affected by the particular form of control selected. Thus, the Layman's exclusive concern with forms of state intervention that seem "law-like," rather than "market-like," is to the Scientist merely a manifestation of deep ignorance which appears a peculiarly unlikely candidate for promotion to the status of constitutional truth.

It is therefore very revealing to recognize that *none* of the government's "behind-the-scenes" efforts to manipulate the price system have generated serious takings issues, while analogous efforts raise acute difficulties as soon as they assume a law-like form on the surface of ordinary life. For example, while modern government has self-consciously manipulated prices in a wide variety of hidden ways without serious challenge, President Nixon's decision [68] to control prices by bureaucratic intervention into ordinary life predictably generated judicial consideration of the takings issue.[69] Indeed, some of the great "hard cases" of takings law can be understood as efforts by the Court to assess the extent to which Layman would associate the state, rather than the market, with the taking of one of his things. Thus, in *Eureka Mines*[70] the Court was obliged to consider whether a wartime bureaucratic order closing the gold mines, so as to free scarce labor for higher priority occupations, constituted a taking requiring compensation. While the majority decided against compensation, I am quite confident that everyone would have found *Eureka* far easier if the government had pursued its objective by behind-the-scenes manipulation of gold prices instead of embarking upon a set of bureaucratic orders that the ordinary citizen naturally associates with the state.[71]

The actions of publicly owned enterprises raise similar difficulties. Once again, while the state regulates enterprise activity in a wide variety of ways, it declares its presence to the Layman in a special way when its own officials actually operate a state-owned firm. Although, from a Scientific point of view, the differences between the Tennessee Valley Authority and a privately owned (but publicly regulated) power company may seem a matter of degree, the Observer will detect a fundamental difference. When Layman interacts with a *public* company in his daily life, he recognizes by the name on the door that he is dealing with the state; in contrast, when dealing with a private (though heavily regulated) company, he perceives the state as playing its normal backstopping role— in which it cannot so readily be held responsible for the content of the "private" transaction. Given our thesis, then, it is significant that with the expansion of state-owned enterprise— most notably in the operation of airports—the courts have been forced to deal with an increasing number of "inverse condemnation" suits [72] initiated by Laymen who claim that action undertaken by one or another state-sponsored activity has triggered the compensation clause.

Here, however, courts have been relatively cautious in extending the compensation requirement—for reasons which are not, I think, difficult to see. It is in dealing with the status of state enterprise that an Ordinary interpretation of the takings

clause most clearly threatens the new economic order wrought
by Roosevelt, whose legitimacy forms the very bedrock of post-
New Deal constitutional law. For is it not a reasonable fear
that requiring compensation whenever Laymen see the state as
involved will cripple—if not kill—the activist policy in-
augurated by the New Deal? Indeed, in one of the great
opinions by Justice Brandeis, shaping post-Roosevelt constitutional jurisprudence, this anxiety can be quite readily detected.[73] As the memories of the Old Court of the 1920s and
1930s fade, judges have, however, gradually expanded the constitutional idea of state involvement even in the takings area [74]
—though the restraint with which the judges work contrasts
sharply to the innovative way they have expanded the concept
of state action in their effort to broaden the scope of the civil
liberties protected by the equal protection and due process
clauses.[75]

It should be emphasized that, as in all else that concerns
Ordinary Observing, we are not dealing here with a judicial
effort to generate a coherent conception of state involvement
from a set of highly abstract principles but an attempt to explicate the evaluative structure into which middle-class Americans are in fact socialized. Doubtless there have been times
and places in which no distinction between state and market
institutions has been made; [76] doubtless the prevailing ordinary conception is itself changing as the economic order de-
parts, in increasingly obvious ways, from the paradigms of
neoclassical political economy. Nonetheless, I think it remains
true that middle-class children are still taught (both by word
and deed) that there is a very great difference in what they
can expect from market and nonmarket institutions; that,
moreover, they cannot hold political authority directly ac-
countable for any and all changes in the market system, but
only for those in which the state seems involved in some
special way. And so long as this is true, the requirement of
special state involvement represents an additional, distinct
burden that must be satisfied before an Ordinary Observer

will recognize that a taking has occurred for which, prima facie, the state bears a constitutional responsibility for compensation.

LAYMAN'S THING HAS BEEN TAKEN BY THE STATE WITHOUT ORDINARY JUSTIFICATION

Once Layman has shown that the state has taken one of his things, he may reasonably expect an Observing judge to recognize that a prima facie case for compensation has been established. In saying that Layman has made out a prima facie case, I mean something that is very familiar to lawyers, however much the concept's structure may legitimately puzzle philosophers.[77] Having advanced a prima facie case, Layman may expect to win provided that nothing more is said by the other side in justification of the taking. If, however, the state does come forward with a justification for its action, then Layman can no longer expect victory without showing why it is that the state's effort at justification is unsatisfactory. To put the point in terms of our framework, a child growing up in middle-class America learns that while he may use his things in many ways, he is not entitled to use them in ways a well-socialized person should recognize as unacceptably harmful to others.[78] Thus, Layman may not properly complain about a taking if the taker can justify his action as necessary[79] to restrain Layman from acting in a way he ought to recognize as unduly harmful. And if this is true in ordinary life, it is—so far as the Observing judge is concerned—also true in constitutional law. The task, then, becomes one of giving a determinate structure to the elusive idea that Layman cannot use his things in ways a well-socialized person ought to recognize as unacceptably harmful. While this formula is even vaguer than the others we have encountered, its practical utility ought not to be discounted. Every day it is called upon by well-socialized Americans as they control themselves on countless occasions in which the use of their possessions would otherwise generate acute social stress.[80]

Nevertheless, it remains true that sometimes social standards are sufficiently ambiguous that one group of self-interested Laymen will believe themselves justified in using their things in ways that another group will consider unjustified. It is at this point that conflict becomes manifest; since the conflicting groups are composed of Laymen who are well-socialized, however, it should be expected that each will seek to interpret dominant communal practices in a way that will put them in the right, their antagonists in the wrong.[81] If the Laymen cannot resolve their dispute by other means, they may ultimately be driven to the legal system to gain relief. If they go directly to the courts, their conflict over the proper interpretation of communal practices will take the form of some kind of tort or contract action; if they go to the legislature, one party or the other will attempt to make more precise, through statutory enactment, the character of the actions that well-socialized Laymen should recognize as unduly harmful to others. This, at any rate, is the relationship between law and social conflict that we shall impute to the judge who thinks like an Ordinary Observer.

Given this understanding, the final interpretative task presented by the takings clause is rather easy to set out in general terms. The problem arises because sometimes Laymen wish to obtain compensation despite the fact that their loss is occasioned by a statute grounded principally in a legislative judgment that they have been acting in ways unbecoming well-socialized individuals. Since, from an Ordinary Observer's point of view, it is quite justified to take somebody's thing away from him if it is necessary to stop him acting in a way he should recognize as socially unacceptable, legislative action capable of Ordinary justification does not require compensation despite the fact that a prima facie taking has occurred. Hence, it is necessary for the judge to discriminate between actions capable of Ordinary justification and those which deprive Layman of his things without suggesting he has been using them in ways a well-socialized person should recognize as unduly harmful.

As should be obvious by now, it is possible to classify judges according to the extent to which they are willing to discern, and defer to, legislative judgments that a taking is capable of Ordinary justification. There are, nevertheless, cases at both poles that seem free from doubt. Consider, for example, the standard highway building case. At Time One, observe Layman engaging in a perfectly legitimate activity on his property —minding his business or tending his garden. Nevertheless, the Highway Department takes his things away from him at Time Two—not because he has been acting badly but because his land is particularly flat and therefore relatively cheap for road building. Since Laymen in their daily lives do not generally condemn each other simply for owning flat land, it follows that the Observing judge will find the taking lacks Ordinary justification and so requires compensation.

At the other pole, consider the takings problem that would be raised by a legislative decision prohibiting the sale or production of cigarettes because of the serious danger they cause to human health. Here, every Layman has from early childhood been taught that he is not entitled to use his things in ways that seriously endanger the lives of others. This recognition may not be enough, of course, to label the sale and manufacture of cigarettes as a plainly improper activity for a well-socialized person, especially when smokers give their consent "freely" to their eventual destruction. The risk of death involved, however, does make the case sufficiently problematic from the Layman's point of view to place it in the gray area of socially questionable conduct. Thus, even though the cigarette traffic is permitted at present (Time One), children are taught that it is better to refrain, smokers are often asked to desist from their habit in public places, sellers are forbidden to hawk their wares on television and are sometimes challenged—both in public and in private—to justify their socially suspect conduct. Consequently, if a ban on the cigarette trade were imposed at some future Time Two, an Observing judge would look at the takings issue far differently from the one generated by the standard highway building case. Viewing the statute against the background of evolving social practice, an Observing judge would have little difficulty understanding it as an attempt by legislators to express the developing concept of socially harmful conduct rather than as an assault on Layman's things without Ordinary justification. Hence the fact that our hypothetical anti-cigarette statute rendered millions of dollars in company plant valueless will be dismissed by Observing judges as merely a noncompensable cost arising from the abatement of a "public nuisance," rather than the source of a legitimate grievance raised on behalf of "unoffending property [that] is taken away from an innocent owner." [82] Or so thought the elder Justice Harlan in 1887, as he denied compensation to the distillers and brewers of Kansas whose plants were transformed into junk by the enactment of a state prohibition statute. And this too will be the fate of cigarette manufacturers today, so long as Ordinary Observing holds sway.[83]

And now for the harder cases. At least for the present, the Supreme Court seems unwilling to question the legislative judgment that a well-socialized person ought not use his property in a way that he has reason to know will cause a great deal of inconvenience to the uses that his neighbors are already making of their things. From *Euclid* v. *Ambler* to *Village of Belle Terre* v. *Boraas,* the Court has been extremely deferential to legislative attempts to define more precisely the Observer's notion of being a good neighbor.[84] Nonetheless, even the most deferential judges have found cause to consider whether the political process has overstepped its rightful bounds. The classic case that presents the problem concerns the brickworks that earlier had been located in the rural outlands within a setting of adjoining uses that were not then inconsistent with industrial activity. A generation or two later, however, the scene has been transformed. Nearby farmers have sold to developers who have sold to suburbanites who wish to restrict the brickyard through zoning in such drastic ways as to terminate its operation. Since a taking of the brickyard has occurred, the only remaining question is whether the owner of the works is using his thing in a way he should, as a well-socialized person, recognize as harming others.

And it is at this point that even a deferential judge may well inquire with some anxiety whether the Layman's notion of being a good neighbor is sufficiently expansive to provide an Ordinary justification for the taking. It is simply not the case that we teach our children, or expect ourselves, to delve deeply into the future in order to satisfy ourselves that we are using our things in a way that will not cause undue harm to others. So long as Layman is not using his things in a way that unduly endangers others in ways *reasonably* perceptible to the person with ordinary foresight, he is commonly entitled to use his things to pursue his own interests. Indeed, if one were to insist upon foresight that spans a generation, this would transform the institution of property as Laymen now know it. For it should be recalled that when something is Layman's, it means that he can appropriately do *lots* of things with it. Yet if any use is to be deemed harmful if it may conceivably harm someone in the remote future, the conscientious Layman must regretfully conclude that he ought in fact do nothing with his things unless he spends a great deal of time gazing into crystal balls far more accurate than those of present manufacture.

This is not to say that a Layman is *never* expected to take account of the harms that his actions will cause in the future. Railroads, for example, will not be heard to complain when they are obliged to construct safe crossings in the towns they themselves were instrumental in bringing into existence.[85] Generally speaking, however, when the future is not clear to ordinary common sense, Layman need not desist from using his thing in the way he desires on the off-chance that time will prove his actions harmful to others. In short, at the time Layman began his brickworks, he could not plausibly be said to be acting in a way inappropriate to the well-socialized, middle-class American. Nor can it be said that the late-coming suburbanites were ignorant of Layman's operation at the time they arrived on the scene. As a consequence, the courts have had great difficulty coming to terms with statutes that seeks to eliminate "nonconforming uses" outright—though they have no trouble at all with legislation that merely requires Layman to refrain from *expanding* the scale of his operations in a way that would further damage the interests of neighbors whose presence is an accomplished fact.[86]

The brickworks problem has been with the law for a very long time. Only recently, however, has a second area even begun to seem problematic to the Ordinary judge. I refer to the notion that a well-socialized Layman ought to desist from using his things not only when they cause harm to the possessions of his human neighbors (as well as their domestic animals) but also that the Layman should be taught to refrain from causing undue damage to things like Nature or Tradition, conceived as entities demanding respect quite apart from the interests of present and future human beings. It is not difficult to detect such strains in the political and legal discourse generated by the movements for environmental and historical conservation.[87] Nonetheless, it is informative that these groups tend to grasp at the *human* interests at stake whenever this seems even remotely plausible. If, however, one turns to the principal means for socializing the next generation, especially the schools and television, conservationist themes—particularly the need to respect Nature in its own right—are presented far more explicitly than is the case in policy discussion amongst the present generation of adults. Given these facts, exceedingly deferential Observing judges may already be willing to endorse legislative action grounded on the idea that well-socialized individuals are not entitled to use their things in a manner that damages Nature (or Tradition) in certain striking ways.[88] Or they may seize upon the merest hint of damage to human interests to declare the taking justified.[89] Those less restrained may, in contrast, continue to demand compensation on the basis of the relatively unproblematic homocentric conception of harm into which they were raised.[90] Or even more significant, the conscientious judge may be sufficiently impressed with the difficulty of identifying dominant social norms at a time of great stress that he may feel called upon to propose a Policymaking answer to the com-

pensation question, at least so far as it deals with environmental regulation. While it is possible to detect movements
in this direction,[91] it is too early to say authoritatively that a
Scientific Policymaking trend has been established. Nonetheless, if there is a Scientific revolution in the making, it is only
to be expected that the first signs should manifest themselves
here, where Ordinary conceptions of justification are most in
flux. And so it is that we come upon one of the deeper legal
paradoxes attendant upon the environmental revolution: a
movement that seeks to restore Nature to its proper place may
well serve as one of the catalyzing events that inaugurates the
triumph of Artifice in legal thought.

LEGAL PROPERTY AND SOCIAL PROPERTY

Thus far, I have avoided needless complexities in order to
present the Ordinary interpretation of the takings clause in
its simplest possible form, in which recovery is granted on a
showing that one of Layman's things has been taken by the
state without Ordinary justification. It is necessary, however,
to discuss several complexities before even a preliminary canvass of the significant practical and theoretical issues may be
concluded. Moreover, it is only by extending the analysis that
we shall come to terms with what is both the most important
and most mysterious writing in takings law—Mr. Justice
Holmes's opinion, for the Supreme Court, in *Pennsylvania
Coal Company* v. *Mahon*.[92]

Before scaling Everest, however, we shall walk more manageable paths that will permit some useful exercise for the
final ascent. Consider, then, an oversimplification that may
well have grated upon some of my readers' legal sensibilities.
Thus far, I have spoken of Layman as if he had an unencum-
bered fee simple estate in his real property and a similarly absolute interest in his personal property. In less technical language, I have assumed that at Time One, Layman has kept
his things to himself and has refused to give permission to
anybody else to use them. Now that we have elaborated the
basic ideas behind the Ordinary Observer's approach, how-

ever, we can afford to abandon such simplicities to take into account the full complexity of modern property relationships.

Let us begin with the easy cases. Imagine that instead of keeping his thing to himself, Layman lets somebody else use it as well. Indeed, imagine that a particular User finds a particular use so attractive that he no longer wishes to use the thing at Layman's sufferance but pays Layman to let him use it as a matter of right. For present purposes it is not important what legal label the lawyers will deploy to guarantee User his rights; [93] to make it an easy case, however, we must stipulate that User is *actually* making use of the thing on a regular basis and is not simply holding his rights for possible future employment. Imagine, for example, that while Layman wishes to continue using the surface of parcel D (for divided) as a factory, he grants a coal company the right to mine under the ground his factory occupies. To assess the significance of the fact of divided ownership, compare the fate of parcel D to that suffered by a second piece of land identical to D in all respects except that this time Layman decides to mine the coal under the factory himself, leaving the ownership of the parcel undivided (hence parcel U).

Having defined their legal relationships during Time One, the owners of parcels U and D find themselves in a familiar situation at Time Two. Both lots, it seems, are in the path of a new road planned by the State Highway Department, which takes full title to them. As a consequence of the state's action, both Layman and User stand as complete strangers to D, while Layman alone has been estranged from U. In each case, the rights-holders have suffered a total loss of a million dollars—though so far as parcel D is concerned, half the loss is borne by Layman and half by User, while U's million dollar loss falls exclusively on Layman. Despite the differing extent in the dimension of *personal* loss, however, American courts insist upon achieving parity between the divided and undivided *parcels,* instructing the state to create a million dollar fund for each parcel payable over to rights-holders as their interests may appear.[94] While this insistence on parity will not always seem justified to a Scientific Policymaker,[95] it makes perfect sense when viewed from the Ordinary Observer's perspective: since Layman has the perfect right to let others use his thing if he wants to, there seems to be no reason to discriminate among things according to the extent to which Layman avails himself of this right. Similarly, the Ordinary judge would experience very little difficulty if the state did not take title to both parcels but imposed a new set of regulations that rendered the mining operations of both User and Layman valueless. Since both mines have been taken, the only question remaining open is whether the takings were justified; if not, both Layman and User would each obtain a half-million dollars in compensation, and parity between the two identical parcels would be maintained.

There is, then, a large class of cases in which the existence of complex patterns of divided ownership do not cause the Ordinary judge any special difficulty in takings law. In these "easy" cases, the holder of a "small" partial interest (like the coal company's right in parcel D) will obtain compensation if, but only if, the owner of a "large," undivided interest (like Layman's in parcel U) would also gain victory under the same circumstances. Yet there comes a point at which the maintenance of this "easy" principle of parity [96] becomes very difficult indeed—where the Ordinary Observer will be sorely tempted to *grant* compensation to the holder of the "small" interest even though he wishes to *deny* it to those who hold the "large" one. This result is, of course, exceedingly peculiar. In constitutional law, as elsewhere, it is not often the case that less is more: that the company should gain constitutional protection *precisely because* it has fewer rights than Layman. It is not for the sake of paradox alone, however, that the consideration of these "hard" cases is worthwhile; for if we press the analysis far enough, we shall finally glimpse one of the deeper perplexities that must afflict the judge who struggles to achieve an Ordinary understanding of the takings clause.

On, then, to the "hard" case of divided ownership. So far we have assumed that both Layman and the coal company have already begun mining operations on their respective parcels at the time the state has passed its anti-mining statute. Assume now, however, that neither has done so, but that each intends to mine the land some time in the future. I should like to persuade you that this single change in the hypothetical facts suffices to transform the case into one where the Ordinary Observer will have great difficulty maintaining parity between U and D.

Up to a certain point, the analysis of these new "hard cases" poses no new difficulties. At least so far as Layman's mining losses on parcel U are concerned, it should be obvious that an Ordinary judge must decide against compensation. Indeed, Layman cannot even advance a prima facie case of a taking since he can point to no thing which has been taken from him by the new regulations. Since there was no mine in existence at Time One, it could not be taken from him at Time Two; and so far as the factory and land are concerned, they are just as much his as they always were. All that was taken from Layman was simply one of the many possible ways he could use his land if he so chose. While the loss of this opportunity did cause the market price of U to plummet by 50 percent to $500,000, this is not enough to induce an Ordinary judge to consider Layman's loss compensable. Instead, Layman's plight seems in all respects identical to that suffered by the unhappy Speculator whose plans for a new Hamburger Heaven were frustrated by the town's zoning board.[97]

Having disposed of Layman's lawsuit so easily, we are now in a position to see why the coal company's analogous suit on parcel D presents a hidden difficulty. In contrast to Layman, the company *can* point to a particular thing which has been taken from it by the state as a result of the passage of its anti-mining legislation. After all, does not the company own a piece of impressive-looking paper granting it mining rights that its lawyers had assured it was a thing of value? And has not this thing been rendered worthless by the state's new law, thereby raising a prima facie case of an Ordinary taking?

An affirmative answer to this question is, of course, suggested by the entire drift of the Ordinary approach. Yet to grant compensation to the company is to breach the parity principle—for we have just shown that so far as Layman's parcel U is concerned, an Ordinary Observer has no difficulty denying compensation for the loss of mining rights. How, then, is the Ordinary judge to respond? Is he to compensate the company for the loss of its thing or maintain parity between parcels U and D?

It is less important to resolve this dilemma than to understand why it arises in the first place. To do this it is necessary to reflect upon the sort of thing that has been taken from the coal company. Since we have stipulated that the company has done nothing to make its mine a social reality, it should be plain that its right to mine parcel D cannot be *social property,* in the sense we have given the term,[98] but only legal property. That is, just as an ordinary person cannot convince a fair-minded friend that he "owns" the air two miles above "his" farm,[99] so too the owners of the coal company could not point to anything in the observable social universe that will substantiate the claim that they stand in a special relationship to parcel D. So far as the unspecialized eye can see, it is Layman, and only Layman, who has a privileged position with respect to D—it is Layman (or his delegate) who is running the factory, using the land for a variety of purposes, and so forth. The company, in contrast, never enters the stage of ordinary social interaction.

It is true, of course, that the non-lawyer will not observe Layman mining "his" land. But there are any number of reasons Layman might refrain from acting in this way—perhaps there is no coal under the land, perhaps mining is not economical, perhaps Layman is just lazy—that are consistent with Layman's owning the mining right as well as the others he *is* exercising in ways that are obvious to nonprofessional eyes. Moreover, even if Layman does not own this particular right, there is nothing in the nonlegal reality that points to the coal company as the true owner—it is not even the case that the company is engaged in a regular habit of paying Layman

a periodic rent for its special rights.[100] Of course, so far as the
legal Scientist is concerned, all this is simply a tribute to the
wonders of the legal system; rather than requiring the coal
company to waste social resources by crudely staking its claim
in the real world of social action, the law simply permits the
company to protect its security of expectation by filing a single
piece of paper in the title registry at a small expense.[101] However efficient this may seem to the Scientist, it is simply magic
to the unprofessional Layman, who must take it *on faith* that
the unfamiliar piece of paper that is the only observable evidence of mining rights says what the company's lawyer says it
says.[102]

As soon as it is recognized that the coal company's rights
are merely legal property, not social property, it is possible to
move beyond one's initial sense of paradox to understand the
fundamental issue raised by the company's effort to obtain
compensation. If the Ordinary judge's concern is restricted to
the taking of social property—Layman's things—then the coal
company can no more point to a thing it has lost on parcel D
than Layman can with respect to parcel U. Both have simply
lost the opportunity to use the land in one of a number of
potentially profitable ways. If, however, the Ordinary judge is
also willing to protect legal property—Lawyer's things as well
as Layman's things—then he will find that the state has taken
the company's property by transforming its legal document to
parcel D into a piece of scrap paper.[103]

Of all the Ordinary ideas we have explored in this essay, the
notion of a Lawyer's thing is perhaps the most difficult for
the Scientific Policymaker to take seriously. To him it seems
quite absurd to imagine that the coal company's case can be
so sharply distinguished from Layman's simply because the
company can point to a particular piece of paper that had become worthless by virtue of the new regulations, while Layman
cannot. Instead, the Scientist will impatiently put the particular pieces of paper to one side and point out that the
bundle of rights to the subsurface held by Layman is the same
as the bundle held by the coal company, regardless of the

documentary ways in which both are packaged. It is only from Layman's point of view that an emphasis on particular pieces of paper seems even remotely plausible. Given his ignorance of the structure of legal discourse, he will grasp at the *physical* existence of a piece of paper in the hope that it will provide him with the Archimedean point from which he can understand his place in the legal universe. Without a piece of paper, Layman must listen passively as his lawyer explains to him his rights and obligations; with a piece of paper, Layman can at least ask pointedly: What is *this?* What does it give me? Similarly, in ordinary life and conversation, he need not idly report his lawyer's talk, but may at least show the piece of paper when called upon by his fair-minded friends to evidence his claim that he stands in a special legal relationship to one or another thing in their common social reality. Thus, it may be quite possible for rather abstruse and unfamiliar legal documents to take on a shadowy social reality which would not exist in the absence of documentation—a phenomenon recently illuminated in the context of more standardized commercial transactions by my colleagues Arthur Leff and Robert Clark.[104] If, then, the Ordinary judge will accord protection to Lawyer's things as well as Layman's things, the fact that the coal company can point to a particular document whose value has been destroyed is a matter of more than ordinary significance.

All this, however, is merely a preliminary to the truly fundamental question—*how* is the Ordinary judge to decide whether he will reserve constitutional protection to Layman's things or extend it further to Lawyer's things? Even upon first approach, it should be plain that the question will prove peculiarly embarrassing to the Ordinary judge. After all, as a matter of basic principle, he is striving to understand the conflict *by using the categories of nonprofessional talk;* yet, by definition, all Layman will say about a Lawyer's thing is that he really must see a lawyer before he can make sense out of it! The Ordinary Observer seems fated by his own methodology to return to his starting place with nothing but an increased sense of frustration, vaguely conscious that his decisionmaking problem can be resolved only at the cost of a deep modification of Ordinary Observing commitments.

Two choices are open. On the one hand, a judge may conclude that the Ordinary methodology is simply inapplicable to legal property and switch to one or another form of Scientific Policymaking to resolve this class of cases.[105] On the other hand, he may seek to devise an Ordinary-looking solution and suppress the perception that the Ordinary forms are no longer rooted in social—as distinct from legal—practice. Thus, the judge may indulge in legal fiction and treat legal property as if it were social property, protecting paper interests like that of the coal company when they are rendered valueless by state action. Or he may conclude that since the untrained citizen could never assess the nature of the coal company's legal rights unaided, the company cannot complain when it is informed that it has been deprived of rights a Layman could not say belonged to it in the first place. In either case, however, the judge has outrun his methodological premises by seeking to derive a determinate legal conclusion from Layman's self-denying recognition that he is incompetent to evaluate legal property claims without consulting a lawyer.

With these options displayed to view, it is possible, I think, to appreciate the deep difficulties confronting Mr. Justice Holmes when he was called upon to write the Court's opinion in the leading case of *Pennsylvania Coal Company* v. *Mahon*. For present purposes, it is enough to describe the case as structurally identical to the hypothetical parcel D which we have been discussing. The coal company sold Layman the surface rights to parcel D, reserving to itself, however, the future right to extract the subsurface anthracite even if this should cause great damage to Layman's surface activities.[106] These mining rights, however, had recently been rendered worthless by a Pennsylvania statute making extraction illegal if it caused subsidence.[107] In response the company went to court to recover compensation for the taking of its Lawyer's thing.

Now, given Holmes's general outlook on constitutional law, it should be clear that he would rebel at the thought of deciding the lawsuit within the Scientific Policymaking framework. For Holmes, nothing could have been less congenial than indulging the Policymaker's notion that the Constitution should be understood as coherently organized around a determinate Comprehensive View.[108] As a result, his only live option was to force an answer out of the Ordinary Observer's methodology: either Lawyer's things were to be treated as if they were Layman's things, and the coal company was to be granted compensation; or Lawyer's things were to be treated as merely legally packaged expectations having no basis in social practice and so beyond the scope of the Ordinary takings clause.

Holmes took the first path. As was to be expected, however, he did not justify his choice by arguing its affirmative attractions but by emphasizing the dangers that might possibly be hidden down the second highway. Down this road, it was claimed, the far-sighted Ordinary jurist could discern the end of all constitutional protection of property, social as well as legal: if the state can take Lawyer's things without compensation, why can it not take Layman's things as well? [109] Pointing out that some Pennsylvania cities had, when laying out their streets, merely purchased rights of way and expressly allowed the sellers to mine the underground coal even if it caused subsidence, Holmes wrote:

> If . . . [the city's] representatives have been so short-sighted as to acquire only surface rights without the right of support, we see no more authority for supplying the latter without compensation than there was for taking the right of way in the first place and refusing to pay for it because the public wanted it very much.[110]

Unfortunately, the navigator who is supremely conscious of the existence of Scylla only succeeds in making his encounter with Charybdis the more certain. Having rejected a position that could possibly be extended "until at last private property disappears," [111] Holmes had no option left but to assume that Lawyer's things should be treated as if they were Layman's things for purposes of takings law. Since the regulation had left a Lawyer's thing worthless, and Holmes could find no Ordinary justification for the state's action,[112] compensation was foreordained within the framework of Ordinary adjudication. Of course, even the most committed Ordinary judge cannot be affirmatively happy with this result, since it is Ordinary only in form and not in substance.[113] As a consequence, it is not surprising to observe Holmes—often so eager to lay down hard and fast objective-looking rules—insisting that the issue before him turns on "a question of degree and therefore cannot be disposed of by general propositions." [114] Having vindicated the constitutional status of Lawyer's things, Holmes senses that he is on uncertain ground and refuses to hand down a rule of any generality to govern the taking of legal, as opposed to social, rights.

Holmes's sense of difficulty has been shared by the generations of Ordinary judges that have succeeded him. *Pennsylvania Coal* has not come down to us today as a ringing affirmation of constitutional protection for interests which do not qualify as social property. Instead of Holmes's aggressive holding, it is his *dicta* disparaging general rules that have proved influential in the courts. While the general embrace of Holmes's ad hoc approach has suppressed the methodological perplexities that would be exposed by an explicit treatment of legal property, the judges have not followed Holmes in according broad protection to the interests of those whose legal rights have been taken from them. Thus, the courts have failed to recognize the relevance of takings law in protecting the expectations of millions who have legal property in the Social Security and welfare programs.[115] Indeed, even so far as more traditional forms of legal property are concerned—like the rights of shareholders and secured creditors—the extent to which the courts will invoke the clause is far from clear.[116]

The continuing judicial uncertainty regarding the proper treatment of legal property is not only of primary practical importance; it is also suggestive of the deeper difficulties that af-

flict the Ordinary Observer as he attempts a credible reading
of the Constitution in a modern setting. Unlike our ancestors,
we no longer count our wealth by looking first to our social
property of land, farms, buildings. Instead, our principal
means of support consist of legal property: stocks, bonds, pen-
sions, an assortment of rights granted by the activist welfare
state. Yet the Ordinary Observer—in principle so sensitive to
the ebb and flow of social mores—is nonetheless peculiarly incapable of grasping the central importance of legal property
in modern life. Since even Laymen recognize that they cannot
make sense of their new forms of property without expert advice, the Ordinary judge is simply without the analytic means
to assess the constitutional significance of the great sea change
that has transformed property in the twentieth century. Instead, he is confronted with two unsatisfactory options: on the
one hand, he may simply reserve the takings clause to social
property only, consigning the new property and its protection
to constitutional limbo; on the other hand, he may approach
the new legal phenomena obliquely by indulging in strained
analogies to the older social forms which his chosen method so
powerfully illuminated. We come, then, to the ultimate paradox: a method of analysis which seeks, above all, to root the
law in dominant social practice finds itself falsifying the structure of this very practice, incapable of coming to terms with an
"everyday" world in which ordinary citizens are increasingly
dependent upon lawyers before they can understand the nature
of their entitlements.

　　Given this methodological dead-end, I doubt that even
Charles Reich's eloquent statement in "The New Property" [117]
will prove sufficient to move Ordinary judges to frame general
rules governing the taking of legal property. Choosing Reich
over Holmes would raise to the surface doubts about the vi-
ability of Ordinary Observing that might be intolerable so
long as the Ordinary interpretation of the clause holds sway.
This is not to say, however, that we are necessarily reduced to
Holmesian shadowplay when it comes to legal property, taking
with one hand what is given with the other. For we can at least

contemplate the move that was unthinkable for Holmes and consider whether it is not best to discard Ordinary Observing and look at the takings problem with the eyes of a Scientific Policymaker. Once this shift is made, the puzzle that overtaxed the skill of a legal genius is transformed, quite remarkably, into the simplest of children's games. Suddenly it becomes perfectly clear that there is no fundamental difference between social property and legal property; that the legally decisive question is not whether a "thing" has been taken, but whether those who lose as a result of the redistribution of property bundles ought to be compensated by those who gain; that the answer to this question is not to be found in the patient elaboration of Ordinary language as a key to legitimate social expectation but in clear and systematic development of the implications of the Comprehensive View that prevails in the legal system; that it is only in this way that the Policymaker has any assurance that he is participating in the larger legal enterprise of settling disputes in a way that makes some overall sense.

By making this transition, of course, the Scientific Policymaker does not pretend that the takings problem has thereby been resolved. Hard work remains: in developing the criteria by which a lawyer is to determine the particular Comprehensive View to be selected as the one dominant in the legal system; in understanding the deep structure of the Comprehensive View that is selected; in elaborating the implications of the Comprehensive View for the problem at hand. It is these tasks—which occupied us in the first half of the book—that, for the Scientific Policymaker, represent the unfinished business of legal thought.

7 On the Nature and Object of Legal Language

ON EXCOMMUNICATION

We are now in a position to pierce the mystery of the takings clause—at least to understand why it is that the guiding principles of compensation law are so obscure to the present generation of lawyers. My essential diagnosis is simple. On the one hand, traditional doctrine is in fact grounded upon the principles of Ordinary Observing. On the other hand, sophisticated lawyers and judges of the present day—especially those apt to write articles or opinions that have a general impact—are increasingly inclined to think about the law in Scientific Policymaking terms. Thus, the Scientific Policymakers are unable to make sense of the law, while the Ordinary Observers have lost their voice and are capable only of manipulating precedents whose deeper structures are lost from view. In short, the subterranean conflict between the two forms of legal thought expresses itself on the surface of professional life by the common perception that takings law is incoherent, its principles altogether mysterious. If I am right, before we can hope to demystify the law it will be necessary to take a self-conscious position on the relative merits of Scientific Policymaking and Ordinary Observing as alternative modes of legal analysis.

It is true, of course, that this call for methodological self-consciousness is an unfamiliar one. At least so far as I can see, our legal culture is sufficiently disorganized (or should I say schizoid?) that many of its principal actors—lawyers, judges, legislators—move back and forth between the perspectives of the Ordinary Observer and Scientific Policymaker quite effortlessly with no sense of impropriety. Consistent with the genius of the common law, advocates are quite happy to indulge either form of argument when it suits their advantage.[1] And judges (as well as legislators) are willing to rule neither kind of argument beyond the pale of legal thought, though they surely have no explicit criteria for determining the contexts in which one or the other legal form should be given preponderant, let alone exclusive, weight.

It takes little foresight, however, to predict that this age of happy ignorance is drawing to a close. It is now a century since the practicing bar began to lose to the law schools control over the education of the new generation of lawyers; as a consequence of this gradual shift, it is now possible to predict with some accuracy the future course of professional concerns by looking to the present state of academic concerns. In saying this, I do *not* mean to claim that the answers given by the future generation of lawyers will be anything like the answers given by the present academic generation. Instead, I only wish to suggest that the concerns into which lawyers are socialized by their teachers will deeply affect the way they think about issues in practice. If this much is conceded, the present academic situation is ripe with significance for crystal-ball gazers. For the muddled form of toleration that is now the rule in legal practice receives an increasingly hostile reception amongst the groves of academe. Nor is the prevailing mood one of coolly dispassionate analysis; instead, partisanship is becoming the rule, with the most theoretically gifted seeming almost eager to excommunicate those who depart from their version of the true faith. At one time, perhaps, intolerance by the Scientific Policymakers was a forgivable failing. Their numbers, their influence on the profession, were so small that sectarianism was necessary for survival.[2] But things are different now. The methods of Scientific Policymaking have made a deep impression upon the generation of law teachers now obtaining positions on important law faculties. Indeed, the Coase Theorem [3] promises to occupy the same symbolic place for this generation that *Erie Railroad* v. *Tompkins* [4] played for the last—an obligatory reference point for sophisticated researchers.[5] While the economic approach to law is currently the most popular,[6] the impulse to Scientific Policymaking can, I think, be detected in many more traditional writers,[7] not to mention the proponents of other interdisciplinary approaches.[8]

As this movement comes to a crescendo, it is all too easy for the triumphant Scientific Policymakers to take an imperialist stance toward the Ordinary natives who formerly tended the vineyards unaided. After expressing their respect for the value of the native tradition in a ritual paragraph or chapter,[9] the Scientists embark on their real work of (a) translating indigenous doctrine into Scientific sense and (b) teaching the natives to think like Policymakers. Needless to say the Scientists may differ as to the state of the traditional legal enterprise. Many will reach the predictable conclusion that by virtue of their analytic failures the natives have made a mess of things; [10] some will argue that the traditional practitioners have reached the "right" results with a frequency that is quite remarkable for folks who so often talk gibberish; [11] a few will even concede that there may be something valuable that is lost in the translation into Scientific terms, to which deference should be given, especially if the natives feel really anxious about its loss.[12] The one thing that is missing however— particularly amongst the now dominant camp of lawyer- economists with whom I am most familiar [13]—is any effort to make sense of the Ordinary Observing tradition *in its own terms* and to confront the task of resolving the conceptual conflict that is then observable.

So long as the Scientists were at the fringe of the teaching profession, their challenge did not need to be taken seriously by the bulk of academics whose instinct was to avoid theoretical questions as much as possible. With the increasing penetration of Scientific Policymaking concepts, however, the time for self-consciousness is coming. Indeed, in fields like torts, which have witnessed a full scale scientific revolution over the past fifteen years, even the traditionalist's counterattack has now been fairly launched.[14] Even more significant is the dawn of professional recognition that lawyers are confronted with a general analytic problem that transcends this or that area of doctrine. Quite recently, two major writers—stimulated in part by the challenge of the lawyer-economists—have launched the first serious efforts to isolate, and reflect upon, the challenge that the new wave of Scientific Policymaking represents.

The first essay, written by Harry Wellington,[15] deals with the phenomenon by trying to convince lawyers that they should be "especially concerned, in the arguments they make or the explanations they give, to distinguish principles from policies . . . —the latter [provide] an instrumental justification for a rule, while the former [do] not.[16] Armed with this distinction, Wellington attempts to define the conditions under which policies, as well as principles, are properly admissible in judicial argument. Speaking very broadly, Wellington's aim is an eclectic one—while his central reliance is on an Observer's methodology,[17] he attempts to find an important (though subordinate) place for Utilitarian Policymakers in adjudication.[18] Unfortunately, however, Wellington fails to elaborate the implications of his eclectic mixture for constitutional law with the same care that he devotes to common law adjudication.[19] Nonetheless, his perception of the need for a systematic treatment of conflicting forms of argument in constitutional law represents an advance of the first importance.

This said, it is also necessary to recognize that Wellington fails to do justice to the complex structure of constitutional argument that has been revealed in our treatment of compensation law. While his definition of a *policy* as an "instrumental justification for a rule" is sufficient, perhaps,[20] to mark out Utilitarian Policymaking from the general run of legal argumentation, Wellington's effort at methodological discrimination ends prematurely at this point. So far as he is concerned, *all* noninstrumental arguments may properly be treated together under the heading of *principles*. This, of course, makes it difficult to recognize that the legal arguments of a Kantian Policymaker are based on very different premises from those advanced by an Ordinary Observer, despite the fact that neither can justly be called instrumental in character. Indeed, when Wellington seeks to deploy his distinction in a valuable series of concrete case discussions, the *only* principles taken seriously are those generated by a sophisticated kind of Ordinary Observing; the power of Kantian Policymaking is never squarely confronted.[21] In short, while Wellington recognizes that traditional forms of legal argument are under attack, he imagines that the challenge comes only from Utilitarian Policymaking. In doing so he mistakes the assault launched by a particularly visible strike force of lawyer-economists for the deeper threat to Ordinary Observing presented by the larger army of Scientific Policymakers.

This certainly cannot be said of Ronald Dworkin's recent report from the battlefield.[22] Indeed, Dworkin's overall conceptual apparatus permits a more just appreciation of the contending parties. Instead of relying on a single distinction to do all the work, Dworkin's battle plan has at least two discrete dimensions. Dworkin first locates judges on the basis of

> the doctrine of political responsibility . . . [which] states, in its most general form that political officials must make only such political decisions as they can justify within a political theory that also justifies the other decisions they propose to make. The doctrine . . . condemn[s] a style of political administration that might be called . . . intuitionistic. It condemns the practice of making decisions that seem right in isolation, but cannot be brought within some comprehensive theory of general principles and policies that is consistent with other decisions also thought right.[23]

It should be plain that this doctrine will have the consequence of distinguishing the Policymakers from the Observers in our present legal culture. For, as we have seen, so long as we remain distant from a Utopia in which a single Comprehensive View is perfectly institutionalized in social practice, Observers will refuse to purchase abstract theoretical consistency at the price of falsifying the structure of dominant social expectation, and so will qualify as "intuitionists" so far as Dworkin is concerned. In contrast, Policymakers will insist upon articulate theoretical consistency, and so will qualify as "politically responsible." [24]

Having sorted Observers from Policymakers in a rough and ready way, Dworkin deploys a second set of distinctions, which permits one to discriminate between the two Comprehensive Views treated in the first half of this book. Unfortunately for the novice, Dworkin has chosen to express this second distinction by using the same verbal opposition between *principle* and *policy* invoked by Wellington for a very different purpose.[25] Thus, for Dworkin: "Arguments of policy . . . [show] that the decision advances or protects some *collective goal of the community as a whole. . . .* Arguments of principle . . . [show] that the decision respects or secures some *individual or group right.*" [26] As I hope my selective emphasis suggests, Dworkin's distinction between principle and policy is far from clear. As he himself recognizes, it requires a powerful way of discriminating between "collective goals" on the one hand and "individual or group rights" on the other.[27] Whatever else remains obscure, however, it seems clear that Dworkin would consider the Utilitarian arguments described in Chapter 3 to provide an archetypal form of policy reasoning; while the Kantian arguments in Chapter 4 are of a paradigmatically principled character.[28] In short, the Kantian arguments Dworkin takes to be paradigmatic of principle, Wellington fails to take seriously; while the Observing arguments Wellington understands to be central to principle, Dworkin would not consider principled at all but rather condemn as "intuitionistic." To compound the confusion, both Wellington and Dworkin agree (though for different reasons) on calling Utilitarian arguments policies. Once we penetrate the smoke, however, it should be plain that Dworkin provides the better battle plan—sorting "intuitionistic" Observers onto one side of the field and grouping on the other side "politically responsible" Policymakers of both the Utilitarian and Kantian kinds.

Unfortunately, Dworkin's superiority in analytic power is overmatched by his peculiar perspective upon the scene of the legal battle. For the picture he presents of the contestants seems sorely at variance with American legal realities. As Wellington's article suggests, the fiercest struggle at present is between Ordinary Observers and Utilitarian Policymakers, with the Kantian Policymakers at best constituting an increasingly ready reserve. Yet one would hardly recognize this from Dworkin's account. So far as the established Anglo-American tradition of Ordinary Observing is concerned, Dworkin conceives it unworthy of any analysis whatever, content to "condemn" it in a paragraph as an "intuitionistic" breach of "political responsibility." [29] This move is especially remarkable in a writer whose stated ambition is to provide "not some new information about what judges do, but a new way of describing what we all know they do." [30] Having disposed of the Observers with a single wave of the hand, Dworkin dispatches the Utilitarian Policymakers with almost equal facility. His thesis is, once again, an extreme one: "that judicial decisions in civil cases . . . characteristically are and should be generated by principle not policy." [31]

While, as we have seen, the distinction between principles and policies is not clear, there can be little doubt that Dworkin intends to ban absolutely from the judicial repertoire forms of Utilitarian Policymaking that serve as the standard perspective for most of the prominent authors who take an economic approach to law—Guido Calabresi and Richard Posner, to name only two.[32] Moving closer to our present subject, Dworkin's position would suggest that the two legal writers who are generally understood to have contributed most to takings law in the past decade—Frank Michelman and Joseph Sax—have, by virtue of their lapses into Utilitarianism, written little that judges should find relevant to their straight and narrow inquiry. Now one would think that such a sweeping excommunication should be accompanied by a thoughtful consideration of the grounds that could be advanced in support of more tolerant views. Unfortunately, however, Dworkin's main energies are devoted to elaborating the terms of his own thesis, rather than defending it against plausible alternatives. Thus, before his report has properly begun, Dworkin has swept the field clear of its major participants, awarding victory to the small but growing band of Kantians by default.[33] Even those attracted to the Kantian approach, however, must doubt the enduring character of a victory that comes so easily.

Our song, then, is one of division and disdain: so far as Dworkin is concerned, there is no room for a Utilitarian like Posner or an Observer like Wellington within the precincts of generally acceptable legal argument;[34] a view with which Posner tends to agree, so long as the parties' identities are suitably reversed.[35] Wellington, in contrast, seems downright catholic in his tastes, since he ignores only the Kantians while attempting to find an accommodation with the Utilitarians that saves for Observing its accustomed central role.

Now if this were some theological dispute between rival Popes temporarily quartered at Oxford, Chicago, and Yale, it would be of no practical importance to lawyers. Yet if, as I suspect, the conflict between Scientific Policymaker and Ordinary Observer is emerging as one of the master issues in the professional practice of law, lawyers cannot afford to view these academic exercises in mutual incomprehension with casual disdain or idle curiosity. For, as our scrutiny of takings law reveals, the conceptual conflict is already taking a form that practical men of the world cannot so easily evade. And when the moment of professional recognition comes, it would be a shame if the academy has nothing better to offer than narrow interpretations of the nature of the conflict that afflicts American law. What is wanted is philosophy, not theology; a sense of wonder rather than certainty when called upon to explain the grounds upon which lawyers may properly choose between the competing forms of legal thought.

PHILOSOPHICAL FOUNDATIONS

Even if it were within my power, it would be premature to attempt a final theoretical solution to our present legal predicament. Instead, the point of my essay is to make enough people (of different sorts) sufficiently uncomfortable with the prevailing schizophrenia that they find themselves driven to philosophy as the only available therapy. Nevertheless, it may not hurt to mark out some of the more obvious paths that must be explored by those who wish to make sense of the legal terrain. I shall attempt this *tour d'horizon* simply by pointing to philosophical doctrines that the partisans of Ordinary Observing and Scientific Policymaking would tend to find congenial, making a special effort to suggest the ways they may be plausibly interrelated into larger patterns. It should be emphasized, however, that in linking doctrines together I do *not* claim that one position necessarily entails any of the others. Partisans of one or another legal analytic may well reject one or another of their potential philosophic allies as unworthy when judged on its own merits. Nor do I imagine that my enumeration of relevant issues is in any sense exhaustive; instead I wish merely to suggest the broad range of relevant inquiry.

Let us begin by noting what is perhaps the most distinctive feature of the Ordinary Observer's approach to law. By insisting on grounding legal concepts upon those developed in daily life, the Ordinary judge (or other Ordinary decision-maker) [36] remains peculiarly close to the disputants before him by thinking and talking in a way that is in principle comprehensible to the general public. This is not to say that the litigants-behind-the-lawyers will necessarily agree with the Ordinary judge's decision. Even apart from self-interest, laymen may conscientiously weigh the competing arguments differently. The critical point is that the concrete *categories of evaluation* used by the typical citizen are the same as those used by the judge. Hence, while particular laymen may well disagree with the decision, they can at least be brought to understand the nature of their disagreement with established authority in the case at hand.

In contrast, there is no such assurance if the judge deploys a mode of Scientific Policymaking. This is not to say that a legal system operated by Scientific Policymakers will be completely obscure to the untrained citizen. Instead, it should be quite possible to state the guiding principles established by the Comprehensive View in a way that is readily grasped by the general public. Indeed, it may well be far easier for the citizen to gain an understanding of the general aspirations of a Policymaking system than it would be to gain a comparable grasp of an Observing system. Nonetheless, when it comes to working out the implications of the Comprehensive View in the resolution of concrete disputes, the layman will often have great difficulty following the details of Scientific argument. This intelligibility problem does not arise because Scientific conceptual frameworks are necessarily more complicated than their Ordinary counterparts—indeed, Ordinary concepts are anything but simple in their structure—but because Scientific types of analysis are *self-consciously esoteric*. They are not intended as mere elaborations of existing social practices but are designed by and for power-wielders who conceive the alteration of existing practices as an option open to them. There is little point in mastering a Scientific language unless one hopes to be a member of the decisionmaking elite oneself—or, at the very least, an enthusiastic spectator of its comings and goings.

Once this is conceded, it would seem that the partisans of Ordinary Observing can make several kinds of philosophic appeal on behalf of their analytic. On the level of philosophy of language, they may claim that the very notion of creating artificial languages, especially in fields like law, is deeply flawed. To the extent the analyst succeeds in liberating himself from the web of ordinary language into which he has been socialized, he succeeds only in rendering himself unintelligible to himself as well as to others. Instead of applauding the effort to construct an esoteric judicial language, the task of philosophy—on this view—is to expose the Ordinary conceptual troubles that so perplex the lawyer as to drive him to seek salvation in an artificial language. It should be apparent that a certain reading of the later Wittgenstein may powerfully be employed in devising such a defense of Ordinary Observing.[37]

But the argument may be pressed on other equally important fronts as well. On the level of ethical theory, the partisan of Ordinary Observing may disparage the effort to construct coherent and complete normative systems (what we have called Comprehensive Views) in any number of familiar ways. Such systems may be called completely meaningless, or denigrated more subtly as merely the expression of intense subjective convictions or preferences.[38] The fundamental objective, however, is to portray *any* effort at normative system-building as intellectual conceit that merely serves to mystify oneself as to the one supreme truth—that there is *no* Truth in ethics, only lots of different opinions. And if this is so, it is easy to view Scientific Policymaking as an arrogant effort by a handful of scholars to dress up their own particular opinions in a form that will give them the most influence. Since scholars are the only people with the time, inclination, and ability to write up positions that look like Comprehensive Views, a commitment to Scientific Policymaking makes it difficult for judges (and other lawmakers) to consider views that have not gained at least some scholarly acceptance. Yet in disdaining normative opinions that are not dressed up in academic trappings, lawmakers will have simply blinded themselves to the one supreme truth—that a normative opinion remains nothing more than opinion, no matter how elaborate it may seem. At least Ordinary adjudication does not give such inordinate power to those who have most blinded themselves to the truth. At least Ordinary concepts can be seen as the product of countless people in countless generations making countless decisions, each of which individually is of no importance.

Needless to say, the Scientific Policymaker would have a very different view of the Observer's paean to the Ordinary concepts of ordinary folk. For him, the Observer, under cover of his appeal to common ideas, may well be announcing his own personal prejudices on the matter without exposing them to the searching and self-conscious scrutiny that comprehensive and exacting analysis provides.

This objection will lead the partisan of Ordinary Observing to more explicit themes in political philosophy. To put the point in terms of modern Western theory, the Observing style of legal thought fits more comfortably into a political theory in which the state is not marked out from society as an institution with a peculiarly important mission. True, people sometimes come to state officials when they are unable to resolve disputes by other means. But the relative frequency with which even this is done can be readily overestimated. Moreover, the success which state officials have in *imposing* a settlement that is inconsistent with the larger social balance is even more limited. Hence, it is wisest even for relatively powerful state officials not to stray from Ordinary concepts in resolving conflicts. At least these concepts have proved themselves consistent, historically, with the evolution of the basic social forces. Otherwise they would not have survived. In contrast, if state officials adopt a Scientific Policymaking approach, it will be too easy for them to lead where others will not follow—with a resulting conflict that may make it impossible for the state to discharge its basic function of supporting the established social order. Needless to say, such views as these are easiest maintained by those who, like Burke, see great value in the dominant cultural tradition into which the general population is socialized.[39] But such views may also be held by the rare thinker who takes a starkly amoral view of history, neither praising nor condemning culturally dominant tendencies, as the example of Holmes established.[40]

Moving finally to explicit jurisprudential theory, it is easy to attribute peculiar characteristics to courts that make the appeal of Ordinary Observing seem even more compelling than the analogous arguments that can be made in the case of other state decisionmakers.[41] The peculiar function of the courts, it may be said, is to settle individual cases on the basis of the parties' socially based expectations *prevailing at some past time at which the dispute arose.* Once this is conceded, the propriety of Ordinary Observing—which seeks to explicate preexisting socially based expectations—seems almost self-evident.[42] Indeed, one can even say that the litigants are entitled to such a method of judicial reasoning, since this conforms to their understanding of the judicial function. And if pressed as to why such an understanding is imputed to the litigants, it is always possible to retrace the paths we have sketched, seeking to root this idea of adjudication in theories of the state, history, ethics, language, perhaps making use of some specific themes we have discussed or variants of them. Unfortunately, while the philosophic materials exist in abundance, it is impossible to be dogmatic as to the best lines of theoretical development. For the harsh fact is that the great book by an American lawyer or philosopher exploring these themes remains to be written.[43]

Even if a mighty champion of Ordinary Observing should suddenly appear, however, there is little reason to suspect that his arguments would reduce his antagonists to silence. For the proponents of Scientific Policymaking are in a position to advance a wide range of philosophical considerations that provide affirmative support for their own position. Perhaps the Policymaker's case can best be introduced by contrasting his likely theory of the state with the position we imputed to the Ordinary Observer. For the Policymaker, it is a deep mistake to look upon the state as merely an institution people sometimes rely upon when other mechanisms of social control are found wanting. While the existence of (great) constraints upon state power need not be denied, the Policymaker can nevertheless assert that the exercise of state power should be governed by principles that do not presuppose the validity of the concrete evaluative notions that happen to be dominant in the well-socialized Layman's upbringing. To put the point in terms of liberal political philosophy, the Policymaker may insist that theorists like Locke and Bentham were right in supposing that the state's actions should be tested by abstract principles whose validity does not depend in any simple way upon existing social practices. In contrast to writers like Burke and Holmes, these thinkers contend that the state does not exist merely to backstop existing institutions but to exercise a *critical* function, providing its support only for those social practices that satisfy the state's own standards of right. The Policymaker's state, in short, is not concerned with muddling through, but with assuring the attainment of a just or good society.

It should be emphasized that, in invoking the notion of the "critical" state, the Policymaker has not yet committed himself on the substantive character of the values the state ought to express. Thus, it is quite possible for someone to take a very modest view of the proper scope of state functions and nevertheless accept a critical conception of the state. For example, there are many laissez-faire liberals amongst us who believe that state officials should self-consciously restrict themselves to night-watchman functions rather than "mindlessly" follow Observing conceptions wherever they may lead.[44] Needless to say, others may hold a more expansive conception of the values the critical state should affirm. The decisive question for us, however, is one that is logically antecedent to the task of identifying the substantive values the state should express. It is whether state officials should think of themselves merely as accommodating conflicts arising within existing institutional structures or whether they are entitled to question the validity of the structures themselves.

If one accepts the notion of the critical state, it is quite possible to develop a set of jurisprudential positions to justify the use of Scientific Policymaking by courts. No longer will the protection of socially based expectations be conceived as the supreme objective of adjudication. For the social institutions or practices that give rise to these expectations may themselves be unjust, inefficient, or otherwise inconsistent with supervening state objectives. As a consequence, it becomes necessary for courts, especially in constitutional litigation, to exercise a critical function, determining the extent to which one or another social practice deserves the support of the state's coercive power. But to discharge this function, Scientific Policymaking seems an absolute necessity—for how is it possible to criticize institutional practice other than by understanding the relationship between the legal rules presently under dispute and the Comprehensive View imputed to the critical state?[45]

This is not to say that the conscientious Scientific Policy-maker thinks himself entitled to impose his personal Comprehensive View on the parties before him. Instead, he will conceive his role to require him to transcend his private opinions and implement the *state's* Comprehensive View in the dispute at hand—for it is only as a state official that the judge is authorized to exercise his critical function. Thus, the master jurisprudential question for Policymakers will center upon the criteria the judge may appropriately use to identify the Comprehensive View which is to be imputed to the state for purposes of legal analysis. Doubtless, this task is an extremely complex one in the American constitutional system based on the separation of powers. Nonetheless, the difficulty of the issues—both in theory and in the practice of interpreting constitutions, statutes, and prior judicial decisions—will not deter the Policymaking judge from the enterprise. For unless he can provide a convincing account of the techniques by which he transcends his private opinions to ascertain the Comprehensive View adopted by the legal system, he will be unable to defend himself against the Ordinary Observer's charge that Scientific Policymaking is but a screen for imposing idiosyncratic or elite judicial preferences on society at large.[46]

Thus far we have sketched some basic moves in jurisprudential and political theory which will tempt the proponent of Scientific Policymaking seeking to ground his legal analytic in a larger theory. As in the parallel treatment of Ordinary Observing, however, it is possible to go beyond these explicit politico-legal concerns and link Scientific Policymaking to more general theories of normative evaluation and communication. Thus, Policymaking will be strengthend by philosophical efforts to provide convincing foundations for abstract talk criticizing established social practices. For example, insofar as John Rawls' account of justice is convincing,[47] it provides important support for the Kantian style of adjudication sketched in Chapter 4; [48] similarly, a latter-day Bentham could provide important services for those Scientific lawyers who wish to recast the law in explicitly Utilitarian terms. Indeed, Policy-makers are not limited to explicitly philosophical texts in their effort to defend the proposition that their talk about the legal system's Comprehensive View reflects more than a projection of their own personal idiosyncratic preferences. To select only the most striking example, a great deal of recent legal writing has attempted to employ the limited, but powerful, notion of Pareto-superiority, developed by welfare economists,[49] as a tool in the normative evaluation of legal rules.[50]

Finally, on the level of philosophy of language, the legal Scientist may gain a limited support for his enterprise from work by philosophers like R. M. Hare,[51] who seek to isolate certain logical properties of normative discourse; and it is possible once again to look beyond philosophy at least to imagine that far greater guidance may one day come from the revolution in linguistics that has reached a new stage with the writings of Chomsky,[52] as well as the larger tangle of tendencies that is associated with the Structuralist movement.[53] Even more than elsewhere, however, everything remains to be done before the areas of potential relationship can be ascertained and appraised.

We have, then, come to a rather unsurprising conclusion. Neither of the competing legal forms can be considered a cultural anomaly for which nothing can be said in a philosophical way. It will solve absolutely nothing to act as if members of one school or the other were willfully blind or perverse. What is required is discussion, not excommunication: while the general character of the larger issues may be dimly perceived, the entire debate must be brought to a far higher stage of self-conscious development before it can be said to be understood, let alone intelligently resolved.

It is even possible that once the arguments on behalf of the competing legal analytics come into sharper focus, promising intermediate positions may appear in view. Thus, it may seem plausible to mark out certain areas and issues as to which the arguments on behalf of one form or the other are relatively strong, thereby providing a philosophical foundation for a discriminating eclecticism qualitatively different from the present legal muddle. Nonetheless, even our brief canvass of competing positions should serve as a caution that the task of the eclectics will not be an easy one. While much that sounds plausible can be said on behalf of each of the different legal styles, even a casual inspection of the competing arguments will suggest that many an attempt to navigate with two compasses will founder on the rock of logical contradiction. Indeed, caution is warranted even among that small band of American legal scholars for whom "dialectical reasoning," of one sort or another, holds some attraction.[54] However eager one may be to synthesize contradictions on a "higher level," it is sobering to recognize that even Hegel's dialectical capacities proved unequal to the task of transcending the analytical conflict with which we are concerned.

Put in Hegelian terms, the Ordinary Observer's conception of property is rooted in the egoistic, individualistic consciousness of a member of civil (or market) society who is only marginally concerned with the ethical content of communal life. In contrast, the Scientific Policymaker's conception is characteristic of Hegel's ideal state official who seeks to reconcile the inevitable conflicts generated by the market society by referring to the community's fundamental ethical principles. Rather than seeking to resolve this conflict at some higher level, the whole of Hegel's philosophy is an attempt to argue, among other things, that state officials should systematically adopt a Scientific Policymaking conception of their mission.[55] Here, for once, Hegel stands foursquare with the most single-minded missionary from Chicago, who with equal fervor insists that the task of legal thought is to isolate—through Scientific analysis—a suitable basic structure within which market transactions may take place. It is, however, possible to detect an element of irony in the Hegelian position altogether absent from the Chicagoan's Scientific effort to reconstruct law from an Efficiency point of view. If there was one thing Hegel thought he *knew*, it was that the present historical period would be dominated by states whose officials were *self-*

consciously attempting to govern the market society by consulting the community's basic values. What, then, would he say upon learning that officials of the leading state of the twentieth century were as uncertain about the value of Scientific Policymaking as in fact they are? [56]

THE FUTURE

But perhaps Hegel was not so wrong as he seems on first encounter. Perhaps the rise of the critical state in America has merely been delayed, not prevented.[57] Though its substantive values are certainly not Hegel's, it is possible to detect an increasingly critical spirit at work in American legal and political institutions over the past generation. At the constitutional level, the Supreme Court has subjected fundamental social practices to a deep moral critique and has attempted revolutionary changes in the name of law. At the legislative level, the state has accepted responsibility for countless problems arising in social life which were formerly left to chance and private adjustment. At the organizational level, a massive bureaucratic machinery has been developed which, for the first time in America at least, makes it possible at least to imagine that a program initiated at the center could be carried out in a systematic fashion. At the technological level, large organizations possess mechanisms of intelligence and control unknown in the past. All these movements provide a social context congenial to the growth and development of Scientific Policymaking.

It is quite true, of course, that Scientific analysis may itself reveal that the ethical promise of the welfare state has not been redeemed; that fundamental changes in course are justified. The fact that social science reveals past failures, however, does not necessarily endanger the future of the critical state. Indeed, no law-trained person could even imagine that Scientific Policymaking—or any other form of reasoning—can of itself lead us to Utopia. Instead, it will be enough if it provides a disciplined way to learn from the past so as to assure sensitive, responsible reform. And it is far too soon to say whether this more modest hope will prove illusory. At any rate, I see little evidence that the attractions of Scientific Policymaking among the country's elite is on the wane, while there is much to suggest its increase.[58]

Nonetheless, it would be a serious mistake to view the Scientific tendency as if it were inexorably fated to master all that came before it and remake the law in its own image. Perhaps this point can best be made by casting a few sidelong glances toward Europe and noting the enormous cultural distance that still separates the new legal world from the old. In speaking of *a* Continental legal culture, I am, of course, indulging in a gross oversimplification. Moreover, it seems plain that, over the course of the twentieth century, the European legal systems of the West have moved a certain distance away from my model of Scientific Policymaking.[59] Nonetheless, to American eyes, the striking fact remains the extent to which the norms of Scientific Policymaking have been institutionalized within the European legal culture. Turning first to legal education, the dominant motifs are precisely those to be expected from our model: on the one hand, great emphasis is placed upon the mastery of a refined, self-consciously technical, legal language; on the other hand, the standard course of lectures strives to present a synoptic view of vast areas of law, each neatly ordered around "fundamental" principles.[60] Similarly, the structure of adjudication suggests parallel tendencies. Thus, judges are not only recruited on the basis of meritocratic examinations, but their promotion depends upon the extent to which their written opinions and actual decisions conform to standard practice.[61] Equally revealing is the difficulty the Europeans have had in accommodating themselves to the Anglo-American jury—imposed upon them by the French Revolution and its aftermath. Rather than glorying in the participation of laymen, the legal profession has waged a long—and quite successful—battle to limit and control this foreign element in the system. The paradigmatic adjudication remains one that is dominated by professional judges, whose decisions are closely reviewed—as to both law and fact—by professionals further up the bureaucratic hierarchy.[62]

Finally, there is the question of dominant symbols. The documents that serve as the ideological center of the legal culture are the civil and criminal codes of the nineteenth century—statutes that attempt a comprehensive view of their subject based upon a formidable tradition of scholarship tracing itself back to the rediscovery of Roman law in eleventh-century Italy.[63] While it is quite true that these nineteenth-century syntheses are under considerable strain at present,[64] the characteristic Continental reaction is not to question the need for synoptic intelligence, but to begin the work of evolving new comprehensive structures better adapted to contemporary ideas concerning the nature of the legitimate state and its role in social life.[65]

One could go on and on. Yet I hope I have said enough to support my main point: at crucial stages in his professional life, the Continental lawyer is taught to distrust his own untrained intuitions as to the merits of particular cases and is instead trained to view each particular dispute through the refracting lenses provided by a technical language and a generalizing set of legal principles. How different all this seems from the traditional framework within which the profession operates in America: where students are taught by the "Socratic method" to recognize the difficulty of applying abstract legal principles to the "hard" cases which find their way into their casebooks; where judges are selected after proving themselves to be people of good sense to politicians who control the judicial patronage; where the triumph of the legal culture is represented by the Constitution, drafted by statesmen in a single summer of insight.[66] In short, the gradual growth of Scientific Policymaking should not blind us to the fact that the American lawyer continues to be surrounded by institutions and symbols that teach him to be skeptical of abstract and systematic thought, encouraging him instead to view himself as a hard-headed problem-solver who reacts to each practical situation in the light of his common-sense understanding of social expectations.

While the Continental parallel makes it clear how far Scientific Policymaking is from total ascendancy in this country, I do not wish to place too heavy a burden upon the Continental analogy. In particular, I am skeptical of any suggestion that the rise of Scientific Policymaking—if it continues apace—will be accompanied by the self-conscious imitation of European institutional forms. The independence of the Anglo-American tradition from Roman law stands as a basic historical reality far more powerful than any of the habits of mind discussed in this essay. Just as the Scientific Policymaking doctrines treated in the first half of this book are entirely indigenous, without the hint of European legal influence, so too new institutional forms will be the product of the English-speaking tradition. Indeed, contemporary Continentals are themselves increasingly aware of the need for fundamental reconstruction of their legal inheritance—cautioning even those who would happily avoid the agonies of creative thought that this may be a peculiarly bad time to foresake our hard-won legal independence.[67]

The European tradition is useful only as a foil to dramatize the fact that the conflict between Ordinary Observing and Scientific Policymaking involves much more than two disembodied forms of thought. What is at stake is the reorganization of an entire sociocultural system that creates powerful professional incentives for the development of one or another frame of mind. Thus, the question of constitutional law we have debated is a part of a larger challenge to Ordinary Observing in many parts of the legal culture—the decline of the "Socratic" method in the classroom; the erosion of the criminal jury by bureaucratic plea-bargaining; the displacement of the civil jury by statutory compensation schemes and the institution of insurance; the rise of the "expert" administrative agency at the expense of politician and juryman alike; and so forth. Indeed, it is only after the breadth of the challenge is recognized that the empty promise of European models takes on its real significance. For it means that we are very much on our own as we struggle with the task of developing a coherent legal stance—be it Ordinary Observing or Scientific Policymaking or some sensible eclectic combination—in a new world.

From this perspective, two points stand out from the mass explored in the course of the essay. On the one hand, it is significant that the Constitution of the United States, as presently construed, contains a principle that requires the state to assess its manipulation of the economic environment not by a critical yardstick of its own devising but by one rooted in established social practice. On the other hand, it is equally significant that this commitment to the Ordinary Observer's point of view is now constitutionally suspect; neither courts nor commentators are now capable of its explicit statement or sympathetic affirmation. It is, then, a moment of reappraisal—of rediscovery and creation—in which law must become philosophical if it is to make sense of the demand for just compensation.

Notes

CHAPTER 1

1. Sibson v. State of New Hampshire, 115 N.H. 124, 336 A.2d 239 (1975).

2. 115 N.H. 124, 125, 336 A.2d 239, 240.

3. Robert Nozick, for example, is attracted to this view in his *Anarchy, State, and Utopia* (1974). It is not clear, however, that even he pursues this line consistently. Thus, in the midst of his principal discussion of the question, Nozick appears to concede the right of the state to permit only "those polluting activities whose benefits are greater than their costs," id. at 79, thereby seeming to deny the need for compensating polluters, so long as the environmental statute can be justified on utilitarian grounds. All in all, James Buchanan's new book, *The Limits of Liberty* (1975), takes a more consistent "full compensation" position.

4. I have found no contemporary American legal author who advocates out-and-out repeal of the compensation clause or a judicial reading of its command amounting to judicial nullification. There do exist a number of interpretations, however, calling for a "strict construction" of the clause; see, e.g., Fred Bosselman et al., *The Taking Issue* 238–55 (1973); John E. Donaldson, "Regulation of Conduct in Relation to Land: The Need to Purge Natural Law Constraints from the Fourteenth Amendment," 16 *Wm. & Mary L. Rev.* 187 (1974).

5. It should be emphasized at the outset that our aim is not an encyclopedic survey of compensation law but rather an intensive scrutiny of basic principles of interpretation. As a consequence, a number of important peripheral issues have been ignored. Two are at least worthy of notice. First, we shall not construe the textual command that takings be made for a "public use." While the modern understanding of "public use" holds that any state purpose otherwise constitutional should qualify as sufficiently "public" to justify a taking (Berman v. Parker, 348 U.S. 26, 32, 1954), Professor Henry Hansmann, of the University of Pennsylvania Law School, has convinced me that there is at least something to be said on the

other side. I shall, however, leave it to him to say it. Second, a large number of state constitutions include compensation clauses whose language suggests a significant modification of the federal standard. These provisions demand compensation not only when property is "taken," but also when it is "damaged." While this textual modification would seem quite significant (especially on the interpretation we shall attribute to the Ordinary Observer), my impression is that it has had a good deal less impact than might be predicted by textual exegesis alone. In any event, I shall not try to determine the extent to which this expanded version of the clause should have, or has in fact had, an impact on judicial doctrine.

6. While the holding in *Sibson* is clear enough, its precise rationale suffers from characteristic common law forms of ambiguity. Thus, the court expressly notes that Sibson had already received permission to develop profitably an adjacent portion of the marsh, only later expressly to deny the relevance of this fact to its decision, 115 N.H. 124, 126, 336 A.2d 239, 241. Similarly, the court expressed doubt that the property had been rendered valueless since it was adaptable to "the normal traditional uses of the marshland including wildlife observation, hunting, harvesting of marshgrass, clam and shellfish harvesting, and aesthetic purposes." Id. at 127, 243. Indeed, it went so far as to deny that the marsh's value had been reduced at all, explaining that "[It] was the same after the denial of the permit as before and it remained as it had been for milleniums [*sic*]." Ibid. But surely a substantial decline in value had occurred—otherwise the costly suit would never have been brought.

Finally, the court minimized Sibson's interest by noting that the development ban merely deprived him of rights that did not have the "substantial character of a current use," ibid., although it also stated that "the importance of wetlands to the public health and welfare would clearly sustain the denial of the permit to fill plaintiff's marshland even were their rights the substantial property rights inherent in a current use of an activity on their land." Id., at 127, 242–43.

7. Recent wetlands regulation cases have divided approximately evenly on the issue of compensation. See chap. 3, n. 54.

8. Pennsylvania Coal Co. v. Mahon, 260 U.S. 393 (1922) and Village of Euclid v. Ambler Realty Co., 272 U.S. 365 (1926) established the present constitutional framework for applying takings law to land use regulation.

9. The approach taken in the text may profitably be viewed as an application of Ronald Dworkin's more general critique of literalism, to be found in his "The Jurisprudence of Richard Nixon," 18 *The New York Review of Books* 27–28 (May 4, 1972).

10. During the process of ratifying the original Constitution, a number of state conventions proposed amendments which ultimately led to the adoption of the Bill of Rights. None of the state proposals, however, suggested a compensation clause. See Edward Dumbauld, *The Bill of Rights and What It Means Today* 173–205 (1957). The concept was first introduced in Madison's draft of June 8, 1789: "no person shall . . . be obliged to relinquish his property, where it may be necessary for public use, without a just compensation." 1 *Annals of Congress* 451–52. This became, after amendment and debate in both houses, the compensation clause of the Fifth Amendment. Madison's reasons for proposing it have never been satisfactorily explained, and the debates in Congress and in the state ratification conventions throw no light on the matter. Although two pre-1789 state constitutions [Massachusetts (1780) and Vermont (1786)] had just compensation provisions, others merely required that property could not be taken except according to the law of the land, or ignored the taking issue altogether. No colonial charter or "fundamental law" required compensation for the taking of property, except the Massachusetts Body of Liberties § 8 (1641) which required it for "cattle or goods."

11. The takings clause, like the rest of the Bill of Rights, was originally understood to control only actions of the federal government, not those of the states. Nonetheless, it was among the first provisions made applicable to the states through judicial interpretation of the due process clause of the Fourteenth Amendment. See Chicago, Burlington & Quincy Ry. v. Chicago, 166 U.S. 226 (1897). This makes it possible for a would-be historicist to claim that, so far as the states are concerned, the abstract concepts in the takings clause should be controlled by the understandings prevailing among lawyers in 1868, the date of the Fourteenth Amendment's enactment, rather than 1791, the year in which the Fifth Amendment came into force. I leave the solution of this question, however, to those who find it interesting.

12. Even Justice Black, who was enamored of this approach, lacked the courage of his convictions when it came to the takings clause. In a revealing opinion in United States v. Causby, 328 U.S.

256, 268 (1946), Justice Black dissented from the majority's decision to grant compensation to a farm owner injured by low-flying military aircraft, warning the court that "old concepts of private ownership of land should not be introduced into the field of air regulation." Id. at 274. Similarly, Black was willing on other occasions to approve congressional actions that would have troubled a determined historicist; see United States ex rel. T.V.A. v. Welch, 327 U.S. 546 (1946) (interpreting "public use"), and United States v. Commodities Trading Corp., 339 U.S. 121 (1950) (interpreting "just compensation").

13. No researcher has discovered either an English or an American case before 1789 that expressly required compensation in the absence of legislative authorization. See William B. Stoebuck, "A General Theory of Eminent Domain," 47 *Wash. L. Rev.* 553, 575 (1972). Nor was there any scholarly discussion of the issue, except for a brief comment of Blackstone at the end of the colonial period. Sir William Blackstone, 1 *Commentaries on the Laws of England* *139. While there was a parliamentary practice under which compensation was granted in some cases, there seems to have been no well-developed notion in the contemporary legal culture defining the scope of the right to compensation. Compare Stoebuck, supra at 577–88 to Joseph L. Sax, "Takings and the Police Power," 74 *Yale L.J.* 36, 54–60 (1964), for conflicting interpretations of the paltry data.

Looking further afield, a fair reader of Locke can only conclude that he had no clear conception of a class of justified governmental actions which nevertheless required compensation. See his *Two Treatises on Government*, book II, sec. 138–40 (1924); a collection of relevant passages may be found in Casimir J. Czajkowski, *The Theory of Private Property in John Locke's Political Philosophy* 90–97 (1941). Seventeenth-century Continental sources, like Grotius and Pufendorf, have slightly more developed notions that fall far short of a developed takings theory. Despite these modest beginnings, state courts had little difficulty erecting, during the first half of the nineteenth century, a very potent takings jurisprudence on a natural law foundation. Stoebuck, supra at 573, n. 66.

14. This is so even for those who wish to temper Charles E. Beard's *Economic Interpretation of the Constitution*, esp. 152–88 (1935), with interpretations that emphasize the importance of noneconomic factors. See Bernard Bailyn, *The Ideological Origins of*

the American Revolution 175–230 (1967), and Gordon S. Wood, *The Creation of the American Republic* 344–80 (1969).

15. The writings of Wesley Hohfeld are a classic example of this view. See his *Fundamental Legal Conceptions* (1919). The idea is not that legal discourse is more elaborate and sophisticated than ordinary language. (Indeed, one of the chief virtues claimed for Hohfeld's proposed language was its conceptual simplicity.) It is rather that legal and ordinary language are different *in kind,* in much the same way that a mathematical and a phenomenological description of a falling object are different. The Scientific apparatus orders the phenomena on the basis of categories that do not depend for their validity on their connection with the language used in everyday life. For more on the contrasting conceptions of language, compare chaps. 2 and 5, infra.

16. For present purposes it will suffice to classify as a *rule* any legal proposition that does not qualify as an element in the legal system's Comprehensive View. It is possible, of course, that this very broad class of rules may be profitably subdivided into different categories for other purposes. But I do not think I need to discuss this question, and the debate it has engendered. See e.g., Ronald Dworkin, "The Model of Rules," 35 *U. Chi. L. Rev.* 14 (1967); Joseph Raz, "Legal Principles and the Limits of Law," 81 *Yale L.J.* 823 (1972); Ronald Dworkin, "Social Rules and Legal Theory," 81 *Yale L.J.* 855 (1972).

17. It is currently popular in legal theory to define the notion of a "principle" narrowly so that it can be distinguished from another class of abstract and general legal standards called "policies." Compare the different definitions proposed by Professors Wellington and Dworkin, discussed at pp. 171–75. My use of the term, however, should be understood to have a far broader range of application. *Any prescriptive and universalizable proposition* will count as a principle so long as it sets forth one of the abstract ideals that the Policymaker understands the legal system to serve. By restricting the class of potentially admissible propositions to those of a *normative* character, moreover, I mean to impose very modest tests, more or less of the kind suggested by Professor Hare in his general analysis of the logical properties of prescriptive language. R. M. Hare, *The Language of Morals* (1952); see also his *Freedom and Reason* (1963). For example, neither "the sky is blue" nor "I like it" count as prescriptive and universalizable propositions and hence cannot

conceivably be admitted as elements in a Comprehensive View. But the proposition, "Society ought to be arranged so as to maximize its citizens' aggregate utility" certainly does satisfy Hare-like tests and would be a candidate for inclusion in the legal system's Comprehensive View. This Utilitarian proposition would be treated as a "policy," rather than a "principle," by both Dworkin and Wellington.

By saying that my principles must be *general,* I mean that each normative proposition must be understood to be applicable to the legal analysis of many classes of cases. How many is enough is, of course, a difficult question, for reasons suggested once again by Professor Hare in his recent essay, "Principles," 74 *Proceedings of the Aristotelian Society* 1, 3 (1973). While there is, I suspect, a good deal more to be said on the subject as it applies to law, I think it would be too much of a detour to attempt anything fancy here.

18. By requiring that my principles describe *abstract* ideals, I imply something more than that they be *general* in the sense adumbrated in the preceding note. The opposite of "abstract" is "concrete," while the opposite of "general" is "specific." Putting the point crudely, a principle is abstract to the extent to which its proper application to concrete cases seems problematic even after it has been exhaustively stated. While much more needs to be done to clarify this notion, I find Dworkin and Gallie suggestive here. See Ronald Dworkin, "The Jurisprudence of Richard Nixon," 18 *The New York Review of Books,* 27–28 (May 4, 1972); W. B. Gallie, "Essentially Contested Concepts," 56 *Proceedings of the Aristotelian Society* 167 (1956).

Even if the notion of abstractness were perfectly clear, it may be suggested that I have arbitrarily restricted the domain of possible Comprehensive Views by requiring that its constituent elements be abstract as well as general. While this is a deep question, as to which much can be said, I do not think a decision provisionally accepting a requirement that principles be relatively abstract is of any practical significance in the analysis of contemporary American law. When we turn to consider in chapters 3 and 4 the statements of principle that American lawyers would take as serious candidates for the position of Comprehensive View, we will find that highly abstract concepts abound in each of them. Consequently, I do not think we need preoccupy ourselves with the abstractness question in a work of applied jurisprudence like the present one.

19. By saying that the Policymaker presumes his principles form a self-consistent whole I mean three things. First, a perfectly satisfactory Comprehensive View is a *whole* in that at least one of its principles may be properly invoked in each dispute that could be brought before the legal system for resolution. Second, it is *self-consistent* in that its principles, if rightly applied, will lead to one, and only one, doctrinal solution in every case. (Note that this does not require the doctrinal solution to specify a unique substantive outcome in every case. It may be, for example, that a proper application of the Comprehensive View leads to the conclusion that a set of outcomes {A,B . . .} will satisfy equally well the ultimate ends of the legal system. This is all right so long as it is not the case that an equally valid analysis reaches the conclusion that A, or one of the other members of the first outcome-set, constitutes an *im*proper substantive response of the legal system.)

Finally, by stipulating that the Policymaker *presumes* the Comprehensive View to be a self-consistent whole, I wish to suggest the requisite decision-procedure that must be followed when a judge's initial consideration of a particular case reveals that the existing legal system falls short of the two formal ideals discussed in the preceding paragraph. That is, when an initial analysis of a case suggests that the judge's understanding of the Comprehensive View is incomplete or self-contradictory, the Policymaker will nonetheless invoke the presumption that the proper state of affairs is otherwise and proceed to refine and elaborate his understanding of the Comprehensive View so that he may generate a final legal analysis which yields a self-consistent and complete conception of the Comprehensive View.

20. The reader trained in welfare economics should recognize that the decision-procedure described in the text is sufficiently general to embrace the approach with which he is familiar. Thus, the standard Bergsonian-Samuelsonian social welfare function would formally qualify as a Comprehensive View; and the standard LaGrangean process of maximizing the social welfare function would provide a technique a Policymaker might use to identify the rule which best fulfilled the Comprehensive View. For an accessible account, see Francis M. Bator, "The Simple Analytics of Welfare Maximization," 47 *Amer. Econ. Rev.* 22 (1957). Since the normal economic optimization techniques are of a mathematical character, which do not depend for their validity upon ordinary ways of talking, it follows that

the economic approach to law provides a paradigmatic instance of Scientific Policymaking, however much particular practitioners may differ concerning the nature of the social welfare function (i.e., the identity of the relevant Comprehensive View) and the kinds of optimization techniques that best permit one to understand the ways the social welfare function can be maximized (i.e. the identity of the relevant Scientific language). It should be emphasized, however, that while the modern economic approach to law represents a paradigmatic instance of Scientific Policymaking, it is hardly the only way of fulfilling the necessary conditions for this form of legal thought. A notable example of an alternative Scientific Policymaking form is, of course, the work of Professors McDougal and Lasswell; see, e.g., their "Criteria for a Theory About Law," 44 *So. Cal. L. Rev.* 362 (1971). These matters will be discussed more extensively in chaps. 2 and 7.

21. I do not think it proper to set down a firm numerical limit and declare that no Comprehensive View may contain more than *x* principles. This is so not only because the determination of which verbal formulations are to count as one principle, rather than many principles, is itself a problematic matter, but for reasons that implicate the nature of the requirement itself. My insistence upon a relatively small number of principles is not motivated by an aesthetic impulse but rather by a fear that the limitless enumeration of principles will make Policymaking an untenable professional activity. To see this on the practical level we can note that with a large number of principles, a Policymaking lawyer or judge will be faced with the formidable task of selecting out of the mass of principles that subset arguably relevant to his particular decision. At a certain point the cost of this preliminary activity will make the entire Policymaking enterprise impractical. It follows that, as the number of principles increases, the Comprehensive View must also contain "search principles" telling practitioners which classes of substantive principles they should consult before completing their practical legal analysis. It should be apparent that this multilevel structure can itself soon become unmanageable.

Putting aside practical difficulties, however, there is a second reason for requiring a certain level of simplicity. In order for a Policymaking system to be functioning coherently, there must be some occasions upon which at least some professional people attempt to appraise the extent to which the various principles said to constitute the Comprehensive View in fact comprise a self-consistent whole that expresses ideals worthy of state support. Yet as principles become more numerous (and less abstract and general), it will become increasingly difficult to perform this function with any credibility. In short, as the number of principles increases, it becomes harder both for practitioners and scholars to assert that their legal system is structured so as to permit them to select and appraise rules on the basis of a set of abstract ideals that form a self-consistent whole. When this claim can no longer plausibly be made, the Comprehensive View violates the requirement that it contain a relatively small number of principles. It is, of course, one of the virtues of Utilitarianism that it permits the easy statement of the legal system's Comprehensive View in terms of a single principle of great abstraction and generality. But I think it apparent that the legal profession could tolerate a much greater degree of complexity if it seemed that an alternative Comprehensive View better expressed the state's ultimate ideals.

22. At most, this recognition will lead the Scientific Policymaker to introduce a new abstract and general principle dealing with the extent to which socially legitimate expectations should be afforded legal protection despite the fact that reliance would not be justified in a world in which the Comprehensive View had been perfectly institutionalized. Even this modification, however, is not always required. For example, the legal status of "non-conforming social expectations" under a Utilitarian Comprehensive View would be tested by the principle of utility just like every other question. That is, if the utility gained by denying legal protection exceeds the utility lost in disappointing social expectations, then the reliance interest should not be protected, while otherwise it should be. The special problems that arise when courts manned by Scientific Policymakers seek to provide constitutional protection to "non-conforming social expectations" will be discussed at pp. 60–64, and 83.

23. Almost every word in this sentence could profitably be defined and discussed at length. This is not the time, however, to make a full-scale attempt, though the words "principle," "abstract," and "general" have been given separate treatment at notes 17 and 18, supra. Moreover, I hope that some of the obscurities that remain will be clarified by the more extensive discussion of Ordinary Observing to be found in chap. 5.

24. As Aristotle put it: "It is the mark of an educated man to look

for precision in each class of things just as far as the nature of the subject admits; it is evidently foolish to accept probable reasoning from a mathematician, and to demand from a rhetorician scientific proofs." *Nichomachean Ethics* I. iii. 1094^{b}24–7 (tr. W. D. Ross).

25. Or as Plato might put it, the Ordinary Observer mistakes rhetoric for justice. Rhetoric is a form of flattery—like cookery— "[aiming] at what is pleasant, ignoring the good, and I insist that it is not an art, but a routine because it can produce no principle in virtue of which it offers what it does, nor explain the nature thereof, and consequently is unable to point to the cause of any thing it offers." *Gorgias* 465a (tr. Lane Cooper).

26. These earlier Scientists also imagined that their historical analysis would yield a body of principles sufficiently abstract and self-consistent to constitute a Comprehensive View. Thus, a special kind of Scientific Observing served as the foundation for Scientific Policymaking during the "Classical" phase of American legal thought at the turn of the century.

Of course, much of legal thought over the past fifty years has sought, in one way or another, to deal with the breakdown of the Classical enterprise. See Duncan Kennedy, "Form and Substance in Private Law Adjudication," 89 *Harv. L. Rev.* 1685, 1713–78 (1976); Bruce A. Ackerman, "Law and the Modern Mind," 103 *Daedalus* 119 (1974). From this point of view, the present essay does more than make the analytic point that the "Classical" kind of Scientific Policymaking is but a special case of a far more general form of legal thought. It also seeks to demonstrate that the present generation of lawyers is *in fact* developing a kind of Scientific Policymaking quite distinct from the Classical one in both vocabulary, methods, and ultimate values. This is not to deny, of course, that there are some similarities between present Policymaking efforts and Classical ones. It is only to say that the modern enterprise cannot be dismissed by casual references to the Classicists' attempt to ground a Comprehensive View on a narrow conception of the common law that had little historical depth and even less power to guide our future. Whatever the failings of the contemporary Policymaking movement, they are at least different from those of the past.

27. See, e.g., Stanley Cavell, "Must We Mean What We Say?" in V. C. Chappell, ed., *Ordinary Language* 75 (1964); Benson Mates, "On the Verification of Statements About Ordinary Language," id., 64. Good anthologies have been compiled by Fodor and Katz, *The*

Structure of Language (1964); and Davidson and Harman, *Semantics of Natural Language* (1972).

28. Or, as J. L. Austin put it, "It seems to be too readily assumed that if we can only discover the true meaning of each of a cluster of key terms, usually historic terms, that we use in some particular field (as, for example, 'right', 'good' and the rest in morals), then it must without question transpire that each will fit into some single, interlocking, consistent, conceptual scheme. Not only is there no reason to assume this, but all historical probability is against it, especially in the case of a language derived from such varied civilizations as ours is. We may cheerfully subscribe to, or have the grace to be torn between, simply disparate ideals—why *must* there be a conceivable amalgam, the Good Life for Man?" "A Plea for Excuses," 57 *Proceedings of the Aristotelian Society* 1, 29, n.16 (1956).

29. In his recent article, "Hard Cases," 88 *Harv. L. Rev.* 1057 (1975), Professor Dworkin quite self-consciously accepts a Policy-making point of view, which "condemns the practice of making decisions that seem right in isolation, but cannot be brought within some comprehensive theory of general principles and policies that is consistent with other decisions also thought right." Id. at 1064. Dworkin's commitment to Ordinary analysis, however, is no less clear. Consider the method pursued by Dworkin's ideal judge, Hercules, as he seeks to elaborate a Comprehensive View in which the concept of dignity is to play an important role: "This is a process that can usefully be seen as occupying two stages. Hercules will notice, simply as a matter of understanding his language, which are the clear settled cases in which the concept holds. He will notice, for example, that if one man is thought to treat another as his servant, though he is not in fact that man's employer, then he will be thought to have invaded his dignity. He will next try to put himself . . . within the more general scheme of beliefs and attitudes of those who value the concept. . . . put[ting] to himself . . . questions about the deep morality that gives the concept value." Id. at 1106–07.

In the context of American society, however, the "deep" questions one asks, and the "deep" values one finds, will depend upon the particular patterns of "surface" talk and action upon which one concentrates at the "first" stage. Thus, the "clear cases" of a breach of dignity in a marriage will very much depend on the class and culture of the couple and may be organized on very different principles than those which structure the concept of dignity in employment relationships of one kind or another. In short, if one were to posit two of Dworkin's ideal judges—Hercules and Ajax—there would be nothing to prevent them from reading very different understandings of the prevailing Comprehensive View on the basis of different sets of "clear, settled cases" selected at the "first-stage" inquiry. It would seem, then, that Dworkin's commitment to Ordinary analysis will lead him to the conclusion that a number of different Comprehensive Views have equal title to recognition as legally binding within the same legal system. While Dworkin apparently recognizes this possibility, see id. at 1105, it is for quite different reasons.

CHAPTER 2

1. Probably the most popular today is the distinctive vocabulary deployed by the practitioners of the so-called economic approach to law; see Guido Calabresi, *The Costs of Accidents* (1970); Richard A. Posner, *Economic Analysis of Law* (1973), Bruce A. Ackerman, ed., *Economic Foundations of Property Law* (1975). This work represents the most recent manifestation of an approach that can trace its antecedents through Bentham back at least to Hobbes. A second, quite different, legal analytic has been developed by Professors McDougal and Lasswell; see Myres S. McDougal and Harold G. Lasswell, *The Jurisprudence of a Free Society: Studies in Law, Science and Policy* (forthcoming); Lasswell and McDougal, "Criteria for a Theory About Law," 44 *So. Cal. L. Rev.* 362 (1971). More pervasive than either of the preceding vocabularies is the set of concepts developed by Wesley N. Hohfeld, *Fundamental Legal Conceptions* (1919). For some comments on the strikingly different technical vocabulary developed on the Continent, see n. 3, infra.

2. A particularly sensitive treatment of the problem of reification may be found in Arthur A. Leff, "Contract as Thing," 19 *Am. U.L. Rev.* 131 (1970).

3. I have attempted in the preceding paragraphs to provide a straightforward account of the bedrock conventional wisdom about property currently prevailing in enlightened legal circles. While it is possible to cite similar accounts, a few citations cannot prove the important point—that my presentation does in fact conform to the conventional thinking on the subject. For what it is worth, none of the many people who have read this book in manuscript form have failed to recognize the account as part of their own tradition. Those who wish to trace the patterns more carefully in the literature could

well begin with Guido Calabresi and A. Douglas Melamed, "Property Rules, Liability Rules, and Inalienability: One View of the Cathedral," 85 *Harv. L. Rev.* 1089, 1090–93 (1972); Myres S. McDougal and David Haber, *Property, Wealth, Land* 1–113 (1948). These themes are carried through in the commonly used property casebooks; see, e.g., Charles Donahue, Jr., Thomas E. Kauper, and Peter W. Martin, *Property* 1–288 (1974); Curtis J. Berger, *Land Ownership and Use* 1–79 (1975). Similarly, those economists concerned with legal issues would find nothing here with which they would disagree. Professor McKean's statement is typical: "The basic things that we exchange are not products' physical features as such but rather packages of rights to do things with those features." Roland N. McKean, "Products Liability: Implications of Some Changing Property Rights," 84 *Q.J. Econ.* 611 (1970).

However broad the agreement amongst Scientists in the Anglo-American legal world, it should be emphasized that my account does not represent the only way to think about property once one has accepted Scientific premises. Indeed, European lawyers—though deeply committed to the development of a technical legal vocabulary —have nonetheless developed a very different technical language to deal with property relationships. Rather than rejecting "ownership talk" as misguided, Continental lawyers take the idea very seriously, trying both to give the concept a technical meaning and to limit quite strictly the ways in which non-owners may have rights in a thing. The difference in the two modern approaches doubtless may be explained in part by history. On the one hand, the modern American Scientist's skepticism about the utility of describing someone as "the" owner of a thing and his delight in the diversity of property packages may be traced to the feudal origins of the common law of property, where the distribution of rights to land among a variety of persons was a central concern. On the other hand, the modern Continental's emphasis on ownership has an obvious relationship to the rather unitary conception of property traditional in Roman law. Moreover, the entire conception of property plays a far less central role in European legal thought than it does in American, which helps explain why the Continentals have got by with a set of notions that seem extraordinarily unsophisticated and rigid to the typical American lawyer. In short, although the Continental conception of property is equally technical in origins, it conforms far more closely to the patterns of nonprofessional talk than does the Anglo-American conception. The result is quite exceptional when viewed from a comparative perspective—for it is a platitude among comparatists that European substantive law is generally far more technically refined than its common-law counterpart. As Llewellyn remarked: "[If] all our legal thinking . . . were the thinking of a skilled conveyancer when conveyancing . . . , then American lawyers would feel less like zoo specimens when present at a gathering of Continental lawyers." Karl N. Llewellyn, "Rule of Thumb and Principle," in W. Twining, ed., *The Karl Llewellyn Papers* 9 (1968). For a fine introduction to the comparative law of property, as well as useful references to the rather limited comparative literature, see John Henry Merryman, "Ownership and Estate," 48 *Tulane Law Review* 916 (1974).

4. In the cases that will concern us, the claimants have suffered a real money loss as a result of the legislative redistribution of property rights. While this requirement of a real loss may seem obvious, claims for compensation are sometimes raised that may be denied for failure to fulfil this threshhold condition. Imagine, for example, that as a result of the general pattern of ecological regulation, Jones's land increases in value from $25,000 to $40,000 because the value to him of the forbearance of other marshowners is greater to him than the cost imposed by the law's demand that he restrict his own development. Nevertheless, if Jones could free himself from the development limitation while the other Marshans continued to be restricted, he would profit even more from the new legislative enactment. For then he would be free to build the only skyscraper on the marsh, increasing the value of his land to a million dollars. Given these facts, it sometimes happens that Jones goes to court to claim that the law's refusal to grant him an exemption has cost him $960,000, for which the Constitution requires compensation. It should be apparent, however, that rather than costing him $960,000, the statute has benefitted him by $15,000 and that Jones's suit is merely an attempt to gain an even greater share of the collective benefit generated by the statute. While this effort raises complex questions deserving sustained analysis, no one has suggested that the efforts of gainers to obtain even greater gains can be grounded on constitutional, rather than statutory, foundations. Consequently, we shall ignore these questions here. To put the point more generally, we shall be assuming that, as a result of a legislative enactment, the claimant has suffered a substantial financial loss that will not be

made up, even in the long run, by the fact that others will be subjected to similar restraints. For a more elegant formulation of this idea, see A. Mitchell Polinsky, "Probabilistic Compensation Criteria," 86 *Q.J. Econ.* 407 (1972).

Some readers have also called to my attention the possibility that property owners may have good reason to anticipate during Time One the possibility that their rights will be reshuffled at Time Two. This may mean that the market value of their rights will already have suffered a depreciation before the formal taking has occurred at Time Two, sometimes leading to a relatively small market drop at that stage. While all this is sometimes true, even someone who anticipates that a taking is a possibility will nevertheless suffer a "real loss" of some size at Time Two, except under the most unlikely conditions. Moreover, there is no reason for the Policymaker to limit his view of the damage to the moment in time that the taking is announced; instead, he may take into account the costs generated during earlier periods if this would further the Comprehensive View he has imputed to the legal system.

All this is not to deny that the ease with which the possibility of a taking may be foreseen, and the property owner's attitude toward risk, is somteimes relevant to a Policymaker's approach to compensation law. Indeed, it is sometimes very relevant, see pp. 43–46, infra, and also n. 33, chap. 4. It is only to say that "partially anticipated" takings cannot be eliminated by the threshold requirement of a "real loss."

5. A sample of the last generation's scholarship would include, among other things: Alexander M. Bickel, *The Least Dangerous Branch* (1962), and *The Supreme Court and the Idea of Progress* (1970); Charles L. Black, Jr., *The People and the Court: Judicial Review in a Democracy* (1960); Jan G. Deutsch, "Neutrality, Legitimacy and the Supreme Court: Some Intersections Between Law and Political Science," 20 *Stan. L. Rev.* 169 (1968); Learned Hand, *The Bill of Rights* (1958); Herbert Wechsler, "Toward Neutral Principles of Constitutional Law," in *Principles, Politics, and Fundamental Law* (1961).

6. See his Holmes Lectures, *The Bill of Rights,* n. 5, supra.

7. John Rawls, *A Theory of Justice* 4–5, 453–62 (1971).

8. Since each of the three role variables can assume two basic values, it is possible to generate eight logically distinct conceptions of judicial role: (C,D,P_1), (C,D,P_2), (C,A,P_1), (C,A,P_2), (R,D,P_1),

(R,D,P$_2$), (R,A,P$_1$), (R,A,P$_2$) where C = conservative, R = reformist, D = deferential, A = activist, P$_1$ = principled and P$_2$ = pragmatic. Even this, however, is a simplification since, as we shall see, there may often be several plausible ways of defining each of the judicial options that tolerate one or another form of innovation.

CHAPTER 3

1. Chap. 7 locates this problem of Policymaking jurisprudence in a wider philosophical setting. See pp. 175–85 infra.

2. Of course, the good Utilitarian will choose the model of judicial role which, in his best judgment, maximizes long-run utility. But to the present generation of lawyers, at least, it may not be at all obvious which role model will in fact generate the long-run utility-maximizing consequences. Hence the necessity of focusing upon the institutional variable as one of independent importance.

3. In ruling upon a particular litigated case, a Utilitarian judge will be free to frame a rule that covers only a very small number of almost identical situations arising in the future or may instead speak more generally and cover a more numerous class under the same rubric. Needless to say, the generality with which the rule is framed is itself a question that a Utilitarian would determine after a sensitive appreciation of the costs and benefits of greater specificity or generality. For some generally enlightening comments, see Isaac Ehrlich and Richard A. Posner, "An Economic Analysis of Legal Rulemaking," 3 *J. of Legal Studies* 257 (1974); Werner Z. Hirsch, "Reducing Law's Uncertainty and Complexity," 21 *U.C.L.A. L. Rev.* 1233 (1974).

4. For present purposes we shall assume that there is nothing our risk-averse citizen can do to reduce the threat of adverse governmental action by himself engaging in political activities—lobbying and so forth—to protect his financial interest. This is, of course, an unrealistic picture. In many cases, denying compensation to the Marshans will induce them to invest more of their time than they otherwise would in political action. Nonetheless, I do not think the costs involved in this political kind of adaptive behavior would be considered by a restrained judge as he weighed the felicific merit of a compensation requirement. Before he may count the Marshans' intensified political action as a *net* cost, a judge must take it upon himself to measure the possible benefits, both to the Marshans and the larger body politic, that may follow upon their greater political

awareness. And it is difficult to imagine a deferential judge concluding that the increased political activity did more harm than good.

This is not to say, however, that the tie between the compensation requirement and the character of political activity will always be irrelevant in legal analysis. Indeed, it will be a central issue for activist adjudication, to be discussed at pp. 49–56 infra.

5. The literature on the failure of insurance markets is vast and rich. A good place to begin is Mark V. Pauly, "Overinsurance and Public Provision of Insurance: The Roles of Moral Hazard and Adverse Selection," 88 *Q.J. Econ.* 44 (1974), which also cites the most important recent work in the field. While the past decade has seen considerable advances in theoretical understanding of insurance market failure, the prevailing theoretical treatments invoke assumptions sufficiently removed from reality as to defeat any simple effort to derive concrete policy applications from them at the present time. Thus, for the present at least, Utilitarian judges would be well advised to pursue a more common sense approach, taking notice of the practical difficulty involved in obtaining insurance against a wide variety of risks, as well as recognizing the many types of informational imperfection which make perfect insurance markets a theorist's dream. For an illuminating discussion, see Guido Calabresi, *The Costs of Accidents,* chap. 4 (1970).

6. In addition, a favorable decision on compensation may induce entry into the compensated activity that could not be justified on Utilitarian grounds if second-order effects were taken into account. For example, a decision to compensate flood victims for their losses may encourage further settlement on the flood plain, inducing the government to respond to the enhanced flood costs through a dam-construction program—whereas the utility-maximizing solution all along was to restrict settlement in the flood plain.

Just as an appeal to second-order effects may sometimes work against compensation, it may sometimes work powerfully in the opposite direction. For example, where it is only the difficulty of constructing a private insurance market that is preventing the development of an activity that would generate substantial felicific benefits, compensation may seem indicated even in the presence of large process costs. Since courts, however, will typically find it quite difficult to assess second-order effects, these points do not warrant further development here.

7. Generally speaking, prevailing judicial norms require the judge either to grant compensation to all claimants within a given class or withhold it altogether. Given this all-or-nothing choice, the formula presented in the text, which speaks in terms of total rather than marginal conditions, will suffice. If, however, the judge moves to a higher level of sophistication to consider the level of generality at which he should categorize the class of claimants deserving of compensation (see n. 3 supra), then marginal calculations will be the appropriate ones. Thus, in choosing between a rule, R_1, that protected a relatively small set of claimants, $\{X\}$, and a rule R_2 that protected a larger group $\{XUY\}$, it could well turn out that both R_1 and R_2 pass the test set out in the text. In this case, the proper R would be the one for which the difference between U and P was greater; in other words, marginal calculations would here be necessary.

8. A complete theory of judicial restraint would, of course, explain why even a "well-ordered" legislature would tend to slight general uncertainty in its effort to maximize utility. This does not seem especially difficult in light of the well-known problems encountered by large groups whose interests are both diffuse and transitory when they seek to organize for political action. See generally, Mancur Olson, Jr., *The Logic of Collective Action* (1965); James Q. Wilson, *Political Organizations* (1973). Although I will not here take the time to assess and appraise the possible sophisticated theories of the "well-ordered" political process, I do not wish to minimize the importance of this enterprise. Indeed, further reflection on this matter —to which I have been led by a particularly fruitful correspondence with Professor Frank Michelman—convinces me that an elaboration of alternative theories of the *legislative* process is a research topic of the highest priority for all those who wish to attain a sophisticated understanding of *judicial* review in both its deferential and activist modes.

9. Nonetheless, a plausible *constitutional* claim for compensation based on the Appeal to General Uncertainty can be made only if it is the state, rather than some private decisionmaker, whose action has increased the level of risk obtaining in the environment. Of course, compensation may sometimes be justified to offset risks generated by private decisionmakers that are expensive to insure against. Under prevailing legal theories, however, the Constitution is understood to provide relief against actions with which the state is

significantly involved. So far as the deleterious actions of private individuals are concerned, conventional legal theory assigns remedial responsibility largely to the discretion of legislatures, rather than the constitutional judgment of courts. For a brief discussion of the distinction between state and private action, see pp. 145–50 infra.

10. Once again the formula is oversimplified in the text when it suggests that the judge should be concerned only with *total* costs and *total* benefits; for the role of marginal conditions see n. 7 supra.

11. For the definition of deference, see p. 37 supra.

12. See Alexander Bickel, *The Least Dangerous Branch* 111–99 (1962).

13. Recall that in ruling on any particular case the Utilitarian judge understands himself to be constructing a rule which will dispose of a stream of cases arising in the future. Since the process costs arising in the case at bar have already been expended, they will not be counted. Instead the formula requires the judge to compare only those benefits and costs arising in the future. Hence a more sophisticated treatment would require the judge to perform a familiar sort of discounting in order to reduce future to present values. For a more important way in which the discussion's sophistication may be enhanced, recall n. 3 supra.

14. For the role of marginal, as opposed to total, conditions in this felicific formula, see n. 7 supra.

15. "Property, Utility, and Fairness: Comments on the Ethical Foundations of 'Just Compensation' Law," 80 *Harv. L. Rev.* 1165 (1967).

16. Indeed, the idea that competing theories of judicial role importantly control doctrine is absent from the bulk of Michelman's discussion, though a deferential tone is struck in a concluding plea for increased legislative creativity on compensation issues; see id. at 1245–57.

17. Instead, these considerations, together with the "second-order" consequences discussed in n. 6 supra, are aggregated under a single concept termed "demoralization" costs, see id. at 1215–16. For another effort to refine the umbrella concept of "demoralization cost" see Oliver E. Williamson, "Administrative Decision Making and Pricing: Externality and Compensation Analysis Applied," in J. Margolis, ed., *The Analysis of Public Output* 115 (1970).

18. Michelman is not altogether unmindful of this factor and contributes a number of valuable insights (80 *Harv. L. Rev.* 1165,

1235). These insights are not developed, however, and Michelman's introductory statement that a judgment of the statute's underlying Utilitarian merits "is not entirely irrelevant to the compensability issue" (id. at 1235) suggests to the unwary reader that the issue is of subsidiary importance.

19. My debt to Michelman extends far beyond his innovative attempt to sketch the outlines of a Utilitarian approach to compensation law. Other elements of his essay were equally important, obliging me to reflect far more deeply on the subject than I could have done unaided. While certain salient points of agreement and disagreement with Michelman will be noted as they arise, these scholarly tokens do not measure the full compensation that would be due in a well-ordered academy.

20. Quite obviously, my effort here has not been to offer a distilled and condensed version of Michelman's complex argument but to indicate the way certain of his basic insights fit into the present theoretical structure. I am offering a self-conscious reinterpretation, for the purpose of reducing the intellectual chaos presently existing in the field, produced in large measure by the fact that each writer eagerly proceeds at once to propound his own special theory without seeking to relate his thesis to those advanced by others. With so many writers proceeding as if the legal world were forever new, it is no surprise that most labor mightily only to rediscover the wheel, while few are at work on the internal combustion engine (not to speak of solar energy).

21. United States v. Carolene Products Co., 304 U.S. 144, 152, n.4 (1938).

22. "Takings and the Police Power," 74 *Yale L.J.* 36 (1964) (hereafter cited as *Sax I*). For more recent Scientific work expressing similar concerns, see Lawrence Berger, "A Policy Analysis of the Taking Problem," 49 *N.Y.U.L. Rev.* 165, 197–98 (1974); William F. Baxter and Lillian R. Altree, "Legal Aspects of Airport Noise," 15 *J. of Law & Econ.* 1, 2–28 (1972).

23. *Sax I* at 61–67.

24. Indeed, over the past decade it has become increasingly fashionable among political scientists to study institutional actors as if they maximized their utility subject to constraints imposed by external forces—precisely the model underlying Proposition B_1, as it is stated in the text. For a sensitive discussion of the increasing prominence of this mode of political science, see David R. Mayhew,

Congress: The Electoral Connection 13–77 (1974). For an application to administrative behavior, see William A. Niskanen, *Bureaucracy and Representative Government* (1971).

25. There may, of course, be other reasons for distrusting the utility-maximizing character of the decisions handed down by local zoning boards. All I am saying here is that the typical zoning board lacks both the bureaucratic and financial power that permits a plausible application of Proposition B_1. For more on zoning boards, see n. 31 infra.

26. *Sax I* at 64–65. See also Joseph L. Sax, "Takings, Private Property and Public Rights," 81 *Yale L. J.* 149, 169–71 (1971) (hereafter cited as *Sax II*).

27. See n. 20, supra.

28. *Sax II,* n. 26, supra.

29. See Olson, *The Logic of Collective Action* 27–32, n. 8, supra. Wilson, *Political Organizations,* n. 8, supra.

30. See *Sax II* at 160.

31. One line of development is so promising that it requires at least a footnote invitation to further work. In treating the activist judge, the text has considered only the easiest and hardest cases along a continuum. On the one hand, it is relatively easy for a judge to refuse deference to "self-aggrandizing" bureaucracies of the sort discussed at pp. 50–52; on the other hand, it is relatively difficult to deny, except in special cases, deference to the central legislative processes of the state or nation, enshrined as these are by democratic ideology. There are, however, intermediate cases of obvious importance to the compensation clause. Consider, for example, the land use regulations imposed by thousands of zoning boards across the country. While these decisions generally have the warrant of democratic ideology behind them, local government does not have the same high status held by the states and the federal government in our constitutional scheme. There are, moreover, reasons to believe that local governments' use of the zoning power may be systematically biased in a non-felicific fashion. See e.g., Susan Rose-Ackerman, "The Political Economy of a Racist Housing Market," 4 *J. Urban Econ.* (forthcoming, 1977), and materials cited in Bruce A. Ackerman, ed., *Economic Foundations of Property Law* 328 (1975). Consequently, it may be perfectly plausible for an activist judge to subject local zoning regulations to special scrutiny, requiring compensation whenever a careful appraisal of the regula-

tion's overall utility seemed doubtful. While this step would, of course, entail a very substantial incursion into local political processes, it is in fact less intrusive than the flat invalidation of "exclusionary" zoning ordinances on similar grounds that has become increasingly common over the past five years, not to mention the massive judicial intervention in local educational policymaking during the generation since *Brown* v. *Board of Education*. A full appraisal of this form of judicial activism, however, would require too elaborate an analysis to undertake here; one would be obliged to examine a number of models of local government decisionmaking to determine the occasions upon which a good Utilitarian would be especially suspicious of its proper functioning. (For an article which suggests the general form of analysis, though I disagree with its conclusions, see Note, "Equalization of Municipal Services: The Economics of *Serrano* and *Shaw*," 82 *Yale L.J.* 89 (1972), reprinted in *Economic Foundations of Property Law* 247, supra.)

In addition, it would be necessary to consider in detail the constitutional status of local governments, developing and appraising in this context many of the themes developed by Charles Black in his important book, *Structure and Relationship in Constitutional Law* (1969).

32. It is logically conceivable, of course, that an agnostic judge may nevertheless take an extremely activist position on judicial competence and assert that the deliberate actions of the other branches of government are less likely to maximize utility than decisions based on a judicial flip of the coin. But this position is just plain silly—reminding us that many of our analytic boxes will—and should—remain empty in the analysis.

33. As the environmental movement reaches maturity, however, it is becoming apparent that environmental issues may sometimes be inextricably interwoven with fundamental questions of distributive justice. To take but one obvious example, environmental values may be invoked to justify zoning ordinances that have the obvious effect of excluding the poor from desirable communities. As trade-offs of this kind are more generally perceived and discussed, it may become increasingly difficult for agnostic judges to determine whether the principal objective of a legislative reshuffling of property bundles is to eliminate the peculiar environmental disutilities associated with one or another activity or instead to redistribute slices in the overall utility pie between contending groups.

34. This is not to say, however, that all tax legislation should be

understood to serve primarily redistributive functions. Instead, the potential efficiency of taxing polluters and other "externality-producers" has become a part of the dominant Scientific Policy-making credo; see, e.g. William F. Baxter, *People or Penguins: The Case for Optimal Pollution* (1974). Hence it is perfectly possible for an agnostic Utilitarian court to recognize that some tax legislation is motivated by efficiency, rather than distributional concerns, and to proceed to analyze the law in a conservative fashion. Speaking broadly, this approach was in fact taken by the Pennsylvania Supreme Court in a recent case involving the city of Pittsburgh's effort to assess a heavy tax upon private parking lots in the downtown area. Since this tax could most readily be justified on efficiency grounds, requiring automobile owners to "internalize" some of their "externalities," there was no need for an agnostic court to suspend all further takings analysis simply because the legislation took the form of a tax measure. Thus the Pennsylvania court felt free to scrutinize the tax measure further, noting that one of its principal beneficiaries would be the city's own parking authority which operated some 6,000 of the available parking spaces. Invoking Sax's activist distinction between entrepreneurial and mediational functions, the court held the tax to be an unconstitutional taking. The Pennsylvania court's judgment was appealed to the U.S. Supreme Court, which reversed in a cloudy opinion that relied heavily on the traditional immunity of tax legislation. See Alco Parking Corporation v. Pittsburgh, 453 Pa. 245, 307 A.2d 851 (1973), rev'd. 417 U.S. 369 (1974). While the Court's judgment is, of course, significant, I do not think it should be considered as a sober assessment of Sax's theory, which provides the basis for Proposition B_1 advanced previously. Not only does the Pennsylvania decision represent a rather problematic application of the theory, but the tradition of extreme deference on taxation questions undoubtedly increased the Court's unwillingness to take seriously a novel doctrinal suggestion in a field where it has acted with exceeding caution for a half-century. See chap. 6 infra. Sax's theory, in short, will get a fair hearing in the Supreme Court only after a much fuller airing in the lower courts. Tax cases like *Parking Corporation* will seem troublesome, at least in Washington, D.C., only at a later stage in the advance of Scientific Policymaking, when the less obvious implications of Sax's approach are subjected to refined elaboration.

35. The theory of statutory interpretation, as well as the role the

theory plays in constitutional adjudication, has been the subject of a number of insightful essays which cry out for synthesis and further elaboration. See Anthony G. Amsterdam, "The Void-for-Vagueness Doctrine in the Supreme Court," 109 *U. Pa. L. Rev.* 67 (1960); John Hart Ely, "Legislative and Administrative Motivation in Constitutional Law," 79 *Yale L.J.* 1205 (1970); Paul Brest, "Palmer v. Thompson: An Approach to the Problem of Unconstitutional Legislative Motive," *1971 Supreme Court Rev.* 95; Duncan Kennedy, "Legal Formality," 2 *J. Leg. Studies* 351 (1973). See also, Paul Brest, *Processes of Constitutional Decisionmaking: Cases and Materials* 9–46, 102–72 (1975).

36. While I believe that no current theory of justice—be it Utilitarian, Kantian, or what-have-you—suggests the desirability of imposing such a quantitative pattern on social outcomes, others may disagree. Robert Nozick, for example, devotes a great deal of energy to refuting theorists who seek to impose such determinate patterns upon the population, his concentration on the subject suggesting that he is doing something more than tilting at windmills. See Robert Nozick, *Anarchy, State, and Utopia,* 150–74 (1974). I am, however, unpersuaded that the theorists Nozick attacks do in fact espouse the simple position he attributes to them.

37. I am here making a distinction between a legal rule and a principle in the way suggested by Ronald Dworkin, "The Model of Rules," 35 *U. Chi. L. Rev.* 14, 22–29 (1967); for a criticism of this approach, see Joseph Raz, "Legal Principles and the Limits of Law," 81 *Yale L.J.* 823, 834–39 (1972).

38. The simple argument is made in A. C. Pigou, *The Economics of Welfare,* 4th ed., I, 8, §§1–4 (1948), while a more sophisticated, if more limited, form of the argument can be found in Abba P. Lerner, *The Economics of Control: Principles of Welfare Economics,* chap. 3 (1944). For a critical appraisal of the effort to make interpersonal comparisons of utility, see Lionel Robbins, *An Essay on the Nature and Significance of Economic Science,* 2d ed., chap. 6 (1952); Walter J. Blum and Harry Kalven Jr., *The Uneasy Case for Progressive Taxation* 49–63 (1953). It should be noted that while economists are apt to deny the possibility of making meaningful interpersonal comparisons of utility, philosophers are more receptive to the plausibility of the enterprise. See I. M. D. Little, *A Critique of Welfare Economics,* 2d ed., chap. 4 (1957); John Rawls, *A Theory of Justice* 321–24 (1971).

39. See, e.g., Guido Calabresi, *The Costs of Accidents* (1970); Guido Calabresi and Jon T. Hirschoff, "Toward a Test for Strict Liability in Torts," 81 *Yale L.J.* 1055 (1972); Peter A. Diamond and James A. Mirrlees, "On the Assignment of Liability: The Uniform Case," 6 *Bell J. Econ.* 487 (1975); Peter A. Diamond, "Accident Law and Resource Allocation," 5 *Bell J. Econ.* 366 (1974).

40. See e.g., Bruce A. Ackerman, ed., *Economic Foundations of Property Law* (1975); Henry G. Manne, ed., *The Economics of Legal Relationships* (1975); Richard A. Posner, *Economic Analysis of Law* 10–102 (1973).

41. See, e.g., Phillip Areeda and Donald F. Turner, "Predatory Pricing and Related Practices Under Section 2 of the Sherman Act," 88 *Harv. L. Rev.* 697 (1975); F. M. Scherer, "Predatory Pricing and the Sherman Act: A Comment," 89 *Harv. L. Rev.* 869 (1976); Phillip Areeda and Donald F. Turner, "Scherer on Predatory Pricing: A Reply," id. at 891; F. M. Scherer, "Some Last Words on Predatory Pricing, id. at 901; Robert H. Bork and Ward S. Bowman, Jr., "The Crisis in Antitrust," 65 *Colum. L. Rev.* 363 (1965); Harlan M. Blake and William K. Jones, "In Defense of Antitrust," id. at 377; Robert H. Bork and Ward S. Bowman, Jr., "Contrasts in Antitrust Theory," id. at 401; Harlan M. Blake and William K. Jones, "Toward a Three-Dimensional Antitrust Policy," id. at 422; Carl Kaysen and Donald F. Turner, *Antitrust Policy: An Economic and Legal Analysis* (1959); Richard S. Markovits, "Oligopolistic Pricing Suits, The Sherman Act, and Economic Welfare" (Part I) 26 *Stan. L. Rev.* 493 (1974), (Part II) id. at 717, (Part III) 27 *Stan. L. Rev.* 307 (1975), (Part IV) 28 *Stan. L. Rev.* 45 (1975); Richard A. Posner, "Natural Monopoly and Its Regulation," 21 *Stan. L. Rev.* 548 (1969).

42. See, e.g., William D. Andrews, "A Consumption-Type or Cash Flow Personal Income Tax," 87 *Harv. L. Rev.* 1113 (1974); Alvin C. Warren, Jr., "Fairness and a Consumption-Type or Cash Flow Personal Income Tax," 88 *Harv. L. Rev.* 931 (1975); William D. Andrews, "Fairness and the Personal Income Tax: A Reply to Professor Warren," id. at 947; Stanley S. Surrey, *Pathways to Tax Reform* (1973); Alvin C. Warren, Jr., "The Corporate Interest Deduction: A Policy Evaluation," 83 *Yale L.J.* 1585 (1974).

43. See, e.g., Ward S. Bowman, Jr., *Patent and Antitrust Law* (1973); Victor Brudney and Marvin A. Chirelstein, *Cases and Materials on Corporate Finance* (1972); Victor Brudney and Marvin A.

Chirelstein, "Fair Shares in Corporate Mergers and Takeovers," 88 *Harv. L. Rev.* 297 (1974); Oliver E. Williamson, *Markets and Hierarchies* (1975).

44. Shepherd's Law Review Citations reveal more than 100 occasions upon which the Sax and Michelman articles have been cited by other commentators. Among the most significant recent essays that attempt to further the analysis in the scientific spirit are William F. Baxter and Lillian R. Altree, "Legal Aspects of Airport Noise," 15 *J. Law & Econ.* 1 (1972); Lawrence Berger, "A Policy Analysis of the Taking Problem," 49 *N.Y.U.L. Rev.* 165 (1974); John J. Costonis, " 'Fair' Compensation and the Accommodation Power: Antidotes for the Taking Impasse in Land Use Controversies," 75 *Colum. L. Rev.* 1021 (1975), and "Development Rights Transfer: An Exploratory Essay," 83 *Yale L.J.* 75 (1973); Zygmunt J. B. Plater, "The Takings Issue in a Natural Setting: Floodlines and the Police Power," 52 *Tex. L. Rev.* 201 (1974); Oliver E. Williamson, "Administrative Decisionmaking and Pricing: Externality and Compensation Analysis Applied" in J. Margolis, ed., *The Analysis of Public Output* 115 (1970).

45. The courts have demonstrated various degrees of sophistication in their treatment of Michelman and Sax. While many citations seem to be windowdressing for analysis of the Ordinary Observing kind, several courts have made a genuine effort to invoke Scientific doctrine. See, e.g., HFH Ltd. v. Superior Court, 15 Cal. 3d 508, 125 Cal. Rptr. 365, 542 P.2d 237 (1975), cert. den., 425 U.S. 904 (1976); Lutheran Church v. City of New York, 35 N.Y. 2d 121, 359 N.Y.S. 2d 7, 316 N.E. 2d 305 (1974); Alco Parking Corporation v. Pittsburgh, 453 Pa. 245, 307 A.2d 851 (1973), rev'd., 417 U.S. 369 (1974), and discussed at n. 34 supra.

46. See, for example, Hasegawa v. Maui Pineapple Company, 52 Ha. 327, 475 P.2d 679 (1970) in which the Supreme Court of Hawaii invoked Sax's entrepreneurial/mediational distinction in striking down a statue requiring employers to pay employees on jury duty the difference between their regular salaries and jurors' pay.

47. See chaps. 5 and 6.

48. For a canvass of the conventional tests of takings law, see Philip Nichols, *The Law of Eminent Domain*, rev. 3d ed., vol. 2, §§ 6.2–6.38 (1970). The tests are discussed critically in *Sax I;* Michelman, "Property, Utility and Fairness"; Arvo Van Alstyne, "Taking or Damaging by Police Power: The Search for Inverse Condemnation

Criteria," 44 *So. Cal. L. Rev.* 1 (1971); Lawrence Berger, "A Policy Analysis of the Taking Problem," *N.Y.U. L. Rev.* 165, 170–77 (1974).

49. See Nichols, *The Law of Eminent Domain,* vol. 2, §§ 6.2–6.21. The point is illustrated in United States v. Dow, 357 U.S. 17 (1958), which held that despite the provisions of the Declaration of Taking Act, a taking was effected at the time of physical possession, which predated the filing and transfer of title under the act.

50. See e.g., Dooley v. Town Plan and Zoning Commission, 151 Conn. 304, 197 A.2d 770 (1964); Morris County Land Improvement Company v. Parsippany-Troy Hills Township, 40 N.J. 539, 193 A.2d 232 (1963). See Nichols, *The Law of Eminent Domain,* vol. 1, § 1.42 [7]. Judicial concern with diminution of market value has its origin in Mr. Justice Holmes's often quoted dicta on the limits of the police power in Pennsylvania Coal Company v. Mahon, 260 U.S. 393, 413, 415–16 (1922), a case which will be discussed at length at pp. 156–65 infra. See also Commissioner of National Resources v. S. Volpe Company, Inc., 349 Mass. 104, 109–10, 206 N.E. 2d 666, 670 (1965); Miller v. City of Beaver Falls, 368 Pa. 189, 197–98, 82 A.2d 34, 38 (1951).

51. See, e.g., Turnpike Realty Company v. Town of Dedham, 362 Mass. 221, 284 N.E. 2d 891 (1972), cert. den. 409 U.S. 1108 (1973), in which the court refused to hold that an 88% diminution in market value was "conclusive evidence of an unconstitutional deprivation of property"; Consolidated Rock Products Company v. City of Los Angeles, 57 Cal. 2d 515, 370 P.2d 342 (1962), appeal dismissed 371 U.S. 36 (1962), in which the court upheld a zoning restriction while stating, "It must be conceded that in relation to its value for the extraction of rock, sand and gravel, the value of the property for any of the [alternative] uses is relatively small, if not minimal, and that as to a considerable part of it seasonal flooding might prevent its continuous use for any purpose." Cf. Goldblatt v. Town of Hempstead, 369 U.S. 590 (1962). For a collection of cases, see Robert M. Anderson, *American Law of Zoning,* vol. 1, § 2.23 (1968).

52. Compare Turnpike Realty Company v. Town of Dedham, 362 Mass. 221, 284 N.E. 2d 891 (1972), cert. den. 409 U.S. 1108 (1973) (upholding flood plain zoning restrictions) with Dooley v. Town Plan and Zoning Commission, 151 Conn. 304, 197 A.2d 770 (1964) (striking down similar restrictions). See Nichols, *The Law of Eminent Domain,* vol. 1, § 1.42 [2]; Ernst Freund, *The Police Power,* § 511 (1904).

53. A picturesque example of this kind of obscurity is provided by Mr. Justice Sutherland in Village of Euclid v. Ambler Realty Company, 272 U.S. 365, 388 (1926), the landmark case upholding zoning ordinances. In analogizing such regulations to the common law of nuisance, the justice remarked, "a nuisance may be merely a right thing in the wrong place, like a pig in a parlor instead of the barnyard." While this may make perfect sense to an Ordinary Observer, the difficulty for the Scientific Policymaker is that it is not obvious a priori whether the pig or the parlor constitutes the noxious use. See Ronald Coase, "The Problem of Social Costs," 3 *J. Law & Econ.* 1 (1960); *Sax I* at 48–50; Michelman, "Property, Utility and Fairness," at 1196–1201; Note, "An Economic Analysis of Land Use Conflicts," 21 *Stan. L. Rev.* 293 (1969); Guido Calabresi and A. Douglas Melamed, "Property Rules, Liability Rules, and Inalienability: One View of the Cathedral," 85 *Harv. L. Rev.* 1089, 1115–24 (1972); William F. Baxter and Lillian R. Altree, "Legal Aspects of Airport Noise," 15 *J. Law & Econ.* 1 (1972); Robert C. Ellickson, "Alternatives to Zoning: Covenants, Nuisance Rules, and Fines as Land Use Controls," 40 *U. Chi. L. Rev.* 681 (1973).

54. A search of the reports indicates that wetland regulations have been upheld and struck down in approximately equal numbers.

Regulation held invalid: Hamilton v. Diamond, 42 A.D. 2d 465, 349 N.Y.S. 2d 146 (1973); Bartlett v. Zoning Commission of Town of Old Lyme, 161 Conn. 24, 282 A.2d 907 (1971); Thompson v. Water Resources Commission, 159 Conn. 82, 267 A.2d 434 (1970); State v. Johnson, 265 A.2d 711 (Me. 1970); Commissioner of Natural Resources v. S. Volpe & Co., 349 Mass. 104, 206 N.E. 2d 666 (1965); Dooley v. Town Plan and Zoning Commission of Town of Fairfield, 151 Conn. 304, 197 A.2d 770 (1964); Morris County Land Improvement Co. v. Parsippany-Troy Hills Township, 40 N.J. 539, 193 A.2d 232 (1963). Cf. MacGibbon v. Board of Appeals of Duxbury, 356 Mass. 635, 255 N.E. 2d 347 (1970) (voiding Board's policy of protecting wetlands by rejecting all applications for development permits as beyond the scope of its authority under a town by-law and the Zoning Enabling Act).

Regulation held valid: Zabel v. Taub, 430 F 2d 199 (5th Cir. 1970), cert. den. 401 U.S. 910 (1971); Coastal Petroleum Co. v. Secretary of the Army, 315 F. Supp. 845 (1970); Sibson v. State, 115 N.H. 124, 336 A.2d 239 (1975); In re Maine Clean Fuels, 310 A.2d 736 (Me. 1973); In re Spring Valley Development, 300 A.2d 736 (Me. 1973); Turnpike Realty v. Town of Dedham, 362 Mass. 221, 284 N.E.

2d 891 (1972), cert. den. 409 U.S. 1108 (1973); Just v. Marinette County, 56 Wis. 2d 7, 201 N.W. 2d 761 (1972); Potomac Sand and Gravel Company v. Governor of Maryland, 226 Md. 358, 293 A. 2d 241 (1972); Candlestick Properties, Inc. v. San Francisco Bay Conservation and Development Commission, 11 Cal. App. 3d 557, 89 Cal. Reptr. 897 (1970). Cf. Golden v. Board of Selectmen of Falmouth, 358 Mass. 519, 265 N.E. 2d 573 (1970) (upholding power of local authority to deny development permit in order to protect wetland ecology, thus restricting rule of *MacGibbon*, supra; taking issue not raised).

55. See, e.g., In re Spring Valley Development, 300 A.2d 736, 749 (Me. 1973); Potomac Sand and Gravel Company v. Governor of Maryland, 266 Md. 358, 375, 293 A.2d 241, 250 (1972). Cf. In re Maine Clean Fuels, 310 A.2d 736 (Me. 1973) in which plaintiff was held not to have carried the burden of proving excessive diminution of value.

56. It is true that even traditionalist courts sometimes accept the suggestion of an early Policymaking essay by Robert Kratovil and Frank J. Harrison, Jr., "Eminent Domain—Policy and Concept," 42 *Calif. L. Rev.* 596, 609 (1954), which suggests that courts "balance" the "private harm" caused by the regulation against the "public benefit" generated by the change in the law. While this "balancing test" may seem on first approach to resemble the Appeal to Citizen Disaffection, it in fact is generally used in a way that confuses two very different questions—first, whether the law is constitutional without regard to compensation; and second, whether, given an affirmative answer to the first question, the takings clause requires compensation. See Michelman, "Property, Utility and Fairness," 1193–96. Generally speaking, "balancing" courts do not in fact distinguish these two very different issues, perhaps because they do not wish to admit that even when they consciously restrict themselves to the takings question, they do not apply the test in a way that would gain the approval of a clear-thinking Utilitarian Policymaker. As we have shown in the text, the Utilitarian judge's concern with the relation of the costs and benefits generated by the statute is closely tied to the concept of Citizen Disaffection. That is, the more plain the statute's net benefits are to a principled judge, the less weight he will give to the Appeal to Citizen Disaffection. Traditional courts, even when they are thinking clearly, do not use the "balancing" test in this way. Rather than considering whether

total benefits are plainly greater than total costs, the courts instead compare (in some unexplained way) the extent to which the property's value has depreciated against the total benefit to the public. See, e.g., Rochester Business Institute v. City of Rochester, 25 A.D. 2d 97, 101, 267 N.Y.S. 2d 274, 279 (1966). If this formula has any meaning at all, it seems to be a slightly more complicated version of the "diminution of value test" discussed in the text rather than a decisive plunge into Policymaking.

57. Indeed, even elaborate technocratic efforts to understand the environment often serve only to reveal the degree of our ignorance and uncertainty. See Bruce A. Ackerman, et al., *The Uncertain Search for Environmental Quality* (1974). This is not to say, of course, that our ignorance should inhibit an aggressive environmental program; it is only to say that decisionmakers will often be forced to impose considerable disaffection upon small groups, since they will not be in a position to demonstrate in a convincing fashion that their *particular* fears are plainly justified in the *particular* area placed under regulation.

58. For a recent Scientific Policymaking opinion that makes precisely this argument, see HFH Ltd. v. Superior Court, 15 Cal. 3rd 508, 521, 542 P.2d 237, 247 (1975), cert. den. 425 U.S. 904 (1976).

59. Moreover, if the ordinance were dramatically underinclusive, the remedy would more likely be judicial invalidation under the spot zoning doctrine—land law's analogue to equal protection doctrine. See Daniel R. Mandelker, "Delegation of Power and Function in Zoning Administration," 1963 *Wash. U. L. Q.* 60 (1963).

60. See Adirondack Park Agency Act, N.Y. Executive Law, Art. 27, §§ 801–19 (McKinney 1974). The mechanisms and impact of the act are discussed in Philip Nichols, *The Law of Eminent Domain,* vol. 1., § 1.42 [18] [4] [6] [ii], and Booth, "The Adirondack Park Agency Act: A Challenge in Regional Land Use Planning," 43 *Geo. Wash. L. Rev.* 612 (1975). For an Ordinary Observer's analysis of its constitutional implications, see Note, "Preserving Scenic Areas: The Adirondack Land Use Program," 84 *Yale L.J.* 1705 (1975).

61. In attempting to skew his compensation decisions in a way favorable to the poor, the reformist should be aware that decisions which at first glance appear to have favorable distributional consequences may seem less attractive on further analysis. Thus, many of the benefits of a flood control measure may not trickle down to the poorer Earthlings but may instead be appropriated by Earth-

ling landlords in the form of higher rents. Moreover, as a Scientist,
our reformer will not be reluctant to take advantage of recent work
trying to make the distributional impact of public programs clearer.
See, e.g., A. Mitchell Polinsky and Steven Shavell, "Amenities and
Property Values in a Model of an Urban Area," 5 *J. Public Econ.*
119 (1976); Susan Rose-Ackerman, "On the Distribution of Benefits
Between Landlords and Tenents," 3 *J. of Environmental Econ. and
Mgmnt.* (forthcoming, 1977).

62. For an attempt to deal with settlement costs as an element in
a general Scientific Policymaking theory of takings law, see Lawrence
Berger, "A Policy Analysis of the Taking Problem", 49 *N.Y.U.L.
Rev.* 165, 201 (1974).

63. Michelman, "Property, Utility, and Fairness," at 1226–29.

64. The precise relationship between Scientific forms of analysis
and existing doctrine will be treated at length in chap. 6.

65. I have in mind principally the position of the extreme reformist judge, discussed supra at pp. 60, 68 which would lead to a
dramatic reduction in the clause's scope.

66. Thus it is easy to criticize Flemming v. Nestor, 363 U.S. 603
(1960) from the Scientific Utilitarian perspective, incorporating many
of the considerations advanced by Charles Reich in "The New
Property," 73 *Yale L.J.* 733 (1964). The difficulties that beset an
Ordinary Observer who attempts to make a similar move will be
discussed at pp. 156–67 infra.

CHAPTER 4

1. John Rawls, *A Theory of Justice* (1971); Robert Nozick,
Anarchy, State, and Utopia (1974); Robert Paul Wolff, *In Defense
of Anarchism* (1973); Robert Paul Wolff, *The Poverty of Liberalism*
(1968); Michael Walzer, *Obligations* (1970); Charles Fried, *Medical
Experimentation: Personal Integrity and Social Policy* (1974);
Charles Fried, *An Anatomy of Values* (1970); Ronald Dworkin, "The
Original Position," 40 *U. Chi. L. Rev.* 500 (1974); Ronald Dworkin,
"Taking Rights Seriously," in E. V. Rostow, ed., *Is Law Dead?* 168
(1971).

2. There are doubtless Utilitarians in the wings, preparing a
counteroffensive. For indications, see Peter Singer, "The Right to
Be Rich or Poor," 22 *The New York Review of Books* 19 (March 6,
1975). Rolf Sartorius, *Individual Conduct and Social Norms* (1975);
J. J. C. Smart and Bernard Williams, *Utilitarianism: For and*

Against (1973). For a good review, see Dan W. Brock, "Recent Work in Utilitarianism," 10 *Am. Phil. Q.* 241 (1973).

3. This is Wolff's view. While Nozick takes anarchist premises seriously, he seeks to show how they permit the legitimation of a "minimal state," discharging very modest functions. See works cited at n. 1 supra.

4. The views advanced by both Rawls and Walzer certainly permit, if they do not necessarily require, a commitment to state ownership of the means of production. See Rawls, *A Theory of Justice,* § 42; Walzer, *Obligations,* 229–38.

5. It should be emphasized that I am speaking here of the tenor of self-consciously philosophical discussion. In the talk of sophisticated lawyers (and economists) who do not have philosophical pretentions, I think one would find that Utilitarian motifs still dominate discourse. This is particularly true among the lawyer-economists whose vocabulary and methodology are increasingly important today. For a further discussion, see pp. 169–70, 272–74 infra.

6. See Immanuel Kant, *Groundwork of the Metaphysic of Morals,* 2d ed. 66–67, tr. H. J. Paton (1964). If, as may well be the case, it is inappropriate to use a great philosopher's name as a label for a legal principle that represents but an isolated fragment of his thought, it should not be too difficult to think of another label, though I must confess that every proposal I have thus far considered seems to me to have even greater disadvantages than the one I have chosen.

7. A hypothetical unit measuring utility. Throughout the present essay we shall be assuming that the Utilitarian theorist can provide a convincing account of the procedures by which individual utility can be measured and summed to a societal total. Whether Utilitarians can provide such an account is of course a very problematic question. See sources cited at note 38, chap. 3. To pursue the issue here with the seriousness it deserves, however, would transform this essay into a work in general political philosophy rather than one which seeks to establish a relationship between philosophy and constitutional law.

8. The Kantian judge depicted in the text is not positively hostile to utility-maximizing moves, but is simply concerned to assure that they do not violate his Principle of Exploitation. It is, of course, quite possible to conceive of a far more severe critic of Utilitarianism who denied the propriety of any effort to make the world a happier

place. Because this extreme view is held by no significant group of contemporary lawyers it may be ignored in the present discussion.

9. It is possible that the settlement costs involved in compensating the Marshans are so high that the entire net gain of 900,000 utiles will be consumed in the compensation effort. We shall, however, consider this "hard case" separately at pp. 75–76 infra.

10. See pp. 47–48 supra.

11. It is quite significant that this fundamental point in Kantian jurisprudence can be readily expressed using the distinctive language of welfare economics that is now having an important impact upon Scientific legal analysis. Within this conceptual framework, a distribution of property rights, X, is said to be *Pareto-superior* to another distribution, Y, when *at least one person is better off* and *no person is worse off* under X than Y. (For a discussion of Pareto-superiority and its relationship to the different idea of Pareto-optimality, see my *Economic Foundations of Property Law,* xi–xii (1975). Given this definition of Pareto-superiority, the Kantian rule developed in the text can be translated: "If it is possible to develop a compensation practice that will transform the situation prevailing at Time Three into one that is *Pareto-superior* to the one which obtained at Time One, then compensation should be constitutionally required by the restrained Kantian judge." The ease with which the point can be made is, I think, suggestive of a deep affinity between the structure of modern welfare economics and a Kantian jurisprudence —an affinity all the more surprising given the historical connection between modern economics and nineteenth-century Utilitarian thinking.

Note that while the Utilitarian must measure costs and benefits in terms of a hypothetical measure of utility ("utiles"), the Kantian can content himself with the more humdrum dollar measures of everyday life. This is because nothing in the Kantian calculus turns on a comparison of utilities; instead, the question is whether it is possible to arrange things so that nobody is worse off than they were at Time One. To determine this it is only necessary to ascertain the number of dollars necessary to compensate the Marshans, the number of dollars spent for process costs, as well as the number of dollars the Earthlings would sacrifice before they are indifferent between the situation existing at Time One and that which obtains after the marsh-filling statute has been enacted at Time Two.

12. The preceding discussion has ignored the fact that the

Marshans, as taxpayers, may in fact be contributing a substantial amount of money into the general revenue fund which ordinarily pays for process costs. Hence, if one refuses to distinguish between the Marshans as taxpayers and the Marshans as claimants, it is possible to argue that a portion of the process costs paid by the Marshans as taxpayers should not be considered in determining whether their's is an easy case. To put the point in terms of the text's example, imagine that the costs of processing the Marshans' valid claims of $100,000 were $950,000. Since $950,000 is greater than the $900,000 net benefit obtained by the Earthlings, this case would not seem to require compensation under the formula presented in the text. Imagine, however, that judges could properly take account of the fact that the Marshans paid 10 percent of the taxes into the general revenue fund. Once this step is taken, one might then deduct 10 percent from total process costs, allocating only $855,000 as the Earthlings' share. Since this figure is lower than the $900,000 gained by the Earthlings, the case would now qualify as one requiring compensation under the Kantian formula. Putting the point more generally, compensation practices will systematically be skewed against claimants if financed out of a general fund rather than a special fund assessed against those individuals actually benefited by the property redistribution under attack. I shall, however, leave unexamined the traditional assumption of compensation law, which treats as irrelevant the fact that the Marshans are in fact contributing to the general revenue fund from which they draw their compensation.

Just as the Marshans' relationship to the general fund has been oversimplified, so too has the Earthlings' relationship. After all, if the Marshans are compensated, this may raise taxes imposed on some of the Earthlings in an amount greater than the benefit they have obtained from the marsh-filling ordinance. For example, while some Earthlings may value their purer water at $100, some may put only a $10 value on this benefit; hence if each Earthling were taxed $15 to compensate the Marshans, those who put the lower value on the cleaner water would suffer net losses in the movement from Time One to Time Three. To avoid this problem I shall be assuming that no individual Earthling's tax bill is increased to such a degree that it is greater than the benefit he obtains from the property redistribution.

It should be emphasized that the assumptions specified in this note in fact conceal issues of the first importance. While the simplifications they allow do permit us to get to the heart of the takings problem, as conventionally understood, they should certainly be the subject of subsequent Scientific scrutiny.

13. It is true, of course, that a second important legal question might well arise for a Utilitarian judge at this point in the analysis. Since a judicial decision demanding compensation requires that:

$$(1)\ U + D > P$$

and we are now only dealing with cases where:

$$(2)\ P > B - C$$

it follows that a judicial decision requiring compensation entails a finding that:

$$(3)\ U + D > P > B - C$$

In other words, a Utilitarian judge requiring compensation would be forced to conclude that the legislature had made a rather bad blunder in passing our hypothetical marsh-filling ordinance in the first place—since the costs of *either* granting *or* refusing compensation to the Marshans outweigh the net benefits of the legislative action.

This perception will lead, naturally enough, to the question whether the judge should not respond to the Marshans' complaint simply by invalidating the statute and reinstituting the legal situation at Time One. This question, however, is quite distinct from the one with which we are concerned. No matter which way it is answered, the Marshans will be granted compensation so long as $U + D > P$. If the statute is simply invalidated, compensation will be in the form of a return of unrestricted development rights; if the statute is not struck down, compensation will be granted in the form of money sufficient to compensate for the loss of development rights. In either case, however, compensation will be assured under restrained Utilitarian principles.

14. The *conservative* role premise informing this account of the restrained Kantian calculus should be emphasized. For the heavy weight granted the status quo is obviously conditioned on an assumption that the general distribution of property rights prevailing at Time One is consistent with Kantian principles, as would be the case in a well-ordered society. For a discussion of the propriety of reformist Kantian approaches, see pp. 80–83.

15. This is not to deny the possibility of developing Kantian conceptions of justice more elaborate than the simple Principle of Exploitation developed in the text under which a unique solution would be reached in the "hard" cases under discussion. Indeed, it may well be possible to elaborate the simple principle in different ways, so that under one version of the principle, the Marshans are understood to be inadmissibly exploiting the Earthlings, while under another version, the Earthlings would be understood to be exploiting the Marshans. Given these two different versions of Kantianism, a Policymaking court might then feel obligated to determine which of the two conceptions was to be considered authoritative for purposes of constitutional interpretation, though even here a court might well decide that it will defer to the legislative decision on such refined matters. At present, however, a Kantian court would have little choice but to defer to the legislature in "hard cases," since the hard conceptual work required to permit lawyers to work beyond the simple principle has not been attempted.

16. Sometimes it may be possible to soften—if not eliminate—this harsh choice by devising a "partial compensation" solution under which those Marshans hurt most severely by the redistribution will be paid, while the others will be obliged to absorb the loss. The utility of such a compromise solution depends, however, on the process costs involved in distinguishing between deserving and undeserving claimants—for unless some easily ascertainable factors exist that roughly mark out the deserving sub-class, it is possible for the process costs involved in "partial compensation" to be even higher than those generated by a full compensation system.

17. Nor does my definition of a Comprehensive View require such a univocal concern. See note 19, chap. 1, supra.

18. The approach is called lexicographic because it resembles the way one uses a dictionary—that is, first looking only for the first letter of the word sought, and, only after this first condition is satisfied without a unique solution, proceeding to the second letter in an effort to refine one's search further. For more, see Rawls, *A Theory of Justice* 42–44.

19. Although it may be possible to generate a moderately plausible philosophical theory which could justify in principle this form of eclecticism, it would divert us from our present task even to attempt such an account here. In addition, even if a philosophically compelling defense of eclecticism were not forthcoming, eclecticism has more to recommend it when one is doing law than when he is

doing philosophy—but this proposition too must remain unelaborated for the present.

20. See p. 36 supra.

21. It is conceivable, of course, that though the Kantian's initial burden of justification is heavier, he will find it easier in the end to discharge this initial burden by fashioning overwhelming Kantian arguments on behalf of deference, whose persuasive power far outmatches those that may be advanced by Utilitarians. While the present state of theory hardly permits certainty on these matters, I can think of no argument which is differentially available to the Kantian that is likely to overcome systematically the fact of his heavier initial burden of persuasion.

22. While it seems quite clear that the activist Kantian would worry about the danger of institutional self-aggrandizement, it is less clear how he would go about defining the concept. On the one hand, it may be that some Kantians would have no serious objection to the Utilitarian's definition and understand a self-aggrandizing agency as one that systematically discounts antagonistic interests in its cost-benefit analysis. On the other hand, it is perfectly possible that a Kantian may repudiate the idea that agencies ought to engage in cost-benefit analysis of the contemporary sort. If this position is taken, the Kantian would have to define a proper administrative decisionmaking procedure before proceeding to explain the manner in which it could be abused by a self-aggrandizing agency. Unfortunately, this is an area which has remained quite unexplored despite the recent rebirth of non-Utilitarian thinking, though there are some interesting suggestions to be found in Rawls, *A Theory of Justice* 195–201.

23. In defense of the "equal protection" dimension the innovative Kantian may argue that even when it is necessary to select a person out to serve merely as a means to another's end, it is particularly invidious to permit a state official to selectively victimize one rather than another person, simply on the basis of whim or caprice. Once again, however, a good deal of basic philosophical work would be required before the sentiment expressed in the preceding sentence could be precisely located within a general Kantian framework.

24. Indeed, to my knowledge, only Frank Michelman has before now considered the potential application of Kantian arguments to compensation law. For a critical discussion of his attempt, see n. 33 infra.

25. For an explicit statement of these basic role propositions, see chap. 2, pp. 37–38.

26. See pp. 57–60 supra.

27. Rawls, *A Theory of Justice* 179–83, 251–57. See also, Oliver A. Johnson, "The Kantian Interpretation," 85 *Ethics* 58 (1974); Stephen C. Darwall, "A Defense of the Kantian Interpretation," 86 *Ethics* 164 (1976).

28. It should be recalled, however, that there is nothing to prevent a judge from mixing his Comprehensive Views, calling upon Bentham to remedy the inadequacies and obscurities of Kant.

29. See pp. 77–79 supra.

30. For hints of this kind see Frank I. Michelman, "In Pursuit of Constitutional Welfare Rights: One View of Rawls' Theory of Justice," 121 *U. Pa. L. Rev.* 962, 978–81 (1973); Ronald Dworkin, "Taking Rights Seriously," n. 1 supra at 176–78.

31. See pp. 60–64 supra.

32. For a variety of views on these fundamental issues of Utilitarian theory, see the sources cited at n. 2 supra.

33. In contrast, Frank Michelman takes the view that it is only in exceptional cases that a non-Utilitarian judge concerned with fairness will disagree with his Utilitarian colleague. Looking to Rawls rather than Kant to specify a non-Utilitarian approach, Michelman advances a version of the well-known Difference Principle as the key to the fairness of a decision denying compensation. According to this principle, a decision refusing compensation in a class of cases is fair only if it works to the long-run advantage of the class to whom payment has been denied. Imagine, for example, that a particular Marshan called Joe has been deprived of property rights worth $1,000; imagine further that if all Marshans were compensated, Joe's tax bill would go up by $1,500 to pay for the extra process costs that are generated; it would follow, then, that it really is in Joe's long-run interest to have his claim denied (provided, of course, that Joe cannot arrange things so that he is the only Marshan who obtains compensation). In this simple case, Rawls's Difference Principle—as Michelman applies it—serves to provide a convincing explanation for why it is fair to deny Joe compensation. Similarly, as Michelman suggests (80 *Harv. L. Rev.* 1165, 1220–24), there may be more complicated stories in which it is not in the class's long-run interest to insist on compensation, thereby legitimating a decision denying payment under the Difference Principle.

This is all very fine so far as it goes, but it does not go very far at all. For it seems a complicated way of saying that unless the claimant stands a serious chance of suffering a *real* financial loss over the long run, there is no point in compensating him for a loss he has not suffered. The law does not need philosophy for propositions so easy as this one. Indeed, as n. 4, chap. 2, indicates, suffering a serious loss, after long-run effects are taken into account, is an essential precondition of both the traditional law and *all* the reform schemes discussed in this book. In this sense, Michelman's "convergence thesis" between fairness and utility seems innocuous enough—indeed, it is probably true that all remotely plausible views "converge" on the proposition that somebody must suffer a significant loss before he can claim compensation.

The real problem for analysis is how to deal with claimants who have suffered real losses. And on this question, Michelman's version of the Difference Principle—if taken seriously—would lead to an extreme position requiring compensation in *all* cases, since in none can Joe be told that denying compensation is in the long-run interest of those raising claims of a type similar to his own. This position (which is not explicitly advanced by Michelman) represents, of course, one that is even more demanding than the Kantian, let alone the Utilitarian, theories considered in this essay.

It would therefore merit substantial discussion but for the fact that since Michelman wrote his essay it has become clearer that Rawls does not intend his principles to apply to issues—like those involved in compensation law—that do not directly affect the "basic structure" of social organization. See *A Theory of Justice* 7–11. To Michelman's credit, his essay explicitly recognized that the Difference Principle can only "be applied by analogy to test the justice of a compensation practice" (80 *Harv. L. Rev.* 1165, 1221). Consequently, until Michelman or someone else wishes to rehabilitate the extreme "Rawlsian" rule in the light of Rawls's further work, I shall assume that this particular line of inquiry has turned out to be a dead-end.

Chapter 5

1. This, most emphatically, is not to say that the untrained person has no ideas dealing with law and politics or that these ideas have no structure whatever. For a notable effort to probe these structures in the American context, see Robert E. Lane, *Political Ideology*

(1962), and see also Lane's review essay, "Patterns of Political Belief," in Jeanne N. Knutson ed., *Handbook of Political Psychology* 83 (1973). Nor is it even to deny that the typical layman's political principles would pass the tests of self-consistency and completeness necessary to meet the formal requirements of a Comprehensive View, though this is my own opinion. For support, see Philip E. Converse, "Public Opinion and Voting Behavior," in Fred I. Greenstein and Nelson W. Polsby, ed., *Handbook of Political Science,* vol. 4, 75 (1975). Instead the narrow claim needed here is that the typical untrained adult—even if he has a coherent political ideology—does not feel in a position to assess the extent to which his *political* ideology has been incorporated into the structure and rules of the *legal* system. For the socio-political foundations for this claim, see n. 3.

2. Oliver Wendell Holmes, "The Path of the Law," 10 *Harv. L. Rev.* 457, 459–64 (1897). For an analysis of Holmes's views and a discussion of their usefulness in legal theory, see William Twining, "The Bad Man Revisited," 58 *Cornell L. Rev.* 275 (1973).

3. While the division of labor may well be a necessary sociological condition for this divorce between the layman's approach to law and the Policymaker's, it is not a sufficient condition. Even in a society characterized by an extensive division of labor, it is possible for the state to make special efforts to train its inhabitants to look upon the legal system as an expression of one or another Comprehensive View. To take one of the most obvious examples, it may be that the typical Russian has—after a half-century—learned to expect that law-makers and law-appliers will attempt to justify their decisions in terms of a Marxist Comprehensive View. While it is true that the Russian who lacks professional training will—like his American counterpart—be unable to form an *independent* judgment as to the extent to which the existing set of legal rules *in fact* conforms to true Marxist principles (however these are understood), it is at least possible that he will accept *on faith* the notion that existing rules do in fact express Marxist principles. Thus, it would seem that before the general population will deny that the law expresses a Comprehensive View, it is not only necessary for there to be a well-developed division of labor; it is also necessary for the state to refrain from indoctrinating the general population into a determinate Comprehensive View which is proclaimed as the sole orthodoxy. Needless to say this condition is amply fulfilled in a

pluralist democracy like the United States, thereby making it obvious to most laymen that they cannot assess the extent to which their personal political principles are legal principles without the assistance of a lawyer—which is precisely the conclusion asserted in the text.

4. See, e.g., Peter L. Berger and Thomas Luckmann, *The Social Construction of Reality* 47–129 (1967).

5. Uniformity may perhaps be usefully treated as the linguistic dimension of the model of a simple society discussed by H. L. A. Hart in *The Concept of Law* 89–96 (1961).

6. See pp. 41 supra.

7. For some relevant commentary, see H. L. A. Hart, *The Concept of Law*, chap. 6 (1961); Joseph Raz, *The Concept of a Legal System*, chap. 8 (1970); Ronald Dworkin, "The Model of Rules," 35 *U. Chi. L. Rev.* 14, 40–46 (1967), and "Social Rules and Legal Theory," 81 *Yale L. J.* 855, 868–81 (1972).

8. The concept of "middle-class society" is of course ambiguous to the extent to which the Ordinary Observer has failed to articulate a "rule of recognition" which provides him with a clear procedure for identifying which of the differing patterns of social interaction observable in society shall be identified as the source of legally decisive norms. Moreover, as an earlier part of this chapter suggested, the present state of learning on this subject leaves much that is obscure. Nonetheless, while a great deal of clarification is required, it seems to be a basic premise of Observing in American law that the legally decisive norms are to be found by scrutinizing the interactions of the (enlightened) "middle-classes" rather than the mores of the "lower" classes on the one hand or the "privileged few" on the other.

9. It would, of course, defeat the entire purpose of this account of dominant social expectations if I were obliged to support it by citation to an assortment of sociological authorities. For Ordinary Observers need no scientific support to legitimate their observations. On a somewhat different level, however, it may prove useful to note that the approach taken here does have a relationship to an important stream of recent sociological work represented by books like: Peter L. Berger and Thomas Luckmann, *The Social Construction of Reality*, n. 5 supra, especially 129–85; Alfred Schutz and Thomas Luckmann, *The Structures of the Life-World*, tr. R. M. Jauer and H. T. Engelhardt, Jr. (1973); as well as Erving Goffman, *The Presentation of Self in Everyday Life* (1959) and *Behavior in Public*

Places (1963). In addition, Claude Levi-Strauss has some valuable things to say about the social psychology of possession in *The Elementary Structures of Kinship* 84–97 (1969).

10. See Ronald Dworkin, "The Jurisprudence of Richard Nixon," 18 *The New York Review of Books* 27–28 (May 4, 1972).

11. For a somewhat similar but more formal discussion of the Ordinary concept of property, see Frank Snare, "The Concept of Property," 9 *Am. Phil. Q.* 200 (1972). Snare analyzes property in terms of constitutive rules, i.e., rules of social behavior that must be observed by the members of a community in order for it to be true that the institution of property exists in that community. [For discussions of constitutive rules, see John R. Searle, *Speech Acts* 33–36 (1970); John Rawls, "Two Concepts of Rules," 64 *Phil. Rev.* 3 (1956). On rules of social behavior, see H. L. A. Hart, *The Concept of Law* 54–59 (1961); but see Ronald Dworkin, 'Social Rules and Legal Theory," 81 *Yale L.J.* 855, 857–68 (1972).]

According to Snare, "A owns P" is true, and the institution of property therefore exists in A's community, if six rules are observed:

> 1. Right of use: A has a right to use P, *i.e.* (a) prima facie it is not wrong for A to use P, and (b) prima facie it is wrong for others to interfere with A's using P.
> 2. Right of exclusion: Others may use P if, and only if, A consents, *i.e.* (a) if A consents, it is prima facie not wrong for others to use P, and (b) if A doesn't consent it is prima facie wrong to use P.
> 3. Right of transfer: A may permanently transfer the rights in rules 1 and 2 to specific persons by consent.
> 4. Punishment rules: If some other person, B, interferes with A's use of P or if B uses P without A's consent, then B may be punished in certain appropriate manners.
> 5. Damage rules: If some other person, B, damages P without A's consent, then certain appropriate damages may be required of B.
> 6. Liability rules: If P results in certain ways in damage to the person or property of some other person, B, then A may be held responsible and damages required.

Snare makes two important qualifications to his analysis. First, he thinks that rules 4–6 are somewhat peripheral to the concept of property; it is conceivable that the institution could exist without them, although it would be a different one from ours. Second, he does not think that his six rules are jointly necessary conditions for the existence of the institution. Rather they define what he calls the "core concept" of property. One or more of rules 1–6 could be modified or excluded in specific cases without thereby abolishing the institution. He gives ownership of a nontransferable theater ticket as an example of property with respect to which rule 3 has been suspended. I shall return to both of these points.

There are obvious similarities between Snare's analysis of property and the one I have advanced. His rules 1 and 2 correspond respectively to my conditions (a) and (b). His prima facie qualification in rule 1 corresponds to my observation that Layman is not entitled to use his thing in ways harmful to others; in rule 2(b), to the exceptional circumstances mentioned in my condition (b); and in rule 2(a), to the obvious fact that there may be independent reasons why it is wrong for others to use Layman's thing even when he consents.

There are, however, important differences between our accounts. First, Snare's rule 3 sets out a separate right of transfer as part of the definition of property. According to my analysis, alienating a thing is simply one of the many ways in which Layman can use it; to use Snare's terms, 3 is not a separate rule, but rather a special case of rule 1. This is important because it is not true, as Snare seems to imply, that alienation is in principle entitled to special importance among the possible uses of a thing. He himself gives the counterexample of a nontransferable theater ticket, and it would be easy to give many more. As we shall see, pp. 136–41 infra, alienation *is* an important use of things, and, in certain very special circumstances, forbidding Layman to alienate his thing would mean that it would simply be a bad joke to say that the thing remained Layman's thing. Thus, if Layman detested Picasso, yet was bequeathed *Guernica* and was forbidden by law to sell it, there *would* be something funny about saying that *Guernica* was Layman's painting. But these are very special circumstances, in which Layman has no use for the thing and someone else who does is willing to buy (or accept) it from Layman. For in that case the prohibition of alienation would extinguish the only use Layman has for his thing, and it would become misleading to say that my condition (a) had been met. But so long as Layman finds his thing useful, there is no reason to deny that he owns it simply because he is not permitted to alienate it.

Snare also fails to point out that the right to alienate, like the right to use a thing in any other way, is a prima facie right.

Second, Snare believes that rules 4–6 are "peripheral" to the concept of property. In this he is wrong, because they are entirely independent of it, although for different reasons. Rule 4 is simply a consequence of the fact that if B interferes with the exercise of *any* of A's rights he may be subjected to some form of negative sanction. Otherwise it would make no sense to say that A had a *right* with which B had interfered. But this tells us something about rights, not about property. It is a constitutive rule of the institution of rights that if A has a right, then B has a duty not to interfere with A's exercise of it. And it is part of the concept of duty that if one breaches his duty, one is properly liable to an appropriate sanction. See Hart, *The Concept of Law*, supra, 79–88. But this does not help us to distinguish between property and, say, the right to personal security. The same may be said of rule 5, holding a breacher for the damages resulting from the breach. Nor does the sixth rule seem necessary for the institution of private property to exist—indeed, if A may *not* be held responsible for the damage his thing causes, he may well have a property right of an exceptionally valuable kind.

Finally Snare wrongly believes that *any* of rules 1–6 could be modified or suspended without eliminating property. We have seen that rules 4–6 should be excluded as having nothing to do with the concept of property. Rule 3 should be regarded as a particular instance of rule 1, and is therefore superfluous. But, for reasons given in the text, rules 1 and 2, which correspond to my conditions (a) and (b), are individually necessary, and jointly sufficient, before some thing can be said to belong to Layman. I take it that my general point is something like what Wittgenstein had in mind when, as Norman Malcom recalls: "On one walk he gave to me each tree that we passed, with the reservation that I was not to cut it down or do anything to it, or prevent the previous owners from doing anything to it: with those reservations it was henceforth *mine*." N. Malcolm, *Ludwig Wittgenstein–A Memoir* 31 (1967).

12. See pp. 29–31 supra.

13. It is possible, of course, that Layman may not be *completely* estranged from his thing but may be permitted to use it as a member of a group in whose welfare the state is interested. Thus Layman, while strolling in a public park, could well report that it used to be his.

14. See H. L. A. Hart, "The Ascription of Responsibility and Rights," in Antony Flew, ed., *Logic and Language,* First Series, 151 (1965), in which the notion of a prima facie case is discussed in terms of "defeasable concepts." Hart's analysis was vigorously attacked by Peter Geach in "Ascriptivism," 69 *Phil. Rev.* 221 (1960), and by George Pitcher in "Hart on Action and Responsibility," id. at 226, and he subsequently repudiated it. Recently Richard Epstein has attempted to rehabilitate Hart's analysis in "Pleadings and Presumptions," 40 *U. Chi. L. Rev.* 556 (1974). For another attempt to save something of Hart's analysis, see Joel Feinberg, *Doing and Deserving* 119–51 (1970).

15. See the parallel treatment in chap. 2, pp. 31–39 supra.

16. As in our treatment of Scientific role theory, our exclusive concern here will not be with the "perfectly" restrained judge who imagines that all challenged actions are consistent with the ultimate standards of legal judgment, but instead with the "realistically" restrained judge who recognizes an occasional aberration without inferring the existence of a systematic malfunction.

17. It may be objected that this project in definition is unfaithful to the spirit of American Ordinary Observing in that it proposes a set of technical role concepts which have no plain relationship to nonprofessional talk. This objection, however, mistakes the range of application of Ordinary Observing methods in the present legal culture. While it is quite true that many of our basic *substantive* doctrines have an Ordinary Observing structure, Anglo-American talk about process has long been dominated by a highly technical discourse. Indeed, the coexistence of this technical process-talk and ordinary substance-talk is one of the most striking paradoxes of American law when viewed in a comparative perspective. See e.g., Mirjan Damaska, "Structures of Authority and Comparative Criminal Procedure," 84 *Yale L.J.* 480, 526–9 (1975). For present purposes, however, we need not analyze this paradox but simply note its existence in order to acquit ourselves of the charge of falsifying the existing structure of Ordinary legal analysis.

18. The extent to which an Observer can be an aggressive reformist without straining his entire methodology is not at all clear. Given the importance of the distribution of wealth in identifying one or another social pattern of expectation as "dominant," it is uncertain how far an Observing judge can go in challenging the prevailing distribution as inconsistent with "dominant" mores without

rendering the notion of Observation incoherent. This important question, however, is best left for more extensive consideration at another time since takings doctrine—unlike other areas—does not call up any strong reformist impulse amongst the Ordinary judiciary.

19. Thus, a *principled* Observer is a judge who assumes that the litigants are well-socialized and so will accept disadvantageous official decisions without a deep sense of grievance, as would be the case in a "well-ordered" society. In contrast, a *pragmatic* Observer is willing at times to make legally relevant the fact that substantial departures from this "well-ordered" social norm are common. As in the case of reformism (see n. 18 supra) an overly large dose of pragmatism may succeed in rendering problematic the central Observing claim that it is possible to identify a determinate set of social expectations as "dominant," but here too takings law is hardly the place to look for actual decisions which probe methodological limits. I have not found any existing judicial opinion whose premises were not of an entirely principled character.

20. See pp. 57–8 supra.

21. See, e.g., City of Pittsburgh v. Alco Parking Corporation, 417 U.S. 369 (1974), which is discussed at length in n. 34, chap. 3 supra.

22. We shall, in our detailed doctrinal discussion, take pains to note the occasions upon which the degree of judicial deference accepted has an impact upon the doctrinal conclusions reached. See, e.g., pp. 139–41, 151–55, 247–48, 260–64 infra.

23. See opinions cited at nn. 45 and 46 of chap. 3 and nn. 25 and 41 of chap. 6.

CHAPTER 6

1. For a more precise statement of the kind of restraint characteristic of the contemporary judiciary, see chap. 5, pp. 109–10.

2. It was Justice Holmes who set the modern style by declaring—with some pride—that takings law dealt only in "question[s] of degree . . . [which] cannot be disposed of by general propositions." Pennsylvania Coal Co. v. Mahon, 260 U.S. 393, 416 (1922). See also his similar sentiments at p. 413. Hundreds of judges have, in a parody of *stare decisis,* invoked Holmes's words as a complete substitute for serious thought. This is not to say, however, that Holmes's opinion was carelessly written. As we shall see, pp. 156–65 infra, his reluctance to be more explicit can be explained by certain unique features of the case before him.

3. For those who would prefer a term more neutral than "obscurantist," perhaps "unreflective" will do. Since Ordinary Observing presupposes a common understanding of certain basic concepts that organize social reality—of which "property" is certainly one—it should not be surprising that Ordinary judges rarely engage, at least in easy cases, in self-conscious examination of those concepts. This tendency toward unreflectiveness is easily carried over to the "hard" cases since reflection will reveal that existing practices do *not* throw a clear light on the judge's difficulty—thereby undermining the appeal of a mode of juridical reasoning whose very charm is its "common-sense" character.

4. See, e.g., Nebbia v. New York, 291 U.S. 502 (1934); West Coast Hotel Co. v. Parrish, 300 U.S. 379 (1937); Lincoln Federal Labor Union v. Northwestern Iron & Metal Co., 335 U.S. 525 (1949).

5. See, e.g., El Paso v. Simmons, 379 U.S. 497 (1965).

6. See pp. 43, 60, 109 supra.

7. Federal Power Commission v. Hope Natural Gas Co., 320 U.S. 591 (1944).

8. 272 U.S. 365 (1926). The Court upheld a local zoning ordinance forbidding certain commercial and industrial uses of appellee's land, resulting in a 75% diminution of its value.

9. The Court has made no important doctrinal advance since Pennsylvania Coal v. Mahon, n. 2 supra. In most recent cases it has not attempted to improve upon Holmes's *obiter* glorification of ad hoc decision making, and has instead proceeded immediately to a particularistic weighing-up of factors whose character and weight are never clearly assessed. Even Professor Dunham, who sees patterns in some Supreme Court decisions, confesses perplexity when confronted with other holdings, declaring, "Older tests and guides have given way, and there is a tendency in the opinions to substitute a vague ethical standard for any objective standard." Allison Dunham, "Griggs v. Allegheny County in Perspective: Thirty Years of Supreme Court Expropriation Law," *1962 Supreme Court Rev.* 63, 73.

10. See chap. 7, pp. 168–70, 270–71.

11. While this effort may be understood as one which moves beyond the surface language of legal opinions in quest of a "deeper structure," it is important to distinguish the enterprise attempted here from those mounted under the Structuralist banner that is so fashionable today in nonlegal circles. In particular, my account of the law as based on the methods of Ordinary Observing does not

require an elaborate set of transformational rules which are said to permit an analyst to move from "deep structure" to "surface talk." Instead, the ideas behind the Ordinary Observer's approach are more a product of Wittgenstein than Chomsky or Levi-Strauss. If there is a Structuralist element in the analysis, it entered at an earlier stage with the development of the two polarities, Scientific/Ordinary and Policymaker/Observer and the subsequent generation of the four legal analytics portrayed in the table at chap. 1, p. 17. In attempting this "structuralist" account of legal mentalities, however, I was not guided by the classic Structuralist literature.

12. This is not to say that all cases are easy for the Scientific Policymaker—only that his hard cases are different from those which perplex the Ordinary Observer. For more on this see pp. 124–29 infra.

13. See pp. 26–29 supra.

14. For a fuller statement of the Observer's conception of property, see pp. 97–100 supra, and n. 11, chap. 5.

15. While the holder of a legal property right must always appeal to the opinion of a legal specialist before he can make out his rights in ordinary conversation, it should be apparent that there are many reasons the views of a specialist may seem required.

For example, there may be a conflict between social practices giving ownership to one Layman, and a legal document awarding it to another; or several legal documents each purporting to give ownership of the same thing to a different Layman; or conflicting sets of practices and documents in various combinations.

The preceding examples all involve cases in which a claim to a thing is currently a matter of ongoing dispute. But in the paradigm case of legal property, the appeal to the specialist is made not in order to resolve a dispute, but simply in order to know just what it is that one owns. An example would be property claimed under an undisputed will. Once the specialist opinion has been rendered *and* the appropriate social practices have been established, the character of Layman's right changes from legal to social—since he no longer requires a specialist opinion to maintain his claim in ordinary conversation.

For the sake of clarity it is worth observing that some types of legal property are based on—or at least closely related to—special forms of social practice. Examples of such practices are to be found in stock exchanges and markets in such things as mineral leases.

These are different from Ordinary social practices in two ways: they are specialized, institutional, and more or less self-contained; and the things with respect to which people interact are items of *legal* property, i.e., things one cannot claim to own without appeal to a legal specialist. For a further discussion of legal property, see pp. 156–67 infra.

16. We are concerned here not with Layman's psychological state, but with the kind of justification he may advance on behalf of his claim to ownership. The point is that Layman can make out a good justification for his claim to social property without appealing to an expert opinion whose merits he cannot evaluate, while this is not so with legal property. This is certainly consistent with Layman feeling a great degree of subjective certainty when making a claim to legal property—he may, for example, have great confidence in his lawyer's ability and judgment and so be very upset if his legal property rights are taken from him without compensation. Hence the thesis that the Ordinary Observer affords greater constitutional protection to social property than legal property should *not* be seen as an application of the Utilitarian's Appeal to Citizen Disaffection (see pp. 46–68 supra). Rather, the Ordinary Observer's difficulty in protecting legal property stems from the fact that laymen themselves recognize the inapplicability of Ordinary concepts in property disputes of this kind. For a further elaboration, see pp. 156–63 infra.

17. See pp. 156–67 infra.

18. But what if Layman's title over the strip was then being contested in good faith by another well-socialized individual? Then Layman's claim to the strip would be merely legal, rather than social, property, whose status under the takings clause will be considered separately at pp. 156–67 infra; see especially n. 96 for a treatment of this particular problem.

19. See pp. 156–67 infra.

20. Thus, despite the *ad coelum* rule, the government may take airspace that is legal property without compensation. United States v. Causby, 328 U.S. 256, 260–61 (1946). But when social property is taken by the use of glide paths close to the earth's surface, compensation is required. *Causby,* supra at 266–67; Griggs v. Allegheny County, 369 U.S. 84 (1962). For a more extended discussion of the airplane cases, see n. 74 infra.

21. See pp. 156–67 infra.

22. The distinction between legal and social property is useful in analyzing the closely related problem of when a use of property "vests," giving rise to property rights that are protected by the takings clause. Suppose that Layman obtains a permit to build a hotel on his property, and shortly thereafter the zoning ordinance is amended so as to prohibit hotels in his district. His permit is revoked, and Layman brings suit. With some rare exceptions, e.g., Hull v. Hunt, 53 Wash.2d 125, 331 P.2d 856 (1958), courts are agreed that an application for, or an issuance of, a building permit, without more, does not set up any right of Layman in his property use despite the monetary loss suffered by the license revocation. See, e.g., Schneider v. Lazarov, 216 Tenn. 1, 390 S.W.2d 197 (1965). In order to acquire such a right, Layman must have made a substantial change in the land, or incurred substantial expenditures or obligations in reliance on the permit, see, e.g., Gulezian v. Manchester, 112 N.H. 135, 290 A.2d 631 (1972); Poczatek v. Zoning Board of Appeals, 26 A.D. 2d 556, 270 N.Y.S. 2d 980 (1966), thereby placing himself in a situation at least analogous to those where Layman's hotel is in *actual existence*—and so qualifies as social property whose protection constitutes the primary concern of the Ordinary Observer. Indeed, some courts insist that Layman must actually begin construction before his hotel qualifies for constitutional protection—declaring that preparation (no matter how costly) is insufficient to justify constitutional protection for the protected use. See Smith v. M. Spiegel and Sons, Inc., 31 A.D.2d 819, 298 N.Y.S.2d 47 (1969), aff'd 24 N.Y.2d 920, 301 N.Y.S.2d 984, 249 N.E.2d 763 (1969); Arden H. Rathkopf, *The Law of Zoning and Planning*, 3d ed., chap. 57. While this line is an intuitively plausible one for an Ordinary Observer, it is only valid under very special conditions for a Scientific Policymaker. For a more extensive discussion of the difficulties the Policymaker confronts, see the text at pp. 129–36 infra.

23. Just as people do not live beneath the surface or in the air, they do not habitually walk on water. Thus the distinction between social and legal property can serve as a key to two leading cases dealing with the taking of water rights that have served to mystify a generation of Scientifically inclined law students and professors. In both cases, the Army Corps of Engineers built a dam that raised the water level in the adjoining river system; in the earlier case, United States v. Cress, 243 U.S. 316 (1917), raising the water level made it

impossible for the claimant to continue operating his mill by water power, thereby rendering the mill valueless and causing a $1,500 loss; in the later case, United States v. Willow River Power Co., 324 U.S. 499 (1945), raising the water level reduced by some three feet the operating head of a hydroelectric plant, resulting in a partial loss of generating capacity whose value was $25,000. Despite the seeming similarity of the cases, the Supreme Court awarded $1,500 to the claimant in Cress, but denied $25,000 damages to the electric company. Mr. Justice Jackson, writing for the Court in the second case, emphatically denied the apparent inconsistency, resting his case on a distinction that seems deeply problematic from a Scientific point of view. Jackson distinguishes *Cress* on the ground that the mill was located on a *non*-navigable tributary whose height had been raised by an improvement on the main stream, while the hydro-electric facility in *Willow River* depended for its power on the fall of water directly into a *navigable* river. While Jackson is factually correct, it is easy for the Scientist to conclude that the distinction between non-navigable and navigable streams is irrelevant to the problem before him. After all, in both cases the Corps of Engineers' actions were intended to further the state's interest in navigation; in both cases, this pro-navigation decision would predictably injure the interests of riparian users of water power. Why should the redistribution of property rights be determined by the happenstance of the dam's location in the river system?

Justice Jackson's response constitutes one of the more self-conscious expressions of the Ordinary Observer's approach to takings issues:

> In general non-navigable streams were small. . . . They were shallow, could be forded and were no great obstacle to tillage or pasturage on two sides of the stream as a single operation. Such streams, like the lands, were fenced in, and while the waters might show resentment by carrying away a few spans of fence in the spring, *the riparian owner's rights in such streams were acknowledged by the custom of the countryside as well as recognized by the law.* 324 U.S. 499, 505 (emphasis added).

To put the point in our terms, non-navigable streams were social property—Layman could point to a pattern of conduct according to which well-socialized people would, except in extraordinary circumstances, ask his permission before using his stream just as they would before using his land. (Note to legal specialists: neither *Cress* nor *Willow River* tries to deal with the special problems that arise under the distinctive "appropriation" system of water rights in seventeen western states.) In contrast, a claim of social property cannot be made with regard to navigable rivers: on these rivers it is possible to observe a group of well-socialized people in boats who are quite obviously using the river for no exceptional purpose and who nevertheless are not asking Layman's permission before doing so. As in the conversation about air rights hypothesized in the text, how can a stretch of navigable river be Layman's thing if well-socialized people are not asking his permission before using it?

Now, Layman may seek to parry this embarrassing fact by invoking a lawyer's specialist opinion to support his claim to the stream. For example, he may report that his lawyers have assured him that the boats are merely exercising a dominant navigation easement, that legal title remains in him and that he is therefore entitled to insist that the river not be raised beyond its "natural" level. But in asserting this claim Layman is claiming merely legal property, not social property. Or, in Justice Jackson's words, it is "irrelevant whether the shore owner did or did not have a technical title to the bed of the [navigable] river." Quoting previous judicial authority, Jackson declared that regardless of legal title, "In neither event can there be said to arise any ownership of the river. Ownership of a private stream wholly upon the lands of an individual is conceivable, but that the running water in a great navigable stream is capable of private ownership is inconceivable." Id. at 508–9.

To whom is such a thing inconceivable? Certainly not to the Scientific Policymaker, who can readily explore the consequences of privatizing a navigable stream, and may in fact conclude that private ownership is sometimes superior to public. Cf. J. W. Milliman, "Water Law and Private Decisionmaking: A Critique," 2 *J. Law & Econ.* 41 (1959). Such a claim is only inconceivable to a Layman, who is incapable of evaluating it without expert assistance. It follows, then, that while *Cress* involved the taking of social property, *Willow River* only involved the taking of legal property—whose status, for reasons explored in detail later, at pp. 157–63 infra, is much more problematic for the Ordinary judge.

24. A striking example of the uncertain status of future interests as legal property is presented by recent changes in the rule against perpetuities. Courts in several jurisdictions have begun to uphold

otherwise valid wills and trusts that violate the rule. Such decisions are sometimes justified by the "wait and see" doctrine, according to which the court considers events occurring after inception of the instrument and which are relevant to the vesting of a future interest. Phelps v. Shropshire, 254 Miss. 777, 183. So.2d 158 (1966); First Portland Natn'l Bank v. Rodrique, 157 Me. 277, 172 A.2d 107 (1961); Merchants Natn'l Bank v. Curtis, 98 N.H. 225, 97 A.2d 207 (1953); Sears v. Coolidge, 329 Mass. 340, 108 N.E.2d 563 (1952). Other decisions are reached under the "cy pres" doctrine, which permits reformation of the instrument to conform to the rule against perpetuities. See In re Kelly's Estate, 193 So.2d 575 (Miss. 1967); Carter v. Berry, 243 Miss. 356, 140 So.2d 843 (1962). The same results have been reached by statute. E.g., 20 Pa. C.S.A. § 6104 (1975); Ky. R.S.A. § 381.216 (1963). These modifications extinguish future interests of those who would benefit if the instruments were held invalid. And yet the courts never consider, let alone reject, the claim that the property of those holding these future interests has been taken.

25. Traditionally, the fact that a governmental seizure might be temporary did not alter the fact that a taking had occurred requiring compensation. Thus, the fact that Layman's car might be returned from Montana one day would not be constitutionally relevant. Beech Forest Hills, Inc. v. Borough of Morris Plains, 127 N.J. Super. 574, 318 A.2d 435 (1974); Lomarch Corp. v. Mayor of Englewood, 51 N.J. 108, 237 A.2d 881 (1968); Miller v. City of Beaver Falls, 368 Pa. 189, 82 A.2d 34 (1951). Recently, however, there have been strong indications of a developing Scientific Policymaking attitude toward temporary taking cases which question the conventional doctrine. See Golden v. Planning Board of Town of Ramapo, 30 N.Y.2d 359, 334 N.Y.S.2d 138, 285 N.E.2d 291 (1972), appeal dismissed 409 U.S. 1003 (1972), which upheld an ordinance forbidding development of residential land for periods of up to eighteen years; Steel Hill Development, Inc. v. Town of Sanbornton, 469 F.2d 956 (1972), in which the court approved severe zoning restrictions as "a legitimate stop-gap measure" on condition that the town undertake "a professional and scientific study" (!) with a view to instituting a comprehensive development plan.

26. The government may acquire possession in several different ways. Most frequently it performs some official act, such as the institution of condemnation proceedings, and physically ejects the owner. See, e.g., Berman v. Parker, 348 U.S. 26 (1954); United States ex rel.

TVA v. Welch, 327 U.S. 546 (1946). But it is not always the case that the owner is ejected—United States v. Pewee Coal Co., Inc., 341 U.S. 114 (1951); Kimball Laundry Co. v. United States, 338 U.S. 1 (1949); nor that an official act is performed—Eyherabide v. United States, 345 F.2d 565 (1965). All that is required is that a state representative effectively assume the owner's right to control the use of the property: this could happen, for example, simply by requiring the owner to obtain official permission before making *any* use of his thing.

27. Village of Euclid v. Ambler Realty Co., n. 8 supra, where a 75% diminution of value was upheld. The so-called "diminution of value" test and criticisms of it are discussed at pp. 142–45, 253–55 infra.

28. See pp. 70, 86 supra.

29. For example, the Scientific Utilitarian will attend to Uncertainty and Citizen Disaffection costs and other factors, such as institutional self-aggrandizement, involved in the various forms of Utilitarian judicial innovation. The Scientific Kantian will concern himself with the relation between settlement costs and net benefits, as well as those innovative arguments he considers consistent with his role. See chaps. 3 and 4 supra.

30. It should be emphasized that throughout this section we are dealing only with the conditions under which a prima facie case can be made out under existing law. Even where there is a good prima facie case, it is still possible for the court to deny compensation on the ground that the taking was necessary to prevent Layman from engaging in conduct he should have recognized as antisocial. For example, if our speed limit law had reduced the value of Layman's cars to zero rather than $3000, there could be no doubt, according to the diminution of value test discussed at pp. 141–45 infra, that the cars had been taken. But the court might still refuse to award payment if it found that driving at more than twenty-five miles an hour during a fuel crisis would be recognized as unduly harmful by a well-socialized individual in our society. Such a finding would, of course, be very dubious, though perhaps an exceedingly deferential Observer would find sufficient basis in social practice to uphold the legislature's taking as capable of Ordinary justification. This aspect of the taking problem is discussed at length at pp. 150–56 infra.

31. The Ordinary Observer finds the distinction between "regulat-

ing" and "taking" property entirely clear in principle. For him, property talk is about relations between people and things. If Layman owns a particular thing, then he stands in a distinctive relation to that thing, and all other members of the community stand in a different distinctive relation to it. Government actions (restricting the use of things) that destroy these relations are takings; actions that leave them intact are regulations. If, after a governmental action restricting Layman's use of one of his things, it remains true that he can use the thing in lots more ways than others can, and others cannot use it without his permission except in special circumstances, then the use of the thing has been regulated. If not, the thing has been taken.

But for the Scientific Policymaker, the distinction between "taking" and "regulating," *in Layman's sense of those terms,* is unintelligible. This is so because he believes (a) that "property" refers to bundles of rights to use things, and (b) that no particular right or combination of rights to use a thing constitutes "ownership" of that thing. Because of his first belief, he is led to think that all governmental actions restricting the use of things are basically similar in that they remove one or more rights from various property bundles. Since all such actions affect the legal situation in the same way, there is no basis for a radical distinction between takings and regulations, unless a certain set of rights constitutes ownership of a thing. If so, then governmental actions that disturb that set would be takings, and those that do not would be regulations. But that possibility is foreclosed by the second belief.

This is not to say that the Scientific Policymaker avoids using the terms "taking" and "regulation." Governmental actions that incur costs that call for compensation according to his Comprehensive View are takings, and those that do not are regulations. But notice that unlike the Ordinary Observer, who exacts compensation because the action would be called a "taking" in ordinary life, the Scientific Policymaker calls the action a "taking" because compensation is required by the Comprehensive View.

32. Note that the text does not claim that *all* Utilitarian judges would find it simple to conclude that it is better to give Layman a thousand dollar bonus than to spend more than a thousand dollars in added fact-finding costs. This is so because a Utilitarian is ultimately concerned with costs and benefits measured in terms of individual happiness (or utility), rather than dollars. Hence, before he

will refuse to look beyond the nominal dollar sums to ultimate utilities, a judge must believe that dollars are generally distributed in our society in a utility-maximizing way. This, of course, is precisely the approach of a Utilitarian judge whose attitude to the distribution of property we have called *conservative*. See pp. 37, 44–9 supra. It is possible to imagine, however, that some *reformist* judges would be willing to pay more than a thousand dollars in fact-finding costs if the dollars were taken out of the pockets of people with low marginal utility for income, while the extra compensation money was taken from a fund drawn from those with high marginal utilities. Since both fact-finding costs and compensation funds usually come out of general appropriations, however, this reformist possibility may safely be kept in a footnote.

33. Normally, when one of Layman's things is taken, he is entitled to compensation only for the value of that thing and not for damages to other things of his. Sharp v. United States, 191 U.S. 341 (1903). In cases where only a part of Layman's thing has been taken, however, he is entitled to compensation for severance and consequential damages to the remainder. United States v. Miller, 317 U.S. 369 (1943); Sharp v. United States, supra. But great restrictions are placed on Layman's right to recover for such damages. Absent special circumstances, it is limited to cases where the property taken and the remainder previously formed a single physical unit. United States v. Miller, supra; Sharp v. United States, supra. When it is possible to separate damages to the remainder due to use of the property taken from damages due to the use of property taken from other owners for the same purpose, only the former is compensable. Campbell v. United States, 266 U.S. 368 (1924); St. Regis Paper Co. v. United States, 313 F.2d 45 (1962). Layman has the burden of proof and is under a duty to mitigate damages. Also, benefits resulting from the use of the taken land are set off against damages. United States v. Miller, supra; Campbell v. United States, supra; United States v. Welch, 217 U.S. 333 (1910); Sharp v. United States, supra. See generally Philip Nichols, *The Law of Eminent Domain* vol. 4A, chap. 14 (1975).

34. Many state statutes, usually passed in the nineteenth century, delegate the power of eminent domain to private corporations such as railroads or public utilities. See generally Nichols, *The Law of Eminent Domain* vol. 1, § 3.21[2].

35. Recently two Scientific Policymakers of a Utilitarian type have

sought to justify a rule which is only superficially similar to the Ordinary one considered in the text. In an important essay, William Baxter and Lillian Altree advocate a solution to the airport noise problem which, roughly speaking, requires governmentally operated airports to pay compensation "for all external costs imposed on land uses developed before the airport was constructed" but not after. See their "Legal Aspects of Airport Noise," 15 *J. of Law & Econ.* 1, 4 (1972). While this formula could perhaps be understood to mean that only Layman, and not Speculator, would get paid, a careful reading of the article makes it clear that they would also pay Speculator to compensate him for the fact that "the land has been made less suitable for uses that were sensitive to the noise level of airplanes." Id. at 5.

Unfortunately, while the Baxter-Altree approach supports my claim about the uncertain Policymaking justification for a line between Speculator and Layman, I cannot return the compliment and give complete endorsement to their approach. At least when viewed from the Utilitarian point of view to which they are attracted, their proposal seems unduly generous to the property owners surrounding the new airport. Even if, as they assume without discussion, a judge ought to adopt an activist role premise and take into account institutional self-aggrandizement when dealing with government-owned airports, the Baxter-Altree rule would be justified only if the airport were clearly the cheapest cost-avoider so far as *all* the costs of the airport-landowner interaction were concerned. While this *may* be true in the airport case often enough to justify a per se rule of the type proposed, the Baxter-Altree article—though lengthy and significant in other respects—does not systematically explore the empirical dimensions of the issue with sophisticated guidelines of the sort to be found in Guido Calabresi, "Transaction Costs, Resource Allocation and Liability Rules—A Comment," 11 *J. Law & Econ.* 67 (1968), and Robert C. Ellickson, "Alternatives to Zoning: Covenants, Nuisance Rules, and Fines as Land Use Controls," 40 *U. Chi. L. Rev.* 681, 724–28 (1973). While this may be a remediable defect so far as the problem of airport noise is concerned, it is a far more formidable deficiency in the proposal, advanced by Professor Lawrence Berger, that the Baxter-Altree approach be generalized to form a Policymaking formulation of takings law that appropriately mixes efficiency and justice concerns. See Lawrence Berger, "A Policy Analysis of the Taking Problem," 49 *N.Y.U.L. Rev.* 165, 195–206 (1974).

36. Zoning restrictions of the sort imposed on Speculator, which forbid one from making certain *future* uses of one's land, were upheld by the Supreme Court in Euclid v. Ambler, n. 8 supra. The Court never addressed the issue presented by Layman's case: the prohibition of *existing* uses. But it was early and generally accepted that such uses, if otherwise lawful, could not be prohibited by zoning ordinances without compensation. See Arden H. Rathkopf, *The Law of Zoning and Planning*, 3rd ed., vol. 2, chap. 58.

To qualify as a protected nonconforming use, it is only necessary that the use exist on the effective date of the ordinance and be substantial. Morris County Land Improvement Co. v. Parsippany-Troy Hills Township, 40 N.J. 539, 550, 193 A.2d 232, 238–39 (1963); compare People v. Miller, 304 N.Y. 105, 106 N.E. 2d 34 (1952), with Town of Somers v. Comarco, 308 N.Y. 537, 127 N.E. 2d 327 (1955). See also n. 22 supra and n. 45 infra. During the past twenty years, however, the constitutional rights of the nonconforming user have suffered a considerable erosion, particularly as a result of the "amortization" doctrine discussed at n. 41 infra. Nonetheless, it remains true that in the case hypothesized in the text, where Layman's use is subjected to immediate termination, his claim to compensation has been questioned by no court. We shall therefore consider only this case in our textual comparison of the Scientific Policymaker and Ordinary Observer, reserving the doctrinal complexities for treatment at n. 41.

37. *Not* "that bundle of rights over there is mine."

38. See pp. 98, 101–02 supra.

39. See pp. 136–45 infra.

40. This is an imaginary judicial utterance. For real ones, see Vartelas v. Water Resources Com'n., 146 Conn. 650, 658, 153 A.2d 822, 826 (1959); Madis v. Higginson, 164 Colo. 320, 323, 434 P.2d 705, 706 (1967); Wright v. City of Littleton, 483 P.2d 953, 956 (Colo. 1971); In re Spring Valley Development, 300 A.2d 736, 749 (Me. 1973); Village House v. Town of Loudon, 114 N.H. 76, 314 A.2d 635, 637 (1974).

41. While the text has only considered the conceptual foundations of the law of nonconforming use, the distinction between Scientific Policymaker and Ordinary Observer also enlightens the finer points of doctrine in this corner of takings law. Thus, while the immediate termination of Hamburger Heaven will raise the most serious constitutional problems, it is well established that the state may—without compensation—forbid Layman from *expanding*

Hamburger Heaven in a zone where its operation is generally prohibited. Chilson v. Board of Appeals of Attleboro, 344 Mass. 406, 182 N.E.2d 535 (1962). From an Ordinary Observer's point of view, of course, this distinction between the right to maintain the *original* Hamburger Heaven in operating condition and the right to *expand* it makes perfectly good sense—despite the fact that Layman has been denied this second right, it still is correct to say that Hamburger Heaven remains Layman's thing, thereby establishing that only a regulation, rather than a prima facie taking, has occurred.

More difficult for the Ordinary Observer to condone is a common zoning provision forbidding nonconforming users to engage in the extensive repair or alteration of their things. While denying Layman his right to renovate may eventually make his nonconforming use economically unjustified, this fact need not prove insuperable, at least for the deferential judge eager to uphold the legislative judgment. Depriving Layman of the right to renovate, after all, does not deprive him of the thing that was his at the time the statute was enacted—indeed, by its very terms, a statute barring renovation simply stops Layman from passing off a new thing for his old one. Hence, a "non-renovation" rule escapes the reach of the Ordinary Observer's takings clause, a result that conforms with the universal judgment of the courts. See, e.g., Jobert v. Morant, 150 Conn. 584, 192 A.2d 553 (1963).

The next class of cases, though building on the last, is far more troublesome. Here, rather than proscribing renovation and letting obsolescence take its course, the state passes a statute giving Layman a few years of grace, after which he must end Hamburger Heaven's operation by command of law. While, as we have suggested, ordering the immediate termination of a nonconforming use constitutes a prima facie case of taking, does the fact that termination is deferred for a few years suffice to place the statute beyond the Ordinary Observer's takings clause?

Perhaps. After all, if the state can forbid Layman from renovating his nonconforming property, thereby assuring its eventual obsolescence, can it not set a reasonable amortization period for nonconforming structures based on the expected life of the structure without major repairs? And if it can do this for nonconforming structures, can it not establish analogous amortization periods for nonconforming uses? This sort of reasoning, reflected in opinions like that of New York's highest court in Harbison v. City of Buffalo,

4 N.Y.2d 553, 561–62, 176 N.Y.S.2d 598, 604–5, 152 N.E.2d 42, 46–47 (1958), may lead a deferential Ordinary judge to uphold the amortization approach, though less deferential courts will disagree. City of Akron v. Chapman, 160 Ohio St. 382, 116 N.E.2d. 697 (1953).

Of course, from a Scientific Policymaking point of view, these Ordinary efforts to ground a decision by analogizing from the "no-renovation" cases proceeds from premises that are profoundly misconceived. For the reasons suggested in the text, the very notion that nonconforming uses mark out a simple category deserving special constitutional protection seems exceedingly suspect. Consequently, one should expect a Scientific court to seize upon the "amortization" concept as an excuse for cutting back protection. Thus, in upholding an amortization scheme, a California court reasoned:

> In essence there is no distinction between requiring the discontinuance of a nonconforming use within a reasonable period and provisions which deny the right to add to or extend buildings devoted to an existing nonconforming use, which deny the right to resume a nonconforming use after a period of nonuse, which deny the right to extend or enlarge an existing nonconforming use, which deny the right to substitute new buildings for those devoted to an existing nonconforming use—all of which have been held to be valid exercises of the police power. . . . The distinction between an ordinance restricting future uses and one requiring the termination of present uses within a reasonable period of time is merely one of degree, and constitutionality depends on the relative importance to be given to the public gain and to the private loss. . . . A legislative body may well conclude that the beneficial affect on the community of the eventual elimination of all nonconforming uses by a reasonable amortization plan more than offsets individual losses. City of Los Angeles v. Gage, 127 Cal. App.2d 442, 459–60, 274 P.2d 34,44 (1954).

The reasoning here is Scientific, of a restrained, vaguely Utilitarian variety. That it is Scientific is shown by the court's refusal to take seriously the difference between present and future uses of land. See note 22, supra. That it is Utilitarian is illustrated by the talk of balancing public benefits against private losses. For similar sentiments, see Grant v. Baltimore, 212 Md. 301, 129 A. 2d 363 (1957). The in-

creasing acceptance of amortization during the past twenty years—
and opinions such as *Gage*—are signs of the increasingly Scientific
Policymaking character of the legal culture. But the existence of
other opinions, like *Harbison,* supra, in which courts resort to arguments by analogy to Ordinary property talk in order to approve
amortization shows the strong hold of Ordinary Observing on the
judicial mind.

42. See, e.g., Commonwealth v. Kastner, 13 Pa. Cmwlth. 525, 320
A.2d 146 (1974), cert. den. 419 U.S. 1109 (1975); Gibson & Perin Co.
v. City of Cincinnati, 480 F.2d 936 (1973); Commonwealth v. Hes-
sion, 430 Pa. 273, 242 A.2d 432 (1968). In the case hypothesized in
the text, the state has done no more than divert traffic from its
accustomed route by affording it a new one. Cases arise, however,
when the state affirmatively obstructs Layman's access to Highway
One itself. See Dougherty County v. Pylant, 104 Ga. App. 468, 122
S.E.2d 117 (1961); People v. Ricciardi, 23 Cal.2d 390, 144 P.2d 799
(1944). We shall discuss this form of taking, in which Layman's thing
is rendered useless, subsequently at pp. 136-45, and n. 48 infra.

43. Imagine now that the opening of the new Interstate had so
reduced the traffic on Highway One that Proprietor was obliged to
go out of business. At this point Proprietor's thing would have been
destroyed and so it would appear that a prima facie case of taking
would be easy to establish. As we shall see later, however, a second
condition must be fulfilled before a prima facie claim for compensation can be maintained: Proprietor will be obliged to show not
only that his thing has been destroyed, but that the state rather
than the market may justly be held responsible for the destruction.
Moreover, the case we have hypothesized—in which the loss has
been visited by a relatively subtle form of state manipulation of the
economic environment—is precisely the area of greatest ambiguity in
the Ordinary theory of state responsibility. Consequently, we shall
defer further treatment of the issue posed by Proprietor's business
failure to pp. 145-50 and especially n. 71.

44. See, e.g., the cases cited in notes 36, 40, and 42 supra.

45. It should be noted that there are cases which require that an
existing use be "substantial" before it can obtain the protection of
the "nonconforming use" doctrine. Thus, compensation has been
denied in cases where the state deprived Layman of a pigeon loft
(People v. Miller, 304 N.Y. 105, 106 N.E.2d 34 (1952). I myself am
unsympathetic to holdings of this kind, which seem exclusively based

on the maxim *de minimis non curat lex.* Litigation costs beng what they are, I see no reason to believe that the plaintiff does not perceive a substantial stake in any lawsuit he is willing to bring to court.

46. In terms of the analysis presented at pp. 129–30 supra, can there be a taking when neither condition (a) nor (b) obtains?

47. To put the point another way: "An ordinance which permanently so restricts the use of property that it cannot be used for any reasonable purpose goes, it is plain, beyond regulation, and must be recognized as a taking of the property. The only substantial difference, in such case, between restriction and actual taking is that the restriction leaves the owner subject to the burden of payments of taxation, while outright confiscation would relieve him of that burden." Arverne Bay Construction Co. v. Thatcher, 278 N.Y. 222, 232; 15 N.E.2d 587, 591 (1938).

48. It should be noted that there are several different ways in which the state can render Layman's thing useless. For example, it can alter the *legal relation* between Layman and his thing, so that Layman is no longer entitled to do anything useful with it. Our hypothetical case is an example: at Time One, Layman has a right to drive and sell his Cadillac; at Time Three he does not. For actual cases of this sort, see: AMG Associates v. Township of Springfield, 65 N.J. 101, 319 A.d 705 (1974); Morris County Land Improvement Co. v. Parsipanny-Troy Hills Township, 40 N.J. 539, 193 A.2d 232 (1963); City of Plainfield v. Borough of Middlesex, 69 N.J. Super. 136, 173 A.2d 785 (1961). A second way of rendering a thing useless is to change the *physical character* of the property so that it no longer serves any purpose for anyone. See, e.g., United States v. Kansas City Life Insurance Co., 339 U.S. 799 (1950), in which a government navigation project impaired the subsurface drainage of claimant's land, thus destroying its value for farming or any other purpose. Yet another way of rendering property useless is to change the physical relation of real property to adjacent land. This problem is posed, for example, when the state diverts traffic from Hamburger Heaven by opening a new highway or destroys or substantially impairs access to an adjoining street. Cf. William B. Stoebuck, "The Property Right of Access Versus the Power of Eminent Domain," 47 *Tex. L. Rev.* 733 (1969). For an even more extreme example, in which Layman is deprived of all practical access to his thing, see Mackie v. United States, 194 F.Supp. 306 (1961).

49. Imagine, for example, that Layman is lucky enough to own a series of paintings by Monet depicting the cathedral at Rouen at various hours of the day. Layman wishes to sell one of the paintings but is forbidden by the (hypothetical) Art Review Board, which finds that the public interest requires that the collection remain intact, and so requires Layman to sell the entire series of paintings or none at all. Before a court could determine whether this regulation constituted a prima facie taking, an inquiry of the most discriminating kind into Layman's tastes would obviously be required.

50. One expects the market value of the thing only to approach, rather than equal, zero since the market will place a positive value on the possibility that the restrictive legislation will be repealed or modified, either by legislative or judicial action, leaving Layman free once again to use his thing in valuable ways. Moreover, since the value of these "repeal rights" will be a function of the market's perceptions as to the probability and nature of legal modification, no hard-and-fast rule can be stated which specifies the market value that a thing can retain and yet qualify as taken under the "diminution of value" test.

This conclusion is strengthened when the problem of "scrap value" is introduced. It is conceivable, for example, that although the Cadillac has been rendered useless, all of its parts may be useful for other purposes. Hubcaps may be used for ashtrays, batteries for a lawnmower, and so forth. If so, then Layman would own a lot of new things which used to be parts of the Cadillac. Nonetheless he would have been deprived of a *Cadillac,* just as Layman was deprived of Hamburger Heaven even though he retained the collection of pots, pans, and hotplates that were used in the store; see pp. 135–36 infra. In both cases, a thing that could be identified in terms of social practices has been destroyed; and it is this destruction of social property that is the gravamen of Layman's complaint. In short, the requisite "diminution of value" must be measured either by the thing's "scrap value" or "repeal value"—whichever is higher. This is a determination which requires sensitivity to the facts of individual cases if the administration of takings law is even to pretend to be a good approxmation of the Ordinary understanding of constitutional requirements.

51. See Bureau of Mines of Maryland v. George's Creek Coal and Land Co., 272 Md. 143, 321 A.2d 748 (1974); Village House, Inc. v. Town of Loudon, 114 N.H. 76, 314 A.2d 635 (1974); In re Spring

Valley Development, 300 A.2d 736 (Me. 1973); Golden v. Planning Board of Town of Ramapo, 30 N.Y.2d 359, 334 N.Y.S.2d 138, 285 N.E.2d 291, appeal dismissed 409 U.S. 1003 (1972); Just v. Marinette County, 56 Wis.2d 7, 201 N.W.2d 761 (1972).

52. Recall that we are speaking here only of cases that do not qualify as prima facie takings under either of the heads previously considered.

53. See State v. Johnson, 265 A.2d 711 (Me. 1970); Commissioner of Natural Resources v. S. Volpe Co., 349 Mass. 104, 206 N.E.2d 666 (1965); Dooley v. Town Plan and Zoning Commission, 151 Conn. 304, 197 A.2d 770 (1964); Morris County Land Improvement Co. v. Parsipanny-Troy Hills, 40 N.J. 539, 193 A.2d 232 (1963).

54. "Property, Utility, and Fairness," 80 *Harv. L. Rev.* 1165, 1233 (1967).

55. The caveat entered at n. 50 supra should be kept in mind in appraising the absolute value a thing may retain and yet fall within the class of prima facie takings. As is made clear there, no hard and fast rule is appropriate to this matter, the judge being obliged to take into account "scrap" value and "repeal" value in making a decision. Ordinary courts have not, I think, been sufficiently sensitive to the fact that market value can conceivably be quite high in absolute terms and yet satisfy the conditions for a prima facie taking. Cf. Note, "Just Compensation and the Assassin's Bequest: A Utilitarian Approach," 122 *U. Pa. L. Rev.* 1012 (1974).

56. See, e.g., Michelman, "Property, Utility and Fairness," n. 54 supra, 1190–93 (1967); Sax, "Takings and the Police Power," 74 *Yale L.J.* 36, 60 (1964).

57. As I have argued in chap. 4, the restrained Kantian would decide both cases under the same test—do process costs involved in compensation exceed the net benefits of the project for which the taking has been undertaken? If so, compensation will be denied; if not, it will be granted. In conducting this inquiry it is only the pragmatic judge who will count as a cost the special grievances suffered by those citizens who have not learned to think about their legal relationships in Scientific terms and so suffer special costs when things they are accustomed to call "theirs" are taken. Yet, as we have shown, this kind of judicial pragmatism seems exceedingly difficult to justify when the political branches have, by hypothesis, refused to give it decisive weight. See pp. 60–64 and 83 supra.

58. 80 *Harv. L. Rev.* 1165, 1234.

59. Though Michelman himself does not make this transition, it is passages from Michelman's article like the one we have quoted that stand out from the enormous legal literature on the takings clause as the most suggestive of the Ordinary interpretation we have taken pains to develop. Allison Dunham's essay, "Griggs v. Allegheny County in Perspective: Thirty Years of Supreme Court Expropriation Law," *1962 Supreme Court Rev.* 63, to which I am generally indebted, also provides helpful clues.

60. While Michelman's discussion of the "diminution of value" test seems to me entirely correct so far as it goes, there is reason to believe that even his sketch of the uneasy Utilitarian case for "diminution of value" seems unduly kind to existing doctrine, at least when it is considered against the background provided by our Scientific theory of judicial role, introduced in chap. 2.

For we have already seen, at pp. 60–64, that even innovative judges who are quite willing to challenge the conservative and deferential aspects of the restrained role will think it quite a different matter when it comes to protecting pragmatically the hurt feelings suffered by those who have not learned that their claims to property rights are justified only so long as they further the general utility. Yet it is precisely this move away from principle to pragmatism which is involved in the acceptance of Michelman's three-step argument, requiring as it does the special protection of those whose feelings are hurt when "their" things are taken from them for the sake of the general utility. While doubtless a deferential judge would provide great leeway for pragmatic legislative attempts to deal with the hurt feelings of those who possess anti-Utilitarian manners of thought and sensibility, it is quite another thing for a judge to endow those who think of their relationship to objects in an un-Scientific way with special *constitutional* rights, at least if he hopes to maintain his standing as a Scientific Policymaker. The present "diminution of value test" not only requires the Scientific Utilitarian to indulge a "suspect" finding of fact, as Michelman suggests; it also requires him to indulge a pragmatic theory of judicial role that is at least equally doubtful from a Scientific Policymaking point of view.

61. While Michelman relies on John Rawls's theory of justice to develop an approach to compensation questions resembling the Kantian one (see chap. 4, n. 25 supra), this non-Utilitarian concep-

tion is not treated with the same care as is the Utilitarian one. In any event, a Scientific Rawlsian judge would seem to be as perplexed as my Scientific Kantian with an insistence upon the extent to which a particular thing diminishes in value, since it is an individual's total wealth and income (rather than his possession of things) which Rawls would use to measure a person's welfare for purposes of distributive justice. See John Rawls, *A Theory of Justice*, § 15 (1971).

62. Michelman looks to the legislature, rather than the courts, for innovation in compensation practices. Existing judicial doctrine is tolerated on the ground that courts cannot be reasonably expected to implement fully either the Utilitarian or Rawlsian Comprehensive Views that in Michelman's opinion represent the two most plausible candidates for the position of Comprehensive View in the American legal system. 80 *Harv. L. Rev.* 1165, 1245-56.

63. In contrast, Sax's embrace of Scientic Policymaking is not so readily suggestive of the decline of Ordinary Observing methods in the academy. Since present doctrine is based on Ordinary methodology, it is only natural that someone who is dissatisfied with existing law will also be prone to reject the conceptual framework giving it structure. Unlike Michelman's effort to justify existing law in Scientific terms, form and substance support one another in Sax's enterprise. See, e.g., "Takings, Private Property and Public Rights," 81 *Yale L.J.* 149, 161-72 (1971).

64. And recall that Layman's Ordinary claim that his Cadillac has been taken from him is not defeated by pointing out that he can sell his Cadillac *as junk* to the neighborhood recycling plant. See pp. 135-36, and notes 50 and 55 supra.

65. The point is sufficiently obvious not to have been discussed in Phillip Nichols, *The Law of Eminent Domain,* and other similar treatises.

66. While the status of the state action doctrine is much mooted in discussions of the constitutional protection of civil rights, compare Charles L. Black, Jr., "The Supreme Court, 1966 Term, Foreword: 'State Action,' Equal Protection, and California's Proposition 14," 81 *Harv. L. Rev.* 69 (1967), with Jackson v. Metropolitan Edison Co., 419 U.S. 345 (1974), and Hudgens v. National Labor Relations Board, 424 U.S. 507 (1976), I know of no self-conscious discussion of the problem as it arises in the present context, dealing with state responsibility for changes in the economic environment.

67. The paradigmatic exponent of this aspect of Scientific Policy-making is Guido Calabresi. See his *Tragic Choices* (forthcoming); "Property Rules, Liability Rules and Inalienability: One View of the Cathedral" (with A. Douglas Melamed) 85 *Harv. L. Rev.* 1089 (1972); *The Costs of Accidents* chaps. 7, 8 (1970).

68. Economic Stabilization Act of 1970, 84 Stat. 799, and associated Executive Orders. The Act and Executive Orders are set forth at 12 USC § 1964, note (Supplement III 1973).

69. Of the many cases arising under the Nixon price stabilization program, the takings issue was dealt with explicitly in Western States Meat Packers Ass'n., Inc. v. Dunlop, 482 F.2d 1401 (T.E.C.A. 1973), and Minden Beef Co. v. Cost of Living Council, 362 F.Supp. 298 (1973). In both cases the court rejected the takings claim, citing Bowles v. Willingham, 321 U.S. 503 (1944)—a case upholding a rent control program against a takings claim by asserting that the existence of the wartime emergency made it unnecessary to pay compensation. While the *Bowles* court rested its decision on the "emergency" theory, it is important to recognize that the facts of the case did not involve a prima facie taking in any of the Ordinary senses we have distinguished. Hence, it is not necessary for the Ordinary analyst to doubt the propriety of the *Bowles* holding in order to raise doubts as to the scope and validity of the "emergency" rationale. These doubts are enhanced by the fact that the Court's holding in United States v. Pewee Coal Co., 341 U.S. 114 (1951), indicates that the mere existence of a wartime emergency is insufficient to suspend the operation of the clause's protection. Thus, the fact that the judges in the recent challenges to price control felt themselves obliged to resurrect the doubtful "emergency" rationale suggests that they found considerable constitutional difficulty with a state price control effort as soon as it took on a bureaucratic, legalistic character. For more on wartime emergencies, see n. 71 infra.

A similar issue has arisen under the Emergency Petroleum Allocation Act, 87 Stat. 627, 15 U.S.C. §§ 751–6 (Supplement IV 1974), which authorizes the mandatory allocation of petroleum products. The Federal Energy Administration promulgated regulations establishing "entitlements" for the use of specific quantities of certain crude oil and requiring refiners who exceeded their entitlements to "purchase" unused entitlements from other refiners by means of cash payments. See 10 C.F.R. § 211.67.

The regulations were immediately challenged under the taking clause as a forced subsidy of competitors. See Marathon Oil Company v. Federal Energy Administration, 516 F.2d 1397 (T.E.C.A. 1975), cert. den. 426 U.S. — (1976); Cities Service Company v. Federal Energy Administration, 529 F.2d 1016 (T.E.C.A. 1975), cert. den. 426 U.S. — (1976).

70. United States v. Central Eureka Mining Co., 357 U.S. 155 (1958).

71. The importance to the Ordinary judge of the form of state intervention is shown by contrasting *Eureka,* n. 70 supra, with United States v. Pewee Coal Co., 341 U.S. 114 (1951). In *Pewee* the government responded to the threat of a wartime strike by issuing an "Order for Taking Possession" of the mine, requiring that mine officials act as government agents, that the American flag be flown at the mine and that the site be posted as "United States Property." Given these facts, the Court had no difficulty finding a taking by transfer of rightful possession.

Despite *Eureka's* similarity to *Pewee* from the Scientific point of view, the Supreme Court had little trouble distinguishing between *Pewee's* seizure of the coal mines and *Eureka's* diversion of labor from the gold mines. Justice Burton, writing for the *Eureka* majority, denied *Pewee's* precedential value on the ground that "the Government [here] did not occupy, use or in any manner take physical possession of the gold mines." 357 U.S. 155, 165–66. While Burton admitted that the order had deprived the owner of "the most profitable use of his property," he concluded that "in the context of war, we have been reluctant to find that degree of regulation which, without saying so, requires compensation." Id. at 168. Mr. Justice Harlan dissented vigorously, arguing that the owners "were totally deprived of the beneficial use of their property" and that "as a practical matter the Order led to consequences no different from those that would have followed from the temporary acquisition of physical possession." Id. at 181.

72. Inverse condemnation is conceived as a remedy against takings that have been effected without recourse to condemnation. The underlying theory is that the constitutional provision against uncompensated takings is self-executing, so that affected owners have a cause of action even in the absence of official proceedings in eminent domain. Actions in inverse condemnation can arise when property has been taken in any of the three ways we have distin-

guished. Pumpelly v. Green Bay Company 80 U.S. (13 Wall.) 166 (1871); United States v. Causby, 328 U.S. 256 (1946); Ackerman v. Port of Seattle, 55 Wash. 2d 400, 348 P.2d 664 (1960).

73. It was in Ashwander v. Tennessee Valley Authority, 297 U.S. 288 (1936), that Justice Brandeis advanced the notion—later developed by Frankfurter, Bickel, and their school—that the Court should make use of a wide range of jurisdictional doctrines in order to avoid the resolution of constitutional questions that were both intellectually difficult and politically sensitive. *Ashwander* involved, among other things, a takings claim by stockholders of a commercial power company, who argued that the failure of the government to pay compensation for lost company profits rendered unconstitutional the newly created Tennessee Valley authority. Id. at 295.

74. Consider, for example, the way in which the courts have dealt with the advent of the airplane. The first cases were easy. In these, airports had marked out glide-paths for arriving and departing airplanes. Those property owners unfortunate enough to have their land located directly under the path were thereby made the victims of a continuing stream of planes, each skimming the treetops, that made it impossible to carry on their accustomed activities. Since the government act marking out the glide-paths had permitted the airplanes to destroy Layman's (social) things, it was easy for Ordinary judges to find that a taking had occurred; see U.S. v. Causby, 238 U.S. 256 (1946) (a case made even easier by the fact that the low-flying planes which destroyed Causby's chicken-farm were military craft). Having gone this far, however, Ordinary judges became fearful of the extent to which imposing a broad compensation requirement would burden the activist state's effort to further air transportation. This, at any rate, is how I would explain cases like Batten v. United States, 306 F.2d 580 (1962), cert. den. 371 U.S. 955 (1963), which denied compensation to landowners near—but not directly beneath—the glide-path. From an Ordinary judge's point of view, this was a distinction without a difference—even though a direct overflight was not in question, the fact remains that Layman's (social) things had been taken (destroyed) by the state decision. It is for this reason, I think, that decisions like *Batten* have proved somewhat unstable, with courts, at least at the state level, increasingly willing to extend the takings clause to represent more adequately common perceptions of growing state involvement. See Nestle v. Santa Monica, 6 Cal.3d 920, 101 Cal. Rptr. 568, 496 P.2d 480 (1972);

Aaron v. Los Angeles, 40 Cal. App.3d 471, 115 Cal. Rptr. 162 (1974), cert. den., 419 U.S. 1122 (1975); Thornburg v. Port of Portland, 223 Or. 178, 376 P.2d 100 (1962); Martin v. Port of Seattle, 64 Wash.2d 309, 391 P.2d 540 (1964), cert. den. 379 U.S. 989 (1965); City of Jacksonville v. Schumann, 167 So.2. 95 (Fla. App. 1964).

Similarly, the problem of "planning blight" in urban renewal projects has led courts to assume a less deferential stance toward the activist state. Frequently, long delays in the implementation of renewal projects result in a serious reduction of property values within the project area. While the Supreme Court in United States v. Miller, 317 U.S. 369 (1943) and United States v. Virginia Electric and Power Co., 365 U.S. 624 (1961) had held that increase or reduction of value caused by the prospective taking should not affect the award in eminent domain cases, some courts have since developed a "de facto taking" theory for urban renewal cases, whereby the property is to be considered for valuation purposes as taken on the date the governmental agency committed itself to the project. Subsequent loss of value due to planning blight is thus included in the condemnation award, or is recoverable in an action for damage by the owner. Amen v. City of Dearborn, 363 F.Supp. 1267 (1973); Madison Realty Co. v. City of Detroit, 315 F.Supp. 367 (1970); Foster v. City of Detroit, 254 F.Supp. 655 (1966), 405 F.2d 138 (1968); Drakes Bay Land Co. v. United States, 191 Ct. Cl. 389, 424 F.2d 574 (1970). See In re Elmwood Park Project, 376 Mich. 311, 136 N.W.2d 896 (1965). There has, however, been some resistance to the "de facto taking" approach by the courts. Housing Authority v. Lamar, 21 Ill.2d 362, 172 N.E.2d 790 (1961); St. Louis Housing Authority v. Barnes, 375 S.W.2d 144 (Mo. 1964).

75. To take but one example, I suspect a contemporary Ordinary judge would not take seriously a takings claim made by a restaurant driven out of business by a private competitor which leased a portion of a state-owned parking garage to serve as the base of its operations. Nonetheless, the Supreme Court succeeded in finding the requisite state action when such a restaurant discriminated against black customers; see Burton v. City of Wilmington Parking Authority, 365 U.S. 715 (1961). It should be emphasized, moreover, that in the civil rights area at least, the state action doctrine has moved far beyond the Ordinary Observer's conception to include many Scientific elements in its doctrinal formulations. Thus, details—invisible to the Layman's eye—concerning an entity's fiscal and regulatory relation-

ship to the state have often been held to be decisive in individual state action decisions. Here, as elsewhere, the takings clause seems a relatively pure Ordinary type—though it is far from clear to what extent the state action notion implicit in the takings cases will retain its integrity after time brings to the surface its apparent inconsistency with the far more familiar (if chaotic) state action notions developed in the great civil rights cases.

76. Indeed, this is true of the system of feudal tenure, from which the modern American law of real property has evolved.

77. See chapter 5, n. 14 supra.

78. See pp. 101–02 supra.

79. I shall not try to deal with the elusive notion of "necessity" as it is understood by the Ordinary Observer. For present purposes, it is enough to say that a taking is *necessary* to achieve the termination of an antisocial use when less drastic means are plainly inadequate to achieve the objective in a reliable way. In short, I have in mind a test with more bite than that formulation of the "less restrictive alternatives test" which would merely require that less drastic forms of regulation be shown to be somewhat less effective than the taking approach. See Paul Brest, *Processes of Constitutional Decisionmaking* 987–94 (1975).

To make matters even more complex, the notion of "necessity" (however it may be more precisely specified) must be filtered by our theory of judicial role before it can be rendered operational. Thus a *deferential* judge would take into account the fact that the non-judicial branches have already found that the requisite degree of necessity obtains and ask himself whether *there is some reason to believe* that the taking is *not* necessary to terminate the offensive use reliably. It may be that when the notion of "necessity" is qualified in this way, the test becomes operationally equivalent to a judicial inquiry whether there is a *minimally rational* relationship between the legislature's objective of terminating a use that may be Observably antisocial. Even if this is so—a point not at all obvious—the notion of "necessity" would come into its own for Ordinary judges of less deferential varieties.

80. For an illuminating analysis of the sociological role of principles of this sort, see Thorstein Eckhoff, *Justice: Its Determinants in Social Interaction* (1974).

81. See the discussion of the Ordinary Observer's role, pp. 93 to 97 supra.

82. Mugler v. Kansas, 123 U.S. 623, 669 (1887).

83. This is not to say that the cigarette manufacturers would necessarily fare better under Scientific Policymaking. Nonetheless, even the most cursory consideration reveals that the manufacturers could launch a far more powerful case. Thus, Utilitarians would recognize that costs to cigarette manufacturers would be extremely high, a fact that would lend cogency to a claim founded on Citizen Disaffection based on whatever felicific doubts remain open at the time on the smoking question. Further, the uncertainty costs generated by closing down an entire industry could well be great. Hence, the rather modest process costs on the one hand, and the sum of uncertainty and disaffection costs on the other, would either be close or favor compensation. Turning to innovative considerations, a reformist judge would not be troubled by distributional considerations, nor would an activist be detained by the "equal protection" aspect. But the activist might take seriously the possibility of institutional aggrandizement depending upon the kind of institution that promulgated the ban.

For the Scientific Kantian, the high costs to manufacturers would tend to reduce the net benefits of the legislation, thus making a comparison of process costs and net benefits difficult. Reformists and activists would be moved in much the same way as their Utilitarian counterparts, rendering the case for compensation stronger for innovative judges. In sum, Scientific Policymakers of both kinds would find the case far harder than it would seem under traditional doctrine.

84. Village of Euclid v. Ambler Realty Co., 272 U.S. 365 (1926); Village of Belle Terre v. Boraas, 416 U.S. 1 (1974). Cf. Goldblatt v. Town of Hempstead, 369 U.S. 590 (1962); Miller v. Schoene, 276 U.S. 272 (1928). For an interesting attempt to adapt the Ordinary concept of neighborliness to a Scientific Policymaking framework of analysis, see Robert C. Ellickson, "Alternatives to Zoning: Covenants, Nuisance Rules, and Fines as Land Use Controls," 40 *U. Chi. L. Rev.* 681, 728–33 (1973).

85. It is not surprising that Sax, using a Policymaking methodology, comes to a different view of the railroad-crossing cases. Noting that state highway building is an entrepreneurial rather than a mediational activity, Sax argues—for reasons discussed at pp. 50–52 —that the state should be obliged to bear the costs involved when its Highway Department subsequently locates a road near an existing

railroad. He therefore urges the courts to overrule their railroad-crossing decisions.

86. See nn. 36 and 41 supra. While lower courts are quite vigilant in the protection of the rights of nonconforming uses, see, e.g., Lyon Sand & Gravel Co. v. Township of Oakland, 33 Mich. App. 614, 190 N.W.2d 354 (1971); Exton Quarrys, Inc. v. Zoning Board of Adjustment of West Whiteland Township, 425 Pa. 43, 228 A.2d 169 (1967); City of Warick v. Del Bonis Sand and Gravel Co., 99 R.I. 537, 209 A.2d 227 (1965), the Supreme Court has been more restrained in its treatment, sensing a serious problem but refusing to mark decisively the outer boundary of the concept of Ordinary justification. Thus, in Hadachek v. Sebastian, 239 U.S. 394 (1915), Justice MacKenna, for a unanimous court, upheld a Los Angeles ordinance in a classic brickyard case in language whose rhetorical overexertion bespeaks a recognition that the legislature is being permitted to act inconsistently with the Layman's concept of Ordinary justification: "A vested interest cannot be asserted against [the police power] because of conditions once obtaining [citing case]. To so hold would preclude development and fix a city forever in its primitive conditions. There must be progress, and if in its march private interests are in the way they must yield to the good of the community." Id. at 410.

Despite such vigorous rhetoric (which, if taken seriously, would render the takings clause a nullity), *Hadacheck* is not settled law today. Not only are lower courts generally protective of the rights of nonconforming uses, but the modern Supreme Court—in a rare show of initiative in takings law—was so troubled by a modern replay of the brickyard scenario that it actually granted certiorari to set things right. See Goldblatt v. Town of Hempstead, 369 U.S. 590 (1962) (involving a sand and gravel pit rather than a brickyard). When *Goldblatt's* moment of decision came, however, the Court disposed of the case on a narrow ground—apparently unwilling to make some large doctrinal pronouncement that would inevitably have engendered a flood of litigation seeking to push the Court down the path of protecting established economic interests. Nevertheless, the mere fact that the Court made some clucking noises on such matters in a time of great judicial restraint is itself an indication of the hold of the Ordinary Observer on the judicial mind as it works out the categories of takings law.

87. See, e.g., Lawrence H. Tribe, "From Environmental Foundations to Constitutional Structures: Learning from Nature's Future,"

84 *Yale L.J.* 545 (1975); Mark Sagoff, "On Preserving the Natural Environment," 84 *Yale L.J.* 205 (1974); Lawrence H. Tribe, "Ways Not to Think About Plastic Trees: New Foundations for Environmental Law," 83 *Yale L.J.* 1315 (1974); Christopher D. Stone, "Should Trees Have Standing?—Toward Legal Rights for Natural Objects," 45 *So. Ca. L. Rev.* 450 (1972).

88. The case of Sibson v. State, 115 N.H. 124, 336 A.2d 239 (1975), with which chap. 1 opened, is of this character; see nn. 2 and 6, chap. 1. In Just v. Marinette County, 56 Wis. 2d 7, 201 N.W.2d 761 (1972), another case upholding the denial of a permit to develop marshland, the Supreme Court of Wisconsin reached an identical conclusion by alternative arguments of an exceptionally deferential character. Thus, while it conceded that "whether a taking has occurred depends upon whether the restriction practically or substantially renders the land useless for all reasonable purposes," id. at 15, 767, it went on to equate "reasonable purposes" with "natural uses": "An owner has no absolute and unlimited right to change the essential natural character of his land so as to use it for a purpose for which it was unsuited in its natural state. The exercise of the police power must be reasonable, and we think it is not an unreasonable exercise of that power to prevent harm to public rights by limiting the use of private property to its natural use." Id. at 17, 768. Admitting that Just's property had severely depreciated in value, it observed that "this depreciation is not based on the use of the land in its natural state." Id. at 23, 771. But the court stopped short of holding that damaging Nature is *in itself* a harmful use of property by basing the state's power to restrict land to its natural uses on a "public trust duty" to "protect and preserve these waters for fishing, recreation and scenic beauty." Id. at 18, 768. See also Candlestick Properties, Inc. v. San Francisco Bay Conservation and Development Commission, 11 Cal. App. 3d 557, 89 Cal. Rptr. 897 (1970), and cases cited at note 54, chap. 3.

For cases involving the preservation of historical districts, see Bohannan v. City of San Diego, 30 Cal. App. 3d 416, 106 Cal. Rptr. 333 (1973); Maher v. City of New Orleans, 256 La. 131, 235 So.2d 402 (1970); McNeeley v. Board of Appeal of Boston, 358 Mass. 94, 261 N.E.2d 336 (1970).

89. For example, during the past ten years there has been a great deal of legislation limiting land use in flood plain areas, encouraged in part by the Flood Insurance Act of 1968, 42 U.S.C. 4001 et seq.

(1970). While some courts find such legislation confiscatory—State v. Johnson, 265 A.2d 711 (Me. 1970); Dooley v. Town Plan and Zoning Commission of Town of Fairfield 151 Conn. 304, 197 A.2d 770 (1964)—other recent decisions uphold their constitutionality: Turner v. County of Del Norte, 24 Cal. App. 3d 311, 101 Cal. Rptr. 93 (1972); Turnpike Realty Co. v. Town of Dedham, 362 Mass. 221, 284 N.E.2d 891 (1972) cert.den. 409 U.S. 1108 (1973).

90. See, e.g., State v. Johnson, 265 A.2d 711 (Me. 1970); Commissioner of Natural Resources v. S. Volpe & Co., 349 Mass. 104, 206 N.E. 2d 666 (1965); Dooley v. Town Plan and Zoning Comm'n, 151 Conn. 304, 197 A.2d 770 (1964); Morris County Land Improvement Co. v. Parsippany Troy Hills Township, 40 N.J. 539, 193 A.2d 232 (1963).

91. See, e.g., Lutheran Church v. City of New York, 35 N.Y. 2d 121, 359 N.Y. S.2d 7, 316 N.E. 2d 305 (1974) (striking down a historical preservation program on the basis of *Sax I*'s entrepreneurial/arbitral distinction discussed at pp. 50–52 supra).

92. 260 U.S. 393 (1922).

93. The common law is rich in labels, so it may be best to call User's right a lease, a profit a prendre, or an easement.

94. The "undivided fee rule" holds that when property is taken in which there exists a diversity of interests, compensation is to be based on the value of the property itself rather than on the sum of the values of the different interests. This approach, of course, plainly reflects the thought processes of an Ordinary Observer. Exceptions to the "undivided fee rule," however, are sometimes tolerated in extremely unusual circumstances. See Philip Nichols. *The Law of Eminent Domain* vol. §§12.36 [1], [2]. For a modern approach, see the Uniform Eminent Domain Code, §1012, and comment (1975).

95. For example, the typical holder of mining rights may be far less risk-averse then the typical owner of undivided parcels. If this is so, owners of undivided parcels could support their claim before a Utilitarian Policymaker by a relatively strong appeal to General Uncertainty. Similarly, a Kantian Policymaker might be convinced that the process costs involved in compensating those with partial interests are higher than the statute's net benefits, thereby failing to pass his basic requirement for compensation.

In making these arguments I do not suggest that they will always be decisive. Indeed, I suspect that the "parity principle" will often seem quite justified for Policymaking reasons. My point here is that only an Ordinary Observer will consider the "parity principle" a fundamental doctrine requiring no further justification, while it will have no such basic status in common Policymaking approaches.

96. This is a good place to note the existence of a second class of "easy" cases, of a very different kind, arising under the Ordinary interpretation of the takings clause. This class arises not because of the subdivision of ownership into a diverse set of user bundles, but because of the existence of a bona fide dispute over the proper legal owner of the thing in question. Layman, for example, may be in possession of parcel U but another will-socialized person, Goodguy, may have gone to court to further his claim that he has a superior title to the property. As we have seen (n. 15 supra), the existence of such a bona fide dispute may make it impossible for anybody to say that he knows the true owner without relying on expert legal advice, thereby transferring Layman's interest into the category of "legal property" during the pendency of the litigation. It is true, of course, that Laymen's ownership will revert to "social property" as soon as his title is reaffirmed in court. But what if the state takes parcel U during the pendency of the Layman-Goodguy litigation, at a time when neither side has social property rights?

The answer does not seem overly difficult. If Goodguy's claim against Layman is later rejected in the courts, Layman should be treated *as if* he were the holder of *social* property at the time of the taking. To hold otherwise would permit the state to profit from a claim that it itself found to be invalid. It was bad enough that Layman was obliged to spend the time and money to defend himself against Goodguy's bona fide (but invalid) assertions; it would be unconscionable for the state to escape liability simply because Goodguy had (misguidedly) challenged Layman's title at the time of the taking. Similarly, if the courts later uphold Goodguy's claim, he should receive the payment that would have been plainly his if the wings of justice had been swifter. In short, in cases of bona fide dispute, the Observer would order the state to pay compensation into a fund on behalf of the party emerging victorious at the end of the pending litigation. This is in fact the prevailing practice. See generally Philip Nichols, *The Law of Eminent Domain* vol. 2, § 5.2 [2].

97. See pp. 130–33 supra.

98. See pp. 116–18 supra.

266   NOTES TO PAGES 160–61

99. See pp. 118–21 supra.

100. The case with which we are dealing is a very pure case of legal property. It is quite clear, however, that there are many relationships that are hybrid combinations of both social and legal elements. Thus, if the company had been Layman's tenant and customarily paid rent, there would be some evidence in observable social reality of the existence of a special relationship between the company and parcel D, though the precise character of the relationship would remain entirely obscure without recourse to specialized legal expertise. We shall not attempt, however, to trace in detail the range of possible responses to these hybrid forms, contenting ourselves with elaborating the serious methodological difficulties that arise from the Ordinary Observer's confrontation with a relatively pure type of legal property.

101. This argument is made, for example, in Richard A. Posner, *Economic Analysis of Law* 15–6 (1973).

102. It is not true that *all* paper representing potential uses of things should properly be classed as legal, rather than social, property. Money and checks, for example, are forms of paper that have come into such common, everyday use that ordinary social practices and expectations have been built around them. Thus, all sorts of people routinely exchange tangible goods for money and personal checks. Laymen are therefore entirely familiar with the paper and have no need for legal advice in order to understand its use.

It is possible to suggest three criteria that any form of paper must meet in order to qualify as social property. First, it must be associated with social practices and expectations. Second, these practices and expectations must be *general,* and not confined to a specialized institution, such as a stock exchange. Third, they must involve in a fairly direct way objects that are clear cases of Layman's things; that is, it must be possible to exchange the paper for a thing, or assume control of a thing upon presentation of the paper, or something similar. In our example, the company's paper does not meet the first criterion. For examples of papers that meet the first, but not the second or third criterion, see n. 15 supra. For a brief remark on the existence of hybrid mixtures of legal and social property see n. 100 supra.

103. In contrast, Layman's legal document to parcel U is still worth half a million dollars and so he will not find it pointless to claim the thing as his. Indeed, the document would be worth some-

thing even if Layman were not operating a factory, for the surface rights would still have potential uses. Hence Layman can point to no legal thing that has been taken from him any more than he can point to a social thing.

104. Arthur A. Leff, "Contract as Thing," 19 *Am. U. L. Rev.* 131 (1970); Robert C. Clark, "Abstract Rights and Paper Rights under Article 9 of the Uniform Commercial Code," 84 *Yale L.J.* 445 (1975); see n. 102 supra.

105. The possibility of this sort of eclectic decision making was discussed at pp. 110–12 supra. Although it seems a natural way of combining the Scientific Policymaking and Ordinary Observer approaches, there are reasons why Ordinary judges would tend to reject it, since any appeal to Scientific Policymaking, even for that limited class of cases to which the Ordinary Observer approach does not provide a clear answer, tends to undermine confidence in the latter approach. This is not to deny that an Ordinary judge may consistently adopt the eclectic method. But it is also possible that eclecticism will prove unstable, merely a transitional phase to a fuller acceptance of Scientific Policymaking.

106. Mr. Justice Holmes emphasizes at several points in his opinion the fact that the mining right is packaged in a distinctive way, since it "is recognized in Pennsylvania as an estate in land." 260 U.S. 393, 414; see also 412, 415. He thus suggests the significance of legal packaging and documentation in the Ordinary interpretation of takings law when applied to Lawyer's things. In the particular case, the coal company had previously owned the fee and had conveyed it to another, reserving to itself the estate in the subjacent coal. It is this estate that had been rendered valueless.

107. The Kohler Act, P.L. 1198 (1921), the statute under which the suit was brought, forbade the mining of anthracite coal if it would cause the surface to collapse or subside, and if the surface was occupied by inhabited structures or various public facilities such as streets or power lines. But it did not apply to parcels owned in fee simple by the mine operator. Thus the parity problem, discussed above, of treating divided and undivided parcels differently did not arise, no doubt making Holmes's decision much easier.

108. Holmes, of course, is one of the most complex of our legal heroes and it would be foolhardy to attempt a capsule summary here which took an appropriately skeptical attitude toward the platitudes that so often masquerade as the received interpretation

of his thought. Nonetheless, I think it does seem clear that Holmes, on the level of constitutional interpretation at least, was deeply suspicious of the effort to interpret problematic legal concepts in terms of a Comprehensive View. Whether this anti-Scientific Policy-making tendency is also characteristic of Holmes's own affirmative work on the common law seems to me far more problematic, best reserved for detailed exploration. For some citations to the leading work on Holmes, see n. 40, chap. 7 infra.

109. 260 U.S. 393, 415.

110. Ibid.

111. Ibid.

112. Conducting mining operations so as to cause the collapse of inhabited surface land is, of course, an unsociable use of one's property. Nonetheless, this general point did not in Holmes's mind justify the particular statute before him. For this statute only applied to situations in which the owner of the surface rights, at the time of the purchase, was on notice that the owner of the subsurface had the right of subsidence. Given the surface owner's conscious assumption of the risk, Holmes did not believe that the coal company was acting in an unduly harmful way in exercising its option, and so found the taking of its rights without Ordinary justification. See id. at 414

113. Indeed, Justice Brandeis sees quite clearly the paradox involved in granting legal property greater protection than social property in his dissent to Holmes's opinion, id. at 419.

114. Id. at 416.

115. The great case here is Flemming v. Nestor, 363 U.S. 603 (1960), where the Court upheld the constitutionality of a statute denying Social Security benefits to certain aliens deported from the country. In order to reach its decision, the Court found it necessary to hold that Social Security rights were not "accrued property rights" subject to takings analysis but merely were entitlements that could be withdrawn if the decision passed a very weak "rational justification" due process test. And when, more recently, the Court has afforded greater protection to welfare recipients, it has done so under rubrics like due process and equal protection which have permitted it to avoid confrontation with the takings clause. Indeed, it is only in cases involving the right to continued employment with a state agency that the Court speaks of "property interests" in specific benefits, and even here the existence of a property right is under-

stood to trigger due process hearing requirements rather than a demand for compensation under the takings clause. Compare Perry v. Sindermann, 408 U.S. 593, 599–603 (1972) with Board of Regents v. Roth, 408 U.S. 564, 576–78 (1972).

In saying all this, I do *not* mean to suggest that a takings analysis—of either a Scientific Policymaking or Ordinary Observing kind—will inevitably require the invalidation of the challenged governmental actions. Far from it. Nonetheless, many will raise serious issues, as soon as the relevance of the takings question is perceived, as a review of chaps. 3 and 4 will make clear. Rather than providing concrete *answers* here, however, I wish to provide an explanation of why the takings *question* is not even perceived by courts or commentators. [But see Charles A. Reich, "The New Property," 73 *Yale L.J.* 733, 785 (1964), who makes a passing suggestion that interests in "governmental largesse" be protected by the takings clause.] My answer is, of course, that the deep methodological difficulties an Ordinary Observer encounters in conceptualizing the "legal property" problem make even reformist judges wary of pursuing a takings analysis so long as they remain committed to Ordinary Observing.

116. The law here consists of a series of scattered decisions capable of a wide range of interpretation. Thus, decisions according great protection to shareholders and creditors—e.g., Armstrong v. United States, 364 U.S. 40 (1960); Louisville Joint Stock Land Bank v. Radford, 295 U.S. 555 (1935); Brooks-Scanlon v. Railroad Commission, 251 U.S. 396 (1920)—can be paired against decisions which call the extent of constitutional protection into great doubt, e.g., New Haven Inclusion Cases, 399 U.S. 392 (1970).

The *New Haven* case provides a graphic example of the present state of uncertainty. There, the Supreme Court rejected a bondholders' claim that a plan for reorganizing the railroad under §77 of the Bankruptcy Act, 11 USC §205, effected a taking of their property. The plan required that the New Haven continue operations during reorganization proceedings that consumed nearly seven and a half years. This resulted in the erosion of at least $60 million of the value of the bankrupt estate. The Court conceded the bondholders' loss, but held it unprotected by the Fifth Amendment: "While the rights of the bondholders are entitled to respect, . . . [t]hey certainly do not dictate that rail operations vital to the Nation be jettisoned despite the availability of a feasible alternative."

Id. at 492. This reasoning, if brought to its logical conclusion, would entirely deny constitutional protection to owners of legal property like bondholders—for it is the essence of the takings clause that it demands compensation even though the state's intervention is justified by a valid public purpose. Recognizing this fact, the Court moved beyond its abstract pronouncements to discover special features of the New Haven's situation that justified denying recovery, id. at 492–93. And more recently, the Court has explicitly expressed concern about the takings problem raised by the New Haven scenario, see Regional Railroad Reorganization Act Cases, 419 U.S. 102, 125–36 (1974).

The legal uncertainty is mirrored in a pair of excellent law review articles on the subject. Thus, shortly after the *New Haven* case, an excellent student Note appeared condemning it, see Note, "Takings and the Public Interest in Railroad Reorganization," 82 *Yale L.J.* 1004 (1973). Further work, however, and a different perspective on the cases, sufficed to demonstrate that the existing status of legal property is far more uncertain than its partisans would allow. This, at least, has been established beyond doubt by another outstanding student Note, "Conrail and Liquidation Value: Creditors' and Shareholders' Entitlement in the Regional Rail Reorganization," 85 *Yale L.J.* 371 (1976). Unfortunately, while this second Note succeeds in destroying any illusions generated by its predecessor, it fails entirely to propose a methodology by which the proper legal stance toward legal property may be ascertained. It is, of course, my thesis that this failure is not accidental—that even the most brilliant lawyer will have an insuperable task dealing with the problem unless he is willing to abandon the premises of Ordinary Observing and ask himself whether compensating the bondholders will serve the efficiency and justice aims that provide the foundation for a Scientific Policymaking interpretation of the clause.

The collapse of the New Haven, of course, served only as a prelude to the collapse of the Penn-Central system and much else besides. And it is only now that the members of a special Railroad Reorganization Court are confronting the constitutional implications of Congress's attempt to reorganize the Eastern railroad system. Moreover, it is uncertain whether Judge Friendly and his colleagues on the special court will use their opportunity to reconsider the constitutional foundations of compensation law, especially as it relates to legal property. Surely it would be hard to imagine a case that better illustrates the importance of the underlying issues at stake.

117. Charles A. Reich, "The New Property," 73 *Yale L.J.* 733 (1964).

CHAPTER 7

1. This eclecticism in argument has been a distinctive feature of the common law since the Middle Ages. As Professor Milsom puts it, in contrast to the Roman lawyer's effort to obtain a Comprehensive View of the *corpus juris,* medieval English lawyers "did not see the law as a system of substantive rules at all." Concentrating on the elaboration of pleading rules, "they never looked up to consider as a whole the substantive system they did not know they were making." S. F. C. Milsom, *Historical Foundations of the Common Law* 32 (1960). At least since Blackstone, however, the Anglo-American tradition has come very gradually to rediscover the importance of substantive law in its own right. Within this context, the question we are raising is whether these historical tendencies toward Scientific Policymaking have now reached a point at which the main line of professional development will set about self-consciously to develop its own indigenous form of Scientific Policymaking, quite independent from previous efforts made on the continent of Europe. For some further comparative observations, see nn. 59–67 infra, and accompanying text.

2. Indeed, the attitude of Scientific Policymakers toward Ordinary Observing has not advanced appreciably since the first English-speaking Policymaker, Thomas Hobbes, wrote *A Dialogue Between a Philosopher and a Student of the Common Laws of England,* J. Cropsey, ed. (1971). Hobbes's book establishes the intolerant model for Scientific Policymaking described in the text. Thus, Hobbes discredits Sir Edward Coke and the common law methods he represents by every rhetorical means available to him. Id. at, e.g., 2–5, 6, 16–17, 118–20. In the alternative, he attempts to establish that the existing legal rules are capable of interpretation and criticism in the light of a Scientific Policymaking approach. Id. at, e.g., 90–95. Indeed, where the common law rules seem incorrigibly inept, Hobbes invokes the powers of equity to make good the law's promise of conformity to reason. Id. at 17, 80. Similarly, he invites the sovereign to frame his laws self-consciously in the light of Hobbesian policy science. Id. at 30.

3. See Ronald Coase's classic article, "The Problem of Social Costs," 3 *J. Law & Econ.* 1 (1960). Along with the simultaneous publication of Guido Calabresi's early writings, this essay signaled

the rise of the idea that economic theory could provide the basis for a comprehensive and scientific form of legal analysis capable of illuminating all sorts of substantive questions rather than serving merely as a specialized technique useful for the understanding of a few legal fields with obvious economic content, like antitrust or regulated industries. For a sensitive, yet succinct, treatment of the roles economic theory now performs in legal analysis, see Alvin K. Klevorick, "Law and Economic Theory: An Economist's View," Papers and Proceedings of the American Economic Association, 65 *Am. Econ. Rev., Papers and Proceedings* 237 (1975).

4. 304 U.S. 64 (1938). The *Erie* case involved the question whether federal or state law governed an otherwise garden-variety accident involving a trespass on railroad property. In considering this question, the lawyer was required to define (a) the difference between substantive and procedural law; (b) the difference between judge-made law and legislative enactments; and (c) the difference between national and state responsibilities in a federal system. These were precisely the issues that preoccupied the intellectually dominant group of academic lawyers rising to maturity during the 1940s and 1950s—a group I have elsewhere described as the Legal Process School; see my "Law and the Modern Mind," 103 *Daedalus* 119 (1974). Justice Brandeis's majority opinion in *Erie* was particularly important for these scholars because it seeks to resolve these questions on the level of constitutional law, thereby permitting professional legal analysis to proceed without an undue concern with the vagaries of the political process.

In saying that *Erie* is losing its symbolic centrality, I do not mean to suggest that the decision—and the countless judicial and academic utterances it has spawned—is threatened with oblivion. *Erie* will remain a star of the first magnitude in the legal universe; it has merely ceased to be the Pole Star.

5. This is only to say that serious scholars increasingly perceive an intellectual obligation to deal with the Coase theorem (and the Scientific Policymaking it represents) in *one way or another*. To establish symbolic centrality (in the law at least), it is enough to indicate that a problem is taken seriously by a broad range of scholars rather than that all answer the problem in a similar fashion.

6. Over the past decade, legal analysts influenced by economic models have had an impact on a wide variety of fields in addition to those, like antitrust and public utility regulation, in which the

relevance of economic reasoning has long been conceded. They have by now produced a vast literature which grows with the publication of each new issue of such reviews as the *Journal of Law and Economics,* the *Journal of Legal Studies,* and the *Bell Journal of Economics,* as well as the standard student-run legal periodicals. For examples of the application of this mode of analysis to a variety of legal problems, see the works cited at chap. 3, nn. 39–43 supra.

7. Consider, for example, the recent essay on the Fourth Amendment by Professor Anthony Amsterdam, perhaps our most distinguished scholar-practitioner. For Amsterdam, the fundamental question is:

> whether the Amendment should be viewed as a collection of protections of atomistic spheres of interest of individualistic citizens or as a regulation of governmental conduct. Does it safeguard *my* person and *your* house and *her* papers and *his* effects against unreasonable searches and seizures; or is it essentially a regulatory canon requiring government to order its law enforcement procedures in a fashion that keeps us collectively secure in our persons, houses, papers and effects, against unreasonable searches and seizures? "Perspectives on the Fourth Amendment," 58 *Minn. L. Rev.* 349, 367 (1974) (emphasis in original).

As this excerpt suggests, Amsterdam's first, "atomistic" approach can be likened to one generated by the Ordinary Observing style of analysis, while his second, "regulatory" approach seems roughly consistent with Scientific Policymaking premises. Even more striking, Amsterdam finds that while the Fourth Amendment is presently construed along "atomistic" (Ordinary Observer) lines, it is necessary to move to a "regulatory" (Scientific Policymaking) model "[i]n an age where our shrinking privacy and liberty would otherwise be enjoyable only at the sufferance of expanding, militaristically organized bodies of professional police." Id. at 439.

8. For a particularly striking essay that unifies seemingly disparate doctrines by taking a relatively explicit Scientific Policymaking approach, see Joseph Goldstein, "For Harold Lasswell: Some Reflections on Human Dignity, Entrapment, Informed Consent, and the Plea Bargain," 84 *Yale L.J.* 683 (1975). The voluminous writings of Professors Lasswell and McDougal and their followers contain Scientific Policymaking analyses of a wide variety of problems. See,

for example, Myres S. McDougal and Florentino P. Feliciano, *Law and Minimum World Public Order* (1961); Myers S. McDougal, Harold D. Lasswell, and Ivan A. Vlasic, *Law and Public Order in Space* (1963); Myres S. McDougal and William Burke, *The Public Order of the Oceans* (1962); W. Michael Reisman, *Nullity and Revision* (1971).

9. See, for example, Richard A. Posner, *Economic Analysis of Law* 98–102 (1973) and "The Economic Approach to Law," 53 *Tex. L. Rev.* 757, 763–64 (1975); Guido Calabresi and A. Douglas Melamed, "Property Rules, Liability Rules, and Inalienability: One View of the Cathedral," 85 *Harv. L. Rev.* 1089, 1124–27 (1972).

10. As already noted, the critique of contemporary legal doctrine has been wide ranging. In addition to the works cited at chap. 3, nn. 39–43 supra, see: Isaac Ehrlich, *The Deterrent Effect of Capital Punishment: A Question of Life or Death* [Working Paper No. 18, Center for Economic Analysis of Human Behavior, 1973; published in a condensed form in 65 *Am. Econ. Rev.* 397 (1975)] as well as a critical discussion of Ehrlich's paper appearing at 85 *Yale L.J.* nos. 2 and 3 (1975–76); numerous articles, constituting a methodological revolution in substantive and procedural criminal law, appearing in the *Journal of Legal Studies;* Robert C. Ellickson, "Alternatives to Zoning: Covenants, Nuisance Rules and Fines as Land Use Controls," 40 *U. Chi. L. Rev.* 681 (1973); and of course Professor Sax.

11. Richard A. Posner, "A Theory of Negligence," 1 *J. Leg. Studies* 29 (1972); *Economic Analysis of Law* 98–102; and "The Economic Approach to Law," 53 *Tex. L. Rev.* 757, 763–64 (1975); and, of course, Michelman's work on just compensation is of this general character.

12. See, for example, Guido Calabresi, n. 9 supra, at 1102–5, and *The Costs of Accidents* 293–300 (1970).

13. It should not be imagined that the economic analysis of law constitutes either the only—or the first—effort at Scientific Policymaking. As I have already indicated, n. 26, chap. 1, the great event of the modern period is the disintegration of the "Classical" form of Scientific Policymaking dominant before the Great Depression. Similarly, a second group of scholars writing after the Second World War also had comprehensive ambitions as they systematically studied something they called the Legal Process. Indeed, my present effort to develop a "Scientific" theory of judicial role owes much to this kind of

work. For those who wish to trace this strand of contemporary Policy-making, I include a sample of Legal Process work: Lon L. Fuller, *The Law in Quest of Itself* (1940); Paul Freund, *Understanding the Supreme Court* (1949); Edward H. Levi, *An Introduction to Legal Reasoning* (1949); Henry M. Hart, Jr., and Herbert Wechsler, *The Federal Courts and the Federal System* (1953); Alexander M. Bickel and Harry H. Wellington, "Legislative Purpose and the Judicial Process: The Lincoln Mills Case," 71 *Harv. L. Rev.* 1 (1957); Henry M. Hart, Jr., and Albert M. Sacks, *The Legal Process: Basic Problems in the Making and Application of Law* (1958); Henry M. Hart, Jr., "The Supreme Court, 1958 Term, Foreword: The Time Chart of the Justices," 73 *Harv. L. Rev.* 84 (1959); Herbert Wechsler, "Towards Neutral Principles of Constitutional Law," 73 *Harv. L. Rev.* 1 (1959); Karl Llewellyn, *The Common Law Tradition: Deciding Appeals* (1960); Alexander M. Bickel, *The Least Dangerous Branch* (1962); Ronald M. Dworkin, "The Model of Rules," 35 *U. Chi. L. Rev.* 14 (1967); Herbert L. Packer, *The Limits of the Criminal Sanction* (1968); Harry H. Wellington, *Labor and the Legal Process* (1968); Louis L. Jaffe, *English and American Judges as Lawmakers* (1969). And, of course, the writings of the McDougal-Lasswell school, see n. 8 supra, represent another significant Policymaking effort.

14. See Richard A. Epstein, "A Theory of Strict Liability," 2 *J. Leg. Studies* 151 (1973); "Defenses and Subsequent Pleas in a System of Strict Liability," 3 *J. Leg. Studies* 165 (1974); "Intentional Harms," 4 *J. Leg. Studies* 391 (1975); George P. Fletcher, "Fairness and Utility in Tort Theory," 85 *Harv. L. Rev.* 537 (1972). For a similar effort in the area of criminal law, see George P. Fletcher, "The Right Deed for the Wrong Reason: A Reply to Mr. Robinson," 23 *U.C.L.A. L. Rev.* 293 (1975).

15. "Common Law Rules and Constitutional Double Standards: Some Notes on Adjudication," 83 *Yale L.J.* 221 (1973).

16. Id. at 223–24.

17. Wellington's commitment to Observing—that is, to the proposition that the ultimate end of legal analysis is the identification of rules that best support dominant social expectations—is first suggested by his claim that arguments from *principle* are *always* admissible in judicial reasoning while arguments from *policy* are admissible only under special circumstances. The methodological significance of this blanket endorsement of principle can be seen in

the strong link Wellington seeks to forge between judicial principles
and the dominant conventional morality:

> I have claimed, in effect, that when dealing with legal princi-
> ples a court must take a moral point of view. Yet I doubt that
> one would want to say that a court is entitled or required to
> assert *its* moral point of view. Unlike the moral philosopher,
> the court is required to assert *ours*. . . . And that is why we
> must be concerned with conventional morality, for it is there
> that society's set of moral principles and ideals are located. (Id.
> at 244; emphasis in original.)

But it is not so clear whether Wellington is an Ordinary or Scientific Observer. The answer depends on his account of how judges
are to recognize conventional morality. And on that point he is
somewhat ambiguous. He rejects "behavioral science methodology"
in favor of "the method of philosophy," i.e., "to live in [conven-
tional morality], to become sensitive to it, experience widely, read
extensively, and ruminate, reflect, and analyze situations that seem
to call moral obligations into play." Id. at 246. Whether the method
of philosophy requires a Scientific or an Ordinary vocabulary, however, depends on the form of the philosophical analysis employed.

18. Although Wellington believes that principles are the type of
justification most suitable to judicial reasoning in common law adjudication, he argues that policies may properly be invoked if they
are widely regarded as socially desirable and are "neutral," i.e., do
not place without good reason disproportionate burdens on a particular segment of society. Id. at 235–41.

19. Wellington provides a general formulation of his views on
constitutional adjudication: "The scope of judicial review should be
sharply restricted when the primary justification for the exercise of
judicial power is a constitutional policy; it should be searching
where the primary justification is a principle." (Id. at 267.) While
this formulation presupposes that policies are *sometimes* admissible
in constitutional law, the essay never presents a treatment, parallel
to that provided for common law adjudication, see n. 18 supra,
defining the general conditions under which policies are admissible
in constitutional interpretation. It should not be inferred from this
absence of theoretical development, however, that Wellington believes that policy argument plays a minor role in constitutional law.
To the contrary, he thinks it plain that both the First and Fourth

Amendments are (and should be?) principally justified on policy grounds. Id. at 268-71. Unfortunately, no views are expressed on the compensation clause.

20. While Utilitarian arguments are a common kind of "instrumental justification for a rule," they are not the only kind. Rather than focusing upon the felicific consequences of a rule, one may instead stress its impact on the future development of other values —like virtue, enlightenment, and so forth—not readily reducible (even in the last analysis) to happiness. To put the point in the standard philosophical way, Utilitarianism is only one species of *consequentialism*, not the entire genus. Wellington's definition of policy in terms of instrumentalism (by which he seems to mean consequentialism) does not, then, mark out a characteristic possessed exclusively by Utilitarian arguments—though it is plain that he generally has them in mind in his discussion of policies.

21. Wellington does admit that Kantian Policymaking may indirectly affect the content of principles by influencing conventional morality. "We may all think somewhat differently about some aspects of morality, for example, after Rawls." 83 *Yale L.J.* 221, 280. But it cannot provide independent justifications for judicial decisions. For Wellington is at great pains to deny that principles can be derived from non-instrumental Comprehensive Views. Indeed, he refers to such theories as "philosopher's morality," by way of contrast with conventional morality, which is the source of principles. See, e.g., id. at 280, 285. Since policies are by definition instrumental, Kantianism has no place at all in the justification of decisions.

The case is very different with respect to utilitarianism. Wellington frequently calls policies "efficiency-type justifications." And as his discussion of, for example, the Fourth Amendment makes clear, he is not thinking of economic efficiency but rather something very much like Bentham's Utility. Id. at 258-61, 270-72. It follows, then, that while Kantian philosophy may only affect the law *indirectly*, through its impact upon conventional morality, Utilitarian philosophy can serve as a *direct* source of law, independent of conventional morality, so long as it meets the (unspecified) tests for the judicial admissibility of policy arguments in constitutional law. In short, Wellington has in fact created a privileged position for Utilitarianism in legal argument—a rather surprising conclusion for someone who, on the surface, seems to be limiting "policy" arguments on behalf of "principle." Unfortunately, however, Wellington is so concerned with reaching an accommodation between Observing and Utilitarian Policymaking that he does not recognize that, implicitly, he has accorded Bentham a legal status that he denies to Kant.

22. "Hard Cases," 88 *Harv. L. Rev.* 1057 (1975).

23. Id. at 1064.

24. Chap. 1, pp. 12–15 supra.

25. Dworkin makes no reference to Wellington's essay, although it was published almost two years before his own; nor does he attempt to deal with Wellington's distinction between principles and policies.

26. 88 *Harv. L. Rev.* 1057, 1059 (emphasis supplied).

27. Dworkin attempts to discharge this formidable task at pp. 1067–70 of his essay. Since nothing in the present discussion depends on his success, I shall not attempt an evaluation of his arguments.

28. In his discussion of particular policies, Dworkin speaks more of appeals to "economic efficiency" than to the quite different notion of social utility. Nevertheless, Dworkin plainly recognizes the existence of other policy arguments, having to do with equality and military strength (88 *Harv. L. Rev.* 1057, 1068), which do not have an obvious relationship to ordinary notions of economic efficiency; moreover, his discussion of the Learned Hand test in the law of torts, id. at 1075–77, employs the expressions "economic efficiency" and "collective utility" almost interchangeably. In short, there can be no doubt that Utilitarianism is the substantive philosophy that Dworkin seeks to capture in his formal definition of policy. For a criticism of the common tendency to make "economic efficiency" a synonym of "collective utility," see my essay, "On the Role of Economic Analysis in Property Law," in B. A. Ackerman, ed., *Economic Foundations of Property Law,* vii–xvi (1975).

So far as Kantianism is concerned, while Dworkin's attempt at a formal definition of principle is very obscure indeed (see 88 *Harv. L. Rev.* 1057, 1067–70), concrete discussions, together with his interesting analysis of rights in "The Original Position," 40 *U. Chi. L. Rev.* 500, 519–20 (1970), make it plain that he understands Kantian notions of individual dignity to provide a suitable (perhaps the most suitable?) source of principles.

29. 88 *Harv. L. Rev.* 1057, 1064. See also "The Original Position," n. 28 supra, at 509–19, where Dworkin discusses competing models of consistency in moral reasoning, giving similarly short shrift to intuitionism.

30. 88 *Harv. L. Rev.* 1057, 1067.

31. Id. at 1060.

32. While at one point Dworkin does allow rule Utilitarianism as an admissible possibility, id at 1072–73, even here he draws the line at any judicial inquiry into the Utilitarian justification of the application of the rule to a particular case or class of cases.

It should be noted, moreover, that Dworkin's "rights thesis" contains a number of escape hatches which, if opened wide enough, will permit an orderly retreat to a less exposed, if less commanding, position. First, Dworkin expressly limits his thesis to "civil" cases, and whether the takings clause fits under this label is far from clear. See his brief discussion of the matter at pp. 1077–78. Second, while an application of the thesis to common-law adjudication seems moderately straightforward, this cannot be said of its application to statutory interpretation and constitutional law—fields which are far more important in contemporary judicial work. Thus, in his illustrative discussion of the way a model judge, Hercules, would deploy the "rights thesis," we find that Hercules is permitted to employ something called the *principle* of federalism, id. at 1086, which seems plainly to qualify as a *policy* in Dworkin's theory, and also to countenance the possibility that the purpose of the First Amendment's guarantee of religious freedom is the reduction of "social tension or disorder," id. at 1084—a goal which, once again, seems most plausibly justified on grounds of collective welfare. See Ronald Dworkin, "On Not Prosecuting Civil Disobedience," in J. Feinberg and H. Gross, ed., *Philosophy of Law* 197, 204 (1975).

Of course it may be said that judges are bound by *principles*(?) of institutional subordination to implement constitutional and statutory policies if such a step is intended by the superordinate authority. But this requires one to unravel the mystery of legislative intention as a necessary condition of understanding the "rights thesis." Moreover, it admits the possibility that vast areas of current American law—perhaps by far the most important—*are* appropriately governed today by self-conscious judicial recourse to policy reasoning. While this apparent escape hatch is at least as important as the first one, it does not seem available in a discussion of compensation law—since we have seen that recourse to the intention of the Framers does not provide significant help in choosing between one or another form of legal thought.

33. Just as Dworkin's abstract arguments move too quickly to a Kantian conclusion, so too does his discussion of particular legal

doctrines. Thus, Dworkin singles out Learned Hand's well-known approach to negligence law as representing one of the "few" potential counter-examples to his thesis and seeks to demonstrate that Hand's doctrine is in fact based on a principle rather than a policy; 88 *Harv. L. Rev.* 1057, 1077–78. Dworkin recognizes, of course, that Hand's test seems at first glance to be justified by a policy, since it explicitly makes a decision in a negligence action turn on whether it advances the collective good by reducing the overall cost of damaging social interaction. But he makes a distinction between the substance of the theory and the language in which it is expressed. He argues that although the theory is expressed in economic terms, it is a formula by which to determine the proper Kantian outcome in negligence cases. The problem for Kantianism in such cases is to balance the respect due the plaintiff by the defendant with the defendant's liberty and autonomy. "It is natural, particularly when economic vocabulary is in fashion, to define the proper balance [between respect and liberty] by comparing the sum of the utilities of these two parties under different conditions." Id. at 1076.

Now it is certainly possible that a Kantian judge might attempt to state his decisions in economic terms. Indeed, as I have suggested at chap. 4, n. 11 supra, the language of welfare economics may turn out to be a most suitable one for expressing some versions of the Kantian Comprehensive View. But none of this justifies Dworkin's conclusion that the Learned Hand test is *in fact* a rule derived from Kantian principles and expressed in economic terms. In order to show that, Dworkin must articulate the Kantian principles more clearly, explain how Kantian arguments are to be translated into an economic vocabulary (if that is not their natural mode of expression), and provide a detailed derivation of the Learned Hand test. It is surely not enough to assert that since a rule derived from Kantian principles *may* be expressed in economic terms, it follows that a given rule expressed in economic terms *is* derived from Kantian principles. Dworkin's claim is particularly remarkable since Utilitarian authors have in fact successfully treated Hand's calculus within their larger framework: see, e.g., Richard A. Posner, "A Theory of Negligence," 1 *J. Leg. Studies* 29 (1972); Guido Calabresi and Jon T. Hirschoff, "Toward a Test for Strict Liability in Torts," 81 *Yale L.J.* 1055 (1972). And authors of a more Kantian persuasion have doubted the propriety of the Hand-type cost-calculus: see George P. Fletcher, "Fairness and Utility in Tort Theory," 85 *Harv. L. Rev.*

537 (1972). Moreover, even if Dworkin were to demonstrate that the Hand test is based on principle, rather than policy, he would have gone only a very small way toward establishing the "rights thesis" as the best descriptive account of existing judicial practice. Rather than being an extraordinarily rare exception to the general rule, self-conscious resort to (seemingly) Utilitarian arguments is quite a common phenomenon in modern American case-law.

34. It should be recalled, however, that Dworkin does allow for exceptional situations in which Utilitarian Policymakers, if not Observers, may be permitted their say; see note 32 supra. Dworkin has not, unfortunately, defined the precise character of these exceptional situations with the care they deserve.

35. See Richard A. Posner, "An Economic Approach to Law," 53 *Tex. L. Rev.* 757, 777–78 (1975), and *Economic Analysis of Law* 6–8, n. 9 supra.

36. While our model of Ordinary adjudication would require revision before it could plausibly be employed by a legislator or other nonjudicial officer, it nevertheless seems likely that an entire family of models could be generated to guide the Ordinary Observer in one or another official task. Indeed the Ordinary judge depicted here has some important resemblances to Charles Lindblom's description of a public administrator who refuses to take a Comprehensive View of his problem and instead responds interstitially to the particular forces at play in his environment. See Charles E. Lindblom, "The Science of 'Muddling Through,'" 19 *Pub. Admin. Rev.* 79 (1959); Lindblom, *The Intelligence of Democracy* (1965). Analogous models of decisionmaking have been developed by a group of distinguished scholars associated with the Carnegie-Mellon School of Public Administration. See, for example, Oliver E. Williamson, *Markets and Hierarchies* (1975); James G. March and Herbert A. Simon, *Organizations* (1958); Herbert A. Simon, "Theories of Bounded Rationality," in C. McGuire and R. Radner, eds., *Decision and Organization* 161 (1972).

Similarly, it is not difficult to find analogies to the Scientific Policymaking mode of adjudication in the more general literature on public choice and decision. Indeed, the effort by economists and systems analysts to revolutionize governmental decisionmaking procedures in the name of Scientific Policymaking is one of the most striking features of contemporary public administration. This movement in turn has engendered a thoughtful literature dealing with

the conflicting forms of decision, which is of the first importance to
lawyers trying to make sense of the analytical tensions in their own
craft. See, in addition to the works already cited, David Braybrooke
and Charles E. Lindblom, *Strategy for Decision* (1963); John D.
Steinbruner, *The Cybernetic Theory of Decision* 3–150 (1974);
Richard Nelson, *The Moon and the Ghetto: An Appreciation of the
Unbalanced Performance of the American Political Economy* (1975);
Laurence H. Tribe, "Policy Science: Analysis or Ideology?" 2 *Phil &
Pub. Affairs* 66 (1972).

37. See Ludwig Wittgenstein, *Philosophical Investigations*,
G. E. M. Anscombe and G. von Wright, eds. (1969); Hanna F.
Pitkin, *Wittgenstein and Justice* 1–168 (1972). Support may also be
found amongst recent European writers in the phenomenological
tradition. See, e.g., Alfred Schutz and Thomas Luckman, *The
Structures of the Life World*, tr. R. M. Jauer and H. T. Engelhardt,
Jr. (1973).

38. See, for example, A. J. Ayer, *Language, Truth and Logic*,
102–20 (1946); Charles L. Stevenson, *Facts and Values* 10–31, 32–54,
138–52 (1963).

39. Michael Oakeshott is, perhaps, the most important contemporary exponent of such views. See his book, *On Human Conduct* (1975) and his collection of essays, *Rationalism in Politics*
(1962).

40. See Yosal Rogat, "The Judge as Spectator," 31 *U. Chi. L. Rev.*
213 (1964); "Mr. Justice Holmes: A Dissenting Opinion," 15 *Stan. L.
Rev.* 3, 254 (1962–63). While a "scientific socialist" of the Marxist
sort also sees the law merely as a reflection of the dominant social
forces of the time, he would probably not be so quick to agree with
Holmes that lawmakers should therefore be expected to adopt an
Ordinary Observer's approach to the disputes they must resolve. For
it is at least possible, I suppose, for the Marxist to view Scientific
Policymaking as an ideological response to the increasingly bureau-
cratized structures of late capitalism, and so an appropriate lawmaking form for present-day America. For a contemporary effort to
marry Marxism and Structuralism in a manner consistent with this
interpretation of Marxism, see Nicos Poulantzas, *Political Power and
Social Classes* 325–61 (1973).

41. For the analogy between the theory of Ordinary adjudication
and important strands in the public administration literature, see
n. 36 supra and the sources cited therein.

42. This is not to say that Ordinary Observing is the only form of thought that is consistent with the retroactive application of laws. So far as the Kantian is concerned, the fact that B did not recognize his duty to respect A will not generally serve as a justification for, or even an excuse of, B's breach so long as the judge is convinced that B did in fact deprive A of his dignity as an autonomous being. Indeed, it is perfectly possible that B's failure to recognize his duty only exacerbates his wrong.

In contrast, retroactively seems far more problematic from a Utilitarian point of view. Given the high premium placed on stability and predictability in a broad range of legal matters, it could well be that net benefits will often be maximized if decisionmakers apply new rules prospectively in the name of reducing uncertainty costs. See Note, "Prospective Overruling and Retroactive Application in the Federal Courts," 71 *Yale L.J.* 907 (1962); Guido Calabresi, "Retroactivity: Paramount Powers and Contractual Changes," 71 *Yale L.J.* 1191 (1962). Indeed, the rise of non-retroactive rulings in modern American law is one of the most striking symbols of the increasing currency of Utilitarian Policymaking.

43. While Professor Alexander Bickel seemed to be evolving in Ordinary Observing directions before his death, he was denied an adequate opportunity to develop a full account of his mature views. For the most complete expression of his later thought, see *The Morality of Consent* (1975) and *The Supreme Court and the Idea of Progress* (1970).

44. See, for example, Milton Friedman, *Capitalism and Freedom* 22–36 (1962).

45. It should be emphasized that I am not making the strong claim that a Scientific Policymaker must *necessarily* accept the validity of a critical state. Indeed, I suspect that such a strong claim cannot be defended. It seems more plausible, however, to suspect that all those who accept the critical state must necessarily prefer Scientific Policymaking (at least on the level of constitutional interpretation)—though I am not at present sufficiently confident even of this weaker claim to do more than invite others to consider it critically.

46. In emphasizing the central importance of developing a set of criteria by which to identify the Comprehensive View that prevails in a given legal system, I do not want to suggest that a Scientific Policymaker is necessarily committed to a form of "legal positivism"

(an expression whose precise meaning I have never got entirely clear). Nor do I wish to argue that the Policymaker's decisive criterion must necessarily refer exclusively to the pedigree, rather than the substance, of the Comprehensive View (if this is what the legal positivist's claim is all about). I merely wish to insist that the judge must develop *some way* of plausibly defending himself against the charge of personal idiosyncrasy in his selection of the Comprehensive View that he has imputed to the legal system. This is not to deny that there are many possible ways of imputing a Comprehensive View to a legal system, and that an adequate Policymaking jurisprudence will explain why its way is the best. But I do not wish to limit discussion of this issue by restricting its scope by some formal device before it has fairly begun. For important work which is relevant to the continuing discussion, see Hans Kelsen, *General Theory of Law and State* 110–23, tr. Anders Wedberg (1945), and *The Pure Theory of Law* 193–221, tr. Max Knight (1970); H. L. A. Hart, *The Concept of Law,* chap. 6 (1961); Joseph Raz, *The Concept of a Legal System,* chap. 8 (1970). Ronald Dworkin has attacked the possibility of a rule of recognition in "The Model of Rules," 35 *U. Chi. L. Rev.* 14, 40–46 (1967) and "Social Rules and Legal Theory," 81 *Yale L.J.* 855, 868–81 (1972).

47. After reading more reviews of the *Theory of Justice* than I care to recall, I must report that the commentators, while eager to admire the ambition of Rawls's enterprise, are generally quite reluctant to concede that Rawls's argument actually succeeds in convincing them in its own right. Indeed, the defects and ambiguities that have been unearthed by the multitude of individual workers add up to a rather prodigious heap. Nonetheless, it is too early to say whether this first round of commentary has simply served to prepare the way for a more precise and convincing reformulation of the contractarian argument or whether it should instead be taken to vindicate the old conventional wisdom which had confidently asserted that the effort to understand the nature of social obligation and social justice by invoking contractarian metaphors was fundamentally misconceived.

48. It should be noted that the extent to which Rawls's work is actually capable of a Kantian interpretation is in fact controversial. See sources cited at n. 27, chap. 4.

49. For introductions to the basic concepts which do not presuppose any great mathematical sophistication, see Bruce A. Ackerman,

"On the Role of Economic Analysis in Property Law," n. 28 supra; William J. Baumol, *Economic Theory and Operations Analysis,* chap. 16 (1972); A. Mitchell Polinsky, "Economic Analysis as a Potentially Defective Product: A Buyer's Guide to Posner's *Economic Analysis of Law,*" 87 *Harv. L. Rev.* 1655 (1974).

50. Perhaps it will provide some hope for the philosophical future of Scientific Policymaking to note that even such a profoundly Ordinary philosopher as J. L. Austin was unwilling to preclude the possibility of its development:

> Certainly ordinary language has no claim to be the last word, if there is such a thing. It embodies, indeed, something better than the metaphysics of the Stone Age, namely, as was said, the inherited experience and acumen of many generations of men. But then, that acumen has been concentrated primarily upon the practical business of life. If a distinction works well for practical purposes in ordinary life (no mean feat, for even ordinary life is full of hard cases), then there is sure to be something in it, it will not mark nothing: yet this is likely enough to be not the best way of arranging things if our interests are more extensive or intellectual than ordinary. And again that experience has been derived only from the sources available to ordinary men throughout most of civilized history: it has not been fed from the resources of the microscope and its successors. And it must be added too, that superstition and error and fantasy of all kinds do become incorporated in ordinary language and even sometimes stand up to the survival test (only, when they do, why should we not detect it?). Certainly then, ordinary language is *not* the last word: in principle it can everywhere be supplemented and improved upon and superseded. Only remember, it is the first word. "A Plea for Excuses," 57 *Proceedings of the Aristotelian Society* 11 (1956).

51. See R. M. Hare, *The Language of Morals* (1952), and *Freedom and Reason* (1963). For some other potentially promising work, see Hilary Putnam, "Meaning and Reference," 70 *J. Phil.* 699, 704–6 (1973), and Eddy M. Zemach, "Putnam's Theory and the Reference of Substance Terms," 73 *J. Phil.* 110, 124–27 (1976).

52. In addition to Chomsky, the writer I have found most suggestive is Basil Bernstein. See his *Class, Codes and Control* (1973).

53. For some recent plunges into the Structuralist fog, see Gerald

Garvey, *Constitutional Bricolage* (1971); Donald H. J. Hermann, "A Structuralist Approach to Legal Reasoning," 48 *So. Cal. L. Rev.* 1131 (1975).

54. I have in mind Duncan Kennedy, "Legal Formality," 2 *J. Leg. Studies* 351 (1973); Laurence H. Tribe, "Ways Not to Think About Plastic Trees: New Foundations for Environmental Law," 83 *Yale L.J.* 1315 (1974); Roberto Mangabeira Unger, *Knowledge and Politics* (1975).

55. See his *Philosophy of Right,* especially §§ 34–71, 182–218, 260–75, together with respective Additions, T. M. Knox, tr. (1952); and *The Phenomenology of Mind,* J. B. Baillie, tr., especially 501–6 (1967). The best English introduction to Hegel's political thought is Shlomo Avineri, *Hegel's Theory of the Modern State* (1972). A number of relevant essays may also be found in Zbigniew Pelczynski's collection, *Hegel's Political Philosophy: Problems and Perspectives* (1971). See Z. A. Pelczynski, "The Hegelian Conception of the State," id. at 1; K. H. Ilting, "The Structure of Hegel's *Philosophy of Right,*" id. at 90; Manfred Reidel, "Nature and Freedom in Hegel's *Philosophy of Right,*" id. at 136.

56. For some sensitive speculations on this subject, see G. A. Kelly, "Hegel's America," 2 *Phil. and Pub. Affairs* 3 (1972).

57. Indeed, Hegel's only significant comments concerning America suggest this very possibility:

> As to the political condition of North America, the general object of the existence of this State is not yet fixed and determined, and the necessity for a finer combination does not yet exist; for a real State and real Government arise only after a distinction of classes has arisen, when wealth and poverty became extreme, and when such a condition of things presents itself that a large portion of the people can no longer satisfy its necessities in the way in which it has been accustomed so to do. But America is hitherto exempt from this pressure, for it has the outlet of colonization constantly and widely open, and multitudes are continually streaming into the plains of the Mississippi. By this means the chief source of discontent is removed and the continuation of the existing civil condition is guaranteed. . . . North America will be comparable with Europe only after the immeasurable space which that country presents to its inhabitants shall have been occupied, and the

members of the political body shall have begun to be pressed
back on each other.

(George W. F. Hegel, *The Philosophy of History* 85–86, J. Sibree, tr.,
1956.)

58. It should be emphasized that the future of Scientific Policymaking among the American elite is not to be judged merely by a
consideration of trends in legal thought. Large proportions of the
elite are now trained by graduate schools of business and public
policy where education is conducted almost exclusively on Scientific
Policymaking premises. Moreover, the increasing use of the computer
in practical decisionmaking is shifting power to those who are at
least superficially acquainted with new forms of Scientific discourse.
Thus, unless lawyers are to lose their hold on public and private
decisionmaking positions, they will be increasingly obliged to be at
least superficially acquainted with the sorts of models which com-
puters manipulate—leading to further pressures toward Scientific
Policymaking in the legal subculture. (This is not to deny that the
rise of the computer will cause lawyers to lose some of their power
to those with more technocratic forms of training; it is only to predict that as a result of the interprofessional struggle for power, legal
thought itself will be powerfully influenced in Scientific Policymaking directions.)

59. The reasons for this development are complex, largely unexplored, and different in different countries. Nonetheless, a few
general remarks should be attempted, lest one too easily infer that
the (modest) decline in Scientific Policymaking on the Continent
portends a similar decline in America. For the fact is that drawing
a straightforward analogy between European and American de-
velopments seems quite unjustified. Modern European legal science
reached its maturity in the nineteenth century and proceeds upon
certain fundamental presuppositions that bear the mark of the
Continental culture of that period. Given the contemporary challenge to some of these presuppositions, it was not surprising that
the Europeans would be obliged to retreat and reconsider their traditional enterprise. Thus, the twentieth century has challenged its
predecessor's failure to confront seriously the problems of lawmaking
in a pluralist democracy, as well as its simple faith in enlightenment rationalism and its implicit assumption of a modest state role
in economic organization. Indeed, even the Continental Scientist's

extraordinary technical vocabulary has begun to seem more than a little quaint in its ignorance of modern economic as well as quantitative concepts essential for intelligent lawmaking in an activist state. Similarly, the Continental model of bureaucracy seems unnecessarily hierarchical and rule-bound, unable to discharge complex lawmaking functions in a rapidly changing environment. Whatever else may be said of American forms of Scientific Policymaking, at least they do not carry with them the heavy weight of an established tradition which so obviously requires renovation. The Americans, in short, have both the advantages and disadvantages of a Scientifically underdeveloped nation—while they are free to take advantage of the newest in technology, they also run the risk of losing touch with their native values in the process. The extent to which American law will resolve this fundamental problem cannot be foreseen by judging the European's success in coming to terms with the very different problems of renovating an historically entrenched form of Scientific Policymaking.

60. On the traditional Continental legal education, see Gerhard Casper, "Two Models of Legal Education," 41 *Tenn. L. Rev.* 13 (1973); Mirjan Damaska, "A Continental Lawyer in an American Law School," 116 *U. Pa. L. Rev.* 1363 (1968); John Henry Merryman; "Legal Education Here and There: A Comparison," 27 *Stan. L. Rev.* 859 (1975). Reform is underway in many Western countries, but strong opposition from defenders of the old paradigm is not surprising. See, e.g., Andreas Heldrich, "Das trojanische Pferd in der Zitadelle des Rechts," 14 *Juristische Schulung* 281 (1974).

61. See, for Germany, Rudolf Schlesinger, *Comparative Law* 118–20 (1970); for France, A. V. Sheehan, *Criminal Procedure in Scotland and France* (1975); and for Italy, Mauro Cappelletti and Joseph M. Perillo, *Civil Procedure in Italy* 74–75 (1965).

62. For a recent discussion, see Mirjan Damaska, "Structures of Authority and Comparative Criminal Procedure," 84 *Yale L.J.* 480, 491–93 (1975) and literature cited therein.

63. The first wave of the codification movement, whose most important works were the French *Code Civil* and the Austrian Code of 1811, worked self-consciously from the comprehensive natural rights theorists of the previous two centuries. See Franz Weiacker, *Privatrechtsgeschichte der Neuzeit*, 2d ed. 249–347 (1967). The second codification wave, whose principal achievement is the German Civil and Criminal Codes enacted at the turn of the century, repre-

sents an even more self-conscious effort to build upon nineteenth-century legal scholarship. See ibid. at 450–513.

64. For a perceptive diagnosis, see Friedrich Kübler, "Kodifikation und Demokratie," 24 *Juristenzeitung* 624 (1969). It is important to note that in the Eastern European countries codification remains the ideal. See, e.g., Imre Szabó, *Les Fondements de la Théorie du Droit* 115, 204–7 (1973).

65. See, for example, the closing pages of Franz Wieacker, *Privatrechtsgeschichte der Neuzeit* 624 ff., n. 63 supra. Or, from a sociologist's point of view, see Niklas Luhmann, *Rechtssystem und Rechtsdogmatik* 19 ff. (1974). It is symptomatic that some Continental lawyers look upon the American system with undisguised despair. For example, André Tunc and Suzanne Tunc, *Le Droit des Etats-Unis d'Amerique* 163 (1955): "L'affaiblissement de l'autorité du précédent, qui, en matière de common law n'est autre que l'affaiblissement du droit lui-même, semble avoir touché le point où il laisse quelque peu désorientés praticiens et théoriciens. Une telle attitude [a l'égard de l'autorité du précédent], poussée a l'extrême, serait la négation du droit. Aux Etats-Unis même, elle ne laisse pas de présenter des dangers." Id. at 183.

66. While for us judicial review represents the paradigmatic instance of a legal decision, it is illuminating to note the difficulty Europeans have had with the notion since it was imported to the Continent. Indeed, there is respectable opinion in favor of the position that constitutional review cannot be considered judicial activity at all, since its premises so plainly challenged received juridical technique. See Joseph Esser, *Vorverständnis und Methodenwahl in der Rechtsfindung* 201 (1970). The conflict between "policy" and "dogmatic" approaches in West Germany—where the constitutional court is very active—is perceptively discussed by Fredrich Kübler, *Über die praktischen Aufgaben zeitgemasser Privatrectstheorie* 27 (1975).

67. See notes 59, 64, and 65 supra. These comparative observations have been greatly influenced by many conversations with my colleague, Mirjan Damaska. While there is much here with which he would disagree, I am greatly indebted to him.

Table of Cases

Page numbers in italics indicate that a particular
case is discussed at some length.

Index

Activism, judicial: definition of, for Scientific Policymaker, 37; relation to institutional competence assumption of well-ordered society, 37, 108; and Scientific Utilitarianism, 49–56, 209, 210–11; and Scientific Kantianism, 77–80, 225–26; definition of, for Ordinary Observer, 108; and existing compensation doctrine, 109, 139–41, 251. *See also* Judicial role *and* Well-ordered society

Activist state, 1–3; and the takings clause, 28, 113–14; and the entrepreneurial/arbitral distinction, 50; conflict between takings clause and, 114, 148–49; legal property and, 165–66; and the notion of the critical state, 181

Ad coelum rule, 120, 238, 258

Administrative process: Utilitarian theory of malfunction of, 50–53; Kantian theory of malfunction of, 226; and local zoning boards, 210–11

Agnosticism, judicial: as a form of judicial reformism, 57–59; and Scientific Utilitarianism, 57–59; and Scientific Kantianism, 81; and existing compensation doctrine, 109

Airspace, 118–21, 238, 258

Altree, Lillian R., 209, 215, 217, 245–46

Appeal to citizen disaffection, 46–48, 49, 67, 69, 218, 238, 243, 261

Appeal to general uncertainty, 44–

46, 49, 67, 69, 205–08, 243, 261, 264

Aristotle, 198

Austin, J. L., 200, 285

Baxter, William F., 209, 212, 215, 217, 245–46

Bickel, Alexander M., 48, 204, 208, 275, 283

Black, Charles L., Jr., 204, 211, 255

Blackstone, Sir William, 193, 271

Calabresi, Guido, 174, 201, 202, 206, 214, 217, 246, 271, 274, 280, 283

Coase, Ronald H., 169, 217, 271, 272

Compensation clause. *See* Takings clause

Comprehensive View: function in Scientific Policymaking, 11; role of principles in, 11, 194–95; abstractness of, 11, 195; completeness of, 11, 195; consistency of, 11, 196; concept of, 11–12; range of admissible, 41–42; theory of judicial role, relation to, 82–83, 105–06; exclusion of legal rules from, 194; welfare economics and, 196–97. *See also* Kantianism, Scientific Policymaker, *and* Utilitarianism

Consequentialism, 277

Conservatism, judicial: definition of, for Scientific Policymaker, 37; relation to distributive justice assumption of well-ordered society, 37, 108; definition of, for Ordinary Observer, 108; and existing